THE
Woman
Road Warrior

An Expert's Guide to Domestic and
International Business Travel

SECOND EDITION

Kathleen Ameche

A B2 BOOK

AGATE

CHICAGO

Second Edition.
ISBN (10-digit) 1-932841-25-3
ISBN (13-digit) 978-1-932841-25-1

Printed in Canada.

The Library of Congress has cataloged the first edition as follows:

Library of Congress Cataloging-in-Publication Data

Ameche, Kathleen.
   The woman road warrior: an expert's guide to domestic and international business travel / Kathleen Ameche.
     p. cm.
   Summary: "Provides practical information, resources, and tips specific to the needs of women business travelers of all ages and levels of experience"—Provided by the publisher.
   ISBN (10-digit) 1-932841-09-1 (pbk.)
   ISBN (13-digit) 9781932841091
   1. Business travel. 2. Businesswomen—Travel. I. Title.
   G156.5.B86A44 2005
   910.2—dc22

                               2004025750

10 9 8 7 6 5 4 3 2 1

B2 Books is an imprint of Agate Publishing.

Agate books are available in bulk at discount prices.
For more information, go to agatepublishing.com.

To Bob,

my husband, advisor, partner, editor,
travel companion, and best friend.

Acknowledgments

When I told people I was writing a book for businesswomen who travel, everyone had a story. A number of their stories are incorporated into this book. My profound thanks to the domestic travelers: Pamela Basone, Pamay Basse, Marea Brichta, Joanne Dobbie, Pam Duffy, Susan Gallagher, Margaret Godfrey, Suzanne Gylfe, Jean Holley, Anne Norris, Sandra Rahill, Susan Rosenstein, Sue Ryan, and Laura Yeager. I also give a sincere thanks to the international travelers: Janet Adney, Lilian Brozek, Lisa Chen, Jennifer Chuang, Nancie Clare, Nancy Eichstadt, Catherine May, Cathy McClain, Rachael McDiarmid, Mona Al-Mehaid, Jennifer Miller, Amy Richards, Judy Samelson, Mary Summons, Holley Thompson, Mary Dale Walters, Annie Wang, Amy Wills, and Winnie Wong.

Many people read all or part of the manuscript and gave valuable comments and feedback. Some of these people also participated in a focus group that helped develop the concept and reviewed an early manuscript. My thanks to Sara Berliner, Amy Berliner, Stephanie Biederman, Marea Brichta, Janet Brookman, Carey Broussard, Debra Cafaro, Pam Duffy, Carol Fowler, Clint Giese, Claudia Jaccarino, Laura Meyer, Mary Lee Montague, Anne Norris, Judy Plummer, Mary Pat Regan, Alejandro Solano, Wendy Strachan, Siobhan Straka, Heather Turk, Michael Vines, Magnus Welsh, and Danielle Zimmerman.

Before I started on this venture, I don't think I had a full appreciation of the hard work and dedication of the people in the travel industry. I send a heartfelt thanks to the people who provided knowledge and insight into its workings: LeeAnn Campbell, John Harris, Kathy Kirk, Beth Nordyke, Cindy Fischer, Dana Forsyth, Nora Gainer, Tracey Galvin, Stephanie Leese, Patty Koehn, Richard Plank, Michael Sands, Rosemary Sollmann, Joe Yeager, and Jeannie Wysoglad.

I also thank the following group, who gave me other support and advice and contributed to my vision: Rita Dragonette, Karen Gordon, Cynthia Kallile, Sandee Kastrul, Cathleen Johnson, Gail Longmore, Laurel McGrath, Annie McLain, Ulysses Smith, Jeannie Walters, Mary Ellen Woods, Argo Tea, and the Your Plan B team.

I have never written a second edition before (or, for that matter, a first edition) and without the knowledge and support from Doug Seibold, my publisher; Ali Douglas, my illustrator; and Jamie Bright Forman, my media coach, I'd still be wondering how to do all of this.

A special thanks to my parents, Don and Carol Ameche—without them, I wouldn't be here. To my loving and growing family, Bob, Sara, Amy, Josh, and Seth—you have all enriched my life more than words can ever express. I'd like to thank my siblings and their families for their continued support.

Of course, any errors or omissions in this book are my responsibility, not anyone else's.

To all the millions of woman road warriors around the world—I hope that you find value and knowledge in this book.

Table of Contents

Introduction

It was the mid-1980s, and I was a twentysomething consultant with a Big Eight (now Big Four) accounting firm. I was told to pack my bags—I was going on the road! When you're young and just getting started in your career, the idea of going out to see the world is exciting. And, after all, consulting and traveling were (and are) synonymous. Having been in the same city for a few years with this company, I was ready for a change.

So, airplane ticket and corporate credit card in hand, I was off for a three-month assignment in Rochester, New York. Travel quickly proved to be far less glamorous than I expected. Okay, so the assignment, the city, and traveling were all new to me. I quickly discovered, though, that getting the hang of the assignment was easy compared to getting the hang of business travel. As the experience unfolded, questions kept popping into my mind; things just weren't the way they seemed. For instance:

- Why were all those people in first class while I was back in coach?
- What did that woman next to me on the plane mean when she said that her ticket cost half as much as mine? Whom did she know?
- What was this thing called the "airline lounge": a travel fraternity or sorority where only the privileged few were accepted? If so, how could I become part of this elite group?
- Why did I always find myself in a less-than-adequate hotel room? It seemed that I was always next to the elevator, below the restaurant, or across from the health club. I kept checking my back to see if I was wearing a sign that said, "New traveler; feel free to dump."
- Whom was I supposed to tip, and how much?
- Why did every trip seem to involve some unexpected event or problem that wreaked havoc on my plans, and how could I learn to anticipate and deal with those kinds of problems?

After all, I was hardly new to traveling. I had already taken many a flight, stayed in different hotels, and managed to navigate airports and schedules just fine. But for some reason, and I wasn't quite sure why, I found myself gazing enviously at other professionals who seemed to be carrying half the amount of luggage I was and behaved as if they didn't have a care in the world. I, on the other hand, was trying desperately to look as if I were composed, yet feeling totally confused and out of sorts.

Before I knew it, I had put on 15 pounds, my face was peeling because of the dryness of airplanes and hotel rooms, and I was constantly feeling bloated after getting off an airplane. As for safety, well, I knew that was just a word used to scare the inexperienced. That attitude quickly changed after my jewelry was stolen from my hotel room, and after I went through a few other similar experiences (some of which I describe in this book).

What I finally figured out was that there is a knack to this thing called "business travel." I learned how to

- travel in first class;
- get that special meal;

- ensure I didn't get stuck with less-than-adequate hotel rooms;
- keep my travel and entertainment reports up to date;
- pack only what I needed, quickly and efficiently;
- stay healthy while on the road.

Just as importantly, as part of the process I learned how to:

- be more assertive;
- ask the right questions;
- juggle the competing demands of work, home, and family;
- let my needs be known, and expect that they be met.

Some estimate that women make up more than 40 percent of today's 41 million business travelers. Although women have made great strides in making our needs known—and, at times, seeing to it that they're met—we still have a long way to go before we are treated as we should be. There may be nearly 17 million of us out there, but I am still amazed when I look around the car rental bus and find that I'm the only female on it. I wonder where the rest of us are.

Much of my education came through trial and error; much came about through talking to people with a lot more experience. Often, I wished that when I joined the firm, instead of receiving a book on how to "dress for success," I'd received a handbook on how to maneuver through the business-travel maze.

My hope is that this book will be that handbook for you. I trust it will help you conquer the challenge of domestic and international business travel, and in the process it will become less daunting and more fun. Each chapter discusses a different aspect of travel and identifies things that may not be obvious or easy to learn. There aren't many real secrets in the travel industry, but there are lots of rules and practices. Some are written and others are not. Discovering them takes time and, in many cases, experience. You can find travel frustrating and costly if you have not learned them; this book will accelerate your education.

I've been traveling consistently for most of my career, and I've learned that yes, there are tricks of the trade, or whatever other cliché you may wish to use; I tend to think of travel as being all about "playing the game" or "beating the system." My aim is to provide you with the knowledge and tools you need to navigate the process. Most of all, I want to help you find your travel voice—the one you need in order to assert yourself in traveling situations and to address the unique issues businesswomen have to face today.

Like many of us, I perfected certain techniques in working with airlines, car-rental agencies, and hotels, and even in terms of packing. Then, on September 11, 2001, the rules changed for everyone. A number of these techniques became obsolete. Gone are the days of carefree travel, with the easy access to airports, cities, and destinations that once was synonymous with business travel. Not only has the travel process become trickier and more time-consuming, but staying healthy and looking your best is also more difficult.

Throughout this book, I've tried to point out some of the areas where things have changed since September 11 and what travelers today need to be aware of in order to have the best travel experience. You will find a heavy emphasis on safety and security. But please do not assume that you should look fearfully for danger around every corner. The point is simply that you need to be alert—which means many different things when you are on the road. In fact, your aura of confidence (which I hope this book will help you create and preserve) is one of your greatest assets. Don't be afraid; be aware. You should think of business travel not as a burden, but as an opportunity to see places you may never see again. Take advantage of it.

As my own years of travel have flown by, I find that I am continuing to learn new things and perfect my various tools and techniques. As a novice, I focused on learning the basics. With a little more experience—and a lot of frequent-flyer miles—I not only attained a higher status with the airlines (more about that later in this book), but I also experienced a "rite of passage." As an intermediate traveler, I learned how to work the system; for example, I learned to use the privileges that came with that higher status (such as upgrades and freebies). As I advanced in my career, my personal and professional responsibilities changed. Although I eventually had someone to assist me with my travel plans, I found myself juggling a spouse, children, and a whole different level of responsibility at work. The guilt of leaving home coupled with my desire to do a good job created a constant tension. Business travel took on a whole new meaning.

As a result, I've tried to organize the information in this book so that you can learn tools and techniques that will help you deal with business travel regardless of the stage of your business-travel career. Each chapter features some tips that I think of as being among the less-obvious tricks of the trade used by the experienced road warrior. I've called them "Woman Road Warrior Tips." I regard these tips as the kinds of things a good friend with more experience would tell you as you embark on the business travel experience. I've also included a handy "Woman Road Warrior Checklist" at the end of each chapter that contains what I think are the most important things you should remember.

I gathered the information in this book not only from my own years of personal experience, but also from a number of true "woman road warriors" who were willing to share their stories with me, and from experienced travel-industry professionals. Remember, many people have gone before you, and while you may feel that you are alone, an entire community of woman road warriors is with you.

Introduction to the Second Edition

Welcome to the second edition of *The Woman Road Warrior*! The world of travel has experienced a great deal of change since our initial publication. Airline travel, in particular, has become more complex, and security procedures have become more burdensome. In addition, some of our enthusiastic readers (we were number one on the Amazon.com bestseller list for business travel for quite a while) have asked us to expand our focus and share the same kind of insights for international travel that the first edition offered for domestic travel. So this second edition includes both—added thoughts relating to international business travel and updates to our advice on the complexities of domestic business travel.

What's different about global travel? A lot. Distances are generally greater, and trips are longer. You may be going someplace where the native language is different than yours. So:

- You may be sitting in an airplane for a much longer time. A coast-to-coast U.S. trip takes perhaps five hours. A trip to Europe will be 6 hours or more; to Asia, 12 hours or more; to Australia, 25 hours or more.
- The food served may have been sitting in storage for hours; the seats probably won't be any more comfortable than they would be on a short flight; and the air won't be any less dry.
- You will probably need to deal with jet lag.
- Distance may require that you stay away from home longer.
- You may break into a cold sweat at the idea of packing for a two-week trip with only one or two suitcases.
- You will need to be prepared (though, like most of us, you may feel woefully unprepared) to tackle the business, social, language, and etiquette issues that will confront you in a different country and a different culture.

Nearly everyone experiences something unsettling when she travels outside her own country—especially for the first time. Even the most seasoned global traveler can have moments of doubt and uncertainty. But you can try to be prepared, and I hope this book will help you. I can still remember my first international business trip. I was a consultant heading off to Paris to work with a multinational client firm. Although I was thrilled about the opportunity, I was quite anxious that I would blunder because I didn't (and, unfortunately, still don't) know the language, and I didn't know what behavior might be expected of me. When I got off the plane, I was pretty groggy (to this day, I don't sleep well on airplanes), so I went to my hotel and promptly went to sleep—exactly what conventional wisdom tells you *not* to do. How was I to know? I was tired.

But global travel can present huge benefits:

- You can be enriched by experiencing different cultures.
- You can forge relationships with new people around the globe.
- You can take advantage of opportunities that may never be presented again.

I've tried to approach international business travel in this second edition in the same way that I approached domestic travel in the first. I want to tell not just my story, but those of other businesswomen. I also want to share more than just an American woman's perspective, so I've spoken with businesswomen throughout the world and have been able to speak with flight attendants and travel agents as well. It has been so much fun and such a pleasure to meet these women; I've learned a great deal about global travel from them. Their anecdotes, perspectives, tips, and tricks have been included in these pages.

My hope continues to be that this book will be a handbook for you. I trust it will help you conquer the challenges of domestic and international business travel. Like the first edition, this isn't a book that needs to be read from cover to cover. Each chapter discusses a different aspect of travel and is written in such a way that you can skip directly to an entire chapter or a certain section.

The world of travel constantly changes. I intend to use our website (www.womanroadwarrior.com) to provide you with even more updates, tips, and anecdotes from other woman road warriors, as well as other sources, and keep you current on the world of business travel. The website will also offer surveys. Your feedback will help educate the travel industry (after all, we *are* its customers) and will provide a constant source of other information that should be of interest to all our readers. The website will also enable you to get information about our line of practical and economical travel products, A-Way Travel Gear, which includes the A-Way Ticket Tote and Travel Treads.

Again, welcome! I hope you will find these pages informative and useful.

CHAPTER 1:

The Basics—Making Arrangements and Paying for Them

For novice travelers or those without a lot of business travel experience, even making your most basic travel arrangements can be a daunting task. Although technology has helped make all of this easier over the past decade or so, you still need to make certain decisions before the process really begins:

- How will you get from point A to point B (e.g., airplane, train, and auto)?
- How will you get around once you reach your destination?
- Where will you stay?
- What other arrangements (meeting logistics, restaurant reservations, etc.) do you need to make in advance?

And that's only the beginning—you still have to decide what and how much to pack, and then consider any additional personal factors (e.g., childcare arrangements) that might affect your plans.

Where to Start: Travel and Entertainment Policy

Your first step is to make travel arrangements. If you work for an organization, you first must find out if it has an internal travel policy. If you familiarize yourself with this policy before making any arrangements, you can save yourself time, stress, and (potentially) money. You can typically find this policy on your company's intranet site (either in the Human Resources or Travel section) or in its employee handbook.

A company's travel policy typically identifies whether your organization has any required or preferred travel agency (whether internal or external) or website, and identifies any particular travel suppliers that your organization either requires or prefers you to use—such as airlines, hotel chains, and car-rental companies. You certainly don't want to make a reservation at one hotel when your company requires that you stay at another in the same city. A travel policy may also tell you the amount of your daily (per diem) living and entertainment allowances and your company's requirements regarding certain expenses you will incur, such as personal phone calls, movies, food and drink from the hotel room minibar, and dry cleaning.

Your company's travel policy should answer questions about reimbursement of various expenses that naturally arise during the travel process. For example, airlines often charge a fee when you make a change to a flight itinerary. Your company's travel policy should tell you when the company absorbs these fees, when they are passed through to a client or customer, and when (if ever) they are your responsibility. Pam, a senior consultant with an international consulting firm, had been traveling for well over a year before she discovered, while talking to a colleague, that their firm routinely billed its clients for the fees airlines charged the consultants for changing a ticket when traveling on client business. Since Pam had been paying the fees herself, she would have saved a lot of money if she'd better understood the policy!

Your company's travel policy won't answer every question that will arise. Accordingly, you need to find the right person to call if you have a question that the travel policy doesn't answer. Finding that person should be a priority—it could be your manager, or someone in the travel department or human resources. And you may have to call different people for the answers to different questions. Don't hesitate to keep asking if the first answer to a question doesn't make sense to you, which may mean asking someone else.

Also, try to find a "travel buddy" or mentor at your company— someone who's been there for a number of years, has traveled extensively, and can help you figure out how to work within the company's travel policy. A travel buddy may also be able to guide you to the person to ask when you need help with your company's travel policy. A new consultant who is working on a large project with a seasoned traveler should ask her counterpart for clarification and assistance in understanding the company's policies. Someone who has lived with the policy is a great resource.

Janet, a director of human resources with a Fortune 100 company, recommends using some common sense—and restraint—when considering how to act in light of your company's policies. For instance:

- Your company may permit you to be reimbursed for your dry cleaning while on the road, but that doesn't mean that you should bring your entire wardrobe for cleaning every week.
- Your hotel room will probably have a minibar, and the charges will appear on your reimbursed hotel bill, but that doesn't mean the food is free.
- Your company will not appreciate constant use of expensive room service. Janet has known people who have earned reputations within their firms as "room service queens," especially when it comes to breakfast. You'd be amazed at what people talk about and how you can be harmed professionally by that kind of gossip.
- Your company may reimburse you for personal calls you make with your cell phone while traveling for business. However, you need to be careful not to abuse this policy. Thus, some of your calls to your significant other or children might best be done on your own dime. You may need to be even more careful when you are traveling internationally, because the costs may be even higher. See Chapter 7 for further discussion.

Your company's travel policy may include different rules for international travel. For example, some companies allow their employees to fly business or first class on trips longer than a certain number of hours. See Chapter 7 for further discussion.

How to Make Travel Arrangements

There are a few other things to keep in mind when you begin the process of making your travel arrangements. First, you must find a personally acceptable balance between safety and cost. The reality for many companies, especially in tough economic times, is that they may feel compelled to ask you to fly on an airline or stay in a hotel with which you are not comfortable. For instance, most hotels, especially in urban areas, require that someone pass through the hotel's lobby, including its reception desk, and through an inner hallway before getting to the door into a guest room. On the other hand, a number of hotels (particularly lower-price motels) provide access to guest rooms through doors that lead directly to the outside of the building. Many woman road warriors believe such a hotel presents a security risk and don't want to stay there, even though the cost may be significantly less. If you find yourself in this kind of situation, talk to your manager or another person you've identified as the one to call when you have a problem with the company's travel policy and see if there's a way to work out a solution. Here is a situation where your travel buddy may be able to give you some guidance as well.

Most of us, but certainly many veteran travelers, often find it difficult to balance cost-savings considerations against the need to get home to children and family. Sometimes you may need to make physical or financial sacrifices to do what you need to do in this respect. Vicki, a partner with an international consulting firm and mother of four, will often suffer a long, grueling day of travel, flying out early in the morning and returning the same day, in order to be home in the evenings with her family.

With company travel policy in hand, you can make travel arrangements in any one of four ways:

Internal travel agency. Find out if your company has an internal travel agency. If so, then your job just became simpler. An internal travel agency exists to bear the burden of making travel arrangements for an organization's employees. It can be either an extension of a company department or a separate company. It exists to serve you, and you should use it; indeed, your company may require that you use it.

Your agency should ask you to complete (and help you complete) a form called a traveler's profile. Your profile would include such information as your airline preferences, frequent-flyer numbers, passport number, seat and special meal preferences, and comparable information for hotels, car-rental agencies, and other travel services. A good agency should rely heavily on this information when making arrangements.

If you have not completed a profile, request one and take the time to complete it. Remember, it's your life that the travel is disrupting; the agency's job is to make the arrangement process easier, but the burden rests with you to let them know how they can be of service. *Therefore, being passive is not an option.*

If you have a family, you may find that there will be times when you will be traveling with one or all of your family members. You should be sure that the internal travel agency has traveler's profiles for all of them on file so that you can make arrangements faster when those times arise. Even children have frequent-flyer and passport numbers and food preferences, and the internal travel agent who has this type of information on file just has fewer questions to ask when you travel with your children.

External travel agency. If your company does not have an internal travel agency, you should consider using an external travel agency. Although similar in function to an internal travel agency, a typical travel agency is an independent company that will have customers ranging from individuals to small- to medium-sized companies. Since the travel agency you pick may have no relationship with your company, you must research the agency to make sure you pick a good one.

Agencies vary in size, which may have a direct impact on the service you receive. For instance, if you work with a small agency,

WOMAN ROAD WARRIOR TIP:

As in any business, travel agency employees vary in skill, experience, and diligence, and do not necessarily remain with one company forever. Do not hesitate to be selective. Also, be persistent in dealing with your travel agent. If you think you know of a better deal or a better way of obtaining what you want, insist that your travel agent pursue your suggestion, and consider changing agents if you are not satisfied with the results.

you may have to wait for service while the agency handles other customers. The last thing you want while you're on the phone with your travel agency is to be on terminal hold while you wait for the resolution to a problem. On the other hand, if the agency is large, you may not get the same kind of personal attention. In either case, you should try to build a rapport with one or two people from the agency you find you can count on. The closer you can get to this ideal, the more satisfied you are likely to be.

You may also want to pick a travel agency that has a particular kind of expertise. For example, if a large part of your travel will be international, make sure that the agency you pick can handle this type of ticketing. If you will be traveling frequently to a specific location that you don't know much about, ask about the agency's experience with booking airline and hotel reservations for that area.

Your travel agent should also ask you to complete a traveler's profile to keep on file. If nobody asks you to fill one out, you may want to consider whether you've picked the right agency. If the agency doesn't have its own form, take the initiative and provide the pertinent information separately. You'll find a generic example of a traveler's profile included in the appendix of this book.

I have been with the same travel agency for more than 20 years, and they not only anticipate my requests, but also look out for my interests. After all these years, I feel as if the travel agency I use is part of my business. My travel agent's phone number is in my cell phone's speed-dial; it's a click away, and as soon as she answers the phone, I begin to get results. I'm not connected to an offshore facility where I have to key in an ID number, wait on interminable hold, explain my itinerary, and, after all that, perhaps get no help at all.

I was in Europe on September 11, 2001, and flew back to the United States several days later on the first day the airports were open. During those long and troubling days, I talked to my travel agent many times, discussing logistics and options. My agent was able to look at flight availability, passenger loads, and different routes in order to help me get back home as quickly and safely as possible. If I had made arrangements by another means (e.g., the Internet or the airline), I could have been subjected to long wait times and limited options. Plus, it was comforting to talk to someone I knew so well in this circumstance. Let's face it: Traveling can be stressful at times, and having a friendly and familiar voice on the phone can make all the difference while you're on the road.

Traditionally, travel agencies derived a large part of their revenue from commissions paid by airlines on tickets sold by the agencies. As airlines continued to look for ways to save money, they first reduced and then eliminated these commissions. In order to stay in business, most travel agencies have started charging a transaction fee for making a reservation or arranging a ticket. Therefore, if you decide to use an external travel agency, be sure to ask about the fee structure. Although my travel agent charges a fee, I feel the benefits far outweigh the cost.

Online travel websites. Bottom-line, the Internet allows the traveler more control over the travel planning process. Digital technology has yielded consumers enormous information about travel choices, and websites that allow you to buy cut-rate tickets and make your own travel arrangements have exploded in growth and popularity in recent years. Internet travel bookings comprise an ever-growing share of the total. It is estimated that business travelers make up over 50 percent of air travel booked online. According to Brian, a senior executive at one of the largest travel websites, the advantages these sites offer to consumers are twofold: first, cost savings, and, second, the ability to see almost all of the available options. Traditional methods of making travel arrangements often left the consumer wondering if she had explored every possible option.

> **WOMAN ROAD WARRIOR TIP:**
>
> Not all travel websites are created equal. Some present unbiased options and others present choices based on revenue and commission deals with airlines. Not all airline options are available on broad travel websites.

Broad, travel-focused websites such as Orbitz and Expedia continue to appear, each making a different claim as to why it is better than the competition. In addition to the broad travel websites, each airline, hotel, and rental-car company has its own site.

Although each travel site is different, you can be sure of several things when you're using the Internet to make arrangements:

- Different sites will quote different prices for similar travel products.
- Transaction fees will vary significantly from website to website.
- You may find better deals (e.g., cheaper tickets, hotel rooms, car rentals) than through a travel agent or from the provider directly.
- No booking site lists every possible travel alternative (for example, the flight schedules of Southwest, AirTran and JetBlue Airlines are posted only on their own websites).
- Smaller carriers that serve specific regions may not be listed on broad travel websites.

Service providers give incentives to customers who make Internet purchases by offering them substantial discounts. Therefore, it pays to shop around.

Each travel site not only offers different prices, but also has different rules for making a reservation. You may find it more difficult to correct an error on a ticket issued through a website than on a ticket obtained through a travel agent. A word of caution: before you conduct any searches, make sure that you are doing just that—*searching*. Some sites require you commit to a purchase before you have seen all the choices and selected a specific option.

A site that does not require you to precommit to a reservation will offer you options as to providers, flight times, and costs. If you're looking for an airline ticket, remember (here's a point worth emphasizing): *Not all travel sites offer all flights*. Therefore, even if you find an acceptable flight, you should look at a competing travel site or go directly to the airline's own site to see if you can find a lower price; similar rules apply to other travel services, such as hotels. The process will only take a few minutes, and price comparison is never a bad thing.

If you decide to select a travel site's offering, you will need a credit card to book the reservation, and an itinerary will be either e-mailed or faxed to you. The itinerary will include a confirmation number, which you can use as proof that you have paid for what you bought. Many travel sites charge a small fee for processing your reservation. Also, if you are booking an airline reservation and want a seat assignment, some sites do not offer that option; you may need to call the airline directly to get an assigned seat.

The earlier you make your plane reservations through a travel website, the greater the cost savings you'll realize. It is not uncommon, however, for airlines to switch flight numbers or schedules within a month or two before a flight's scheduled departure. If a change should occur, the airline is supposed to alert the website, and the website, in turn, is supposed to alert the passenger. Unfortunately, there are times when a breakdown occurs. Jessica, an executive with a manufacturing company, experienced this situation on a domestic flight. The website did not alert her that her flight departure had changed to an earlier time. Fortunately, she arrived at the airport early enough to make the new flight time. You should always check directly with the airline before the departure date to reconfirm the flight schedule—especially if you made your reservation far in advance.

Although travel sites allow you to book several different travel-related reservations (e.g., airlines, hotel, and car rental) at the same time, each reservation is a separate transaction. This means that all of the information you need to complete your reservations (such as your name and credit card number) is not necessarily transferred from one transaction to another. Each transaction also requires a separate transaction fee, and making a series of related changes to your arrangements (such as changing your travel date, which requires you to change the dates of your flights, hotel, and car rental) may require you to pay a series of transaction fees. Booking reservations using a travel site is close to one-stop shopping, but it still requires you to hunt for good deals—particularly when it comes to fees.

WOMAN ROAD WARRIOR TIP:

When making reservations through an online travel website, consider whether you should establish a separate e-mail address exclusively for travel purposes. Travel sites may share information with other suppliers. If you have a separate e-mail address for travel, promotions and advertisements from travel suppliers will go to your travel address, not your primary account.

Direct purchases. If you don't use a travel agent or a travel site, you can contact the various travel-service suppliers (airline, hotel, etc.)

directly. You can either call the suppliers you select (almost all will have toll-free phone numbers) or use their dedicated websites. Some travelers might use the Internet to research alternatives and then make reservations by phone, but be aware that some suppliers—especially some of the airlines—have started to charge travelers a fee for making a reservation over the phone, rather than through their websites. Of course, like all airline business practices, this practice could change—the charge could increase, or it could go away—at any time, and you should pay attention.

The *Official Airline Guide* (OAG), a monthly publication available in paper or CD, lists virtually every scheduled flight on every airline in the world. OAG also maintains a website that will allow you to obtain the same information online for a fee. Other guides exist for hotels and other travel services. You may want to take the time to consider the various options offered by the guides. On the other hand, if you already know your preferences and have the time to contact each supplier directly, then you may wish to do so. You also may pick some suppliers because they sponsor or tie-in with your frequent-user rewards program. On the other hand, being brand-loyal can come at a cost—you may pay more and limit your choices.

For a summary of the pros and cons of using the different methods for securing reservations, see the appendix on page 221.

Technology and the Travel Process

Every woman road warrior has felt—and continues to feel—the positive impact that advances in technology have had on the travel process. I often wonder how we managed to survive without cell phones, PDAs, laptops, e-mail, the Internet, and the like. It wasn't that long ago that I was constantly searching for my paper ticket, hoping that I didn't lose it in my briefcase or, worse, in some place I had no chance of finding it. Now that "ticket" is stored in some airline's computer, and I can use my PDA or my laptop or both to record the numbers that will identify me and my ticket to that airline, if necessary. Data concerning hotel and car rental reservations can be kept in the same manner, and no one has to worry about losing various scraps of paper containing that information. I remember standing in long lines at the airport to check in for my flight—now I can do it almost instantly online or at an electronic kiosk. I recall constantly running to a pay phone (remember them?) to call the client, my office, or home with updates on flight delays.

Recently I had an experience that brought this into sharp focus for me. I was trying to get from Atlanta to my home in Chicago just after a heavy snowfall there (yes, that does sometimes happen in winter in the upper Midwest). Here's what unfolded:

- Because I knew that many flights would be cancelled, putting a big strain on those that weren't, I used my laptop to check in for the flight online before I left for the airport.
- On my way to the airport, I called my travel agent on my cell phone (the first of many such calls). She reserved spots for me on later flights, in case my flight was cancelled, and reserved a hotel room for me in case no flights went to Chicago until the next day.
- At the airport, I went to the airline's lounge, which has wireless Internet service. Using that service on my laptop, I kept track of the status of all the flights by logging onto the airline's website. I noticed that the airline's website posted changes in flight status even before the video monitors in the airport.
- Using the wireless service, my laptop, e-mail, and my cell phone, I was able to establish a "virtual office" at the airport, enabling me to keep up on client commitments and correspondence, as well as maintain constant communication with my travel agent and my family.

As technology continues to advance, undoubtedly those advances will change the travel process. You will benefit if you keep up with changes in technology in the travel context, just as in every other aspect of your business life.

International travel presents additional technology challenges. For example, not all cell phones will work in every country. For a more thorough review of these issues, see Chapter 7.

Methods of Travel

Until September 11, 2001, if a businesswoman needed to make a trip and her final destination was more than a few hours away, she almost always went by plane. Now, given the time needed to maneuver through the air travel process, it's not a foregone conclusion that flying is the swiftest or most convenient way to get where you're going. Increasingly, people are looking for alternative means to get from one place to another. These alternatives could include cars, trains, or even buses. Therefore, before you automatically assume you'll fly, ask yourself if it would be quicker or easier to use some other means of transportation.

When evaluating alternatives to flying, be sure that your projected travel time by air includes:

- the time to get to the airport;
- the time to wait for and pass through airport security;
- the extra time you spend in the airport because you allowed yourself more time than you needed to get through security and to the gate;
- the actual time spent on the plane;
- the time to get from the destination airport to your hotel or business destination.

Let's say you're considering flying to a destination for which the flight time is just an hour. Add the following:

- the 45 minutes it takes you to get to your home airport;
- the 90 minutes you allow yourself to wait in line and check in for your flight, pass through security, and get to the gate;
- the 60 minutes of actual flying time; and
- the 60 minutes it takes to reclaim your luggage, pick up your rental car, and get from the airport to your ultimate destination;

and you've spent more than four hours in transit for a very short (one hour) flight. And consider that this four-hour figure assumes no flight delays or difficulties reclaiming a checked bag. You need to ask yourself if it's quicker and/or easier to go a different way.

For instance, if a city is less than, say, a four-hour drive away, and you know you're going to require a rental car at your destination, it may be quicker, more convenient, and less expensive just to rent the car at home and drive it to your destination and back. In those situations, rail service can be another good option: For example, the corridor between Boston and Washington is well served by fast and convenient trains. And often trains will take you to urban stations that might be much closer to your end destination than an airport based well outside a city.

Many European and some Asian countries have efficient, convenient rail service that is considered a staple in the lives of many business travelers. For more information on this type of travel, see Chapter 7.

Paying for the Trip

Paying for business travel begins and ends with one essential tool: the credit card. Although you can pay for travel expenses with cash (except for rental cars), I don't advise it. You will either be walking around with a lot of cash in your pocket or be running back and forth to the bank or ATM.

Consider these alternatives:

- **Find out if you can get a company credit card.** A number of large companies have corporate credit cards for their employees. If this option is available to you, use it. Traveling is expensive, and if you utilize your own credit card, you can quickly reach your credit limit.

  If you use a company credit card, find out how and when payments are made and who is liable for the charges. Although the card is issued to your company, some companies will expect you to pay your bills directly and seek reimbursement when you file your expense report. If you fail to pay the bill within the credit card company's prescribed period, your name could appear on a report submitted by the credit card company to your company's senior management. Even if your company's policy provides that the company pays the bills directly, you will be legally responsible if the company fails to do so. I know of too many cases where someone with a company credit card incorrectly thought her company would pay her bills directly, but later received a notice threatening to suspend the card because of a large overdue balance. You should also avoid using a company credit card for personal items. It may be against company policy and, even if it's not, it can be confusing trying to keep the items straight.

  Whatever happens, *don't get caught on the road with a suspended credit card!* I can tell you from personal experience that you do not need to be dealing with a suspended card while juggling travel, meetings, client commitments, and other responsibilities.

- **Use a personal credit card.** If your company doesn't provide a corporate card, using your own is the next-best choice. If you do not have one, either check with your bank or obtain one from a nationally known name (e.g., Visa, MasterCard, American Express). Websites for financial institutions and credit card companies are listed in the appendix of this book.

Again, take the time to familiarize yourself with the terms and conditions, such as when the account is charged, the payment terms and credit limits, and what happens if you exceed the limits. Certain kinds of credit cards (technically called "charge cards") do not have credit limits, but do require that you pay your balance each month; typically American Express and Diners Club cards work this way. Remember that travel expenses add up quickly, so you need to be sure that if you have a credit card with limits, your limits are adequate and that your company will reimburse you quickly enough that you won't exceed them. If you think you might exceed your limits, ask your company for an advance.

Designating one card solely for business travel may be the best way for you to keep expenses straight. Some people also set up a separate checking account to pay travel expenses and receive expense reimbursements in order to keep this process cleaner. I suggest that you take no more than two credit cards with you on any trip—one for business and one for personal use. Leave any other credit cards at home in case your wallet or purse is stolen or lost. The best advice I received on my first international trip was to empty my wallet of everything except two credit cards, my health insurance card, some identification, and my airline/hotel/car-rental cards.

> **WOMAN ROAD WARRIOR TIP:**
>
> The travel industry works primarily with credit cards. A separate credit card that you use only for travel will help you keep business and personal expenses separate.

- **Use a debit card.** You use a debit card much as you use a credit card, but instead of receiving a monthly bill with an accumulation of charges, the funds used to pay for the service are immediately withdrawn from your checking or savings account. Using a debit card can deplete your personal funds very quickly while you wait for expense reimbursement. Therefore, I suggest using a debit card only as an interim or emergency solution.
- **Have expenses paid by the company, if possible.** Since airline and hotel charges are usually the largest components of travel expenses, some companies arrange to pay the costs incurred by their employees directly to the suppliers. Check with your company to see if such an arrangement is possible. When traveling internationally, this procedure comes in very handy, because you will not have to be troubled with an exchange rate. Note that car-rental agencies typically will not make such arrangements (see Chapter 4, Renting a Car).

  If your work requires billing to a client or project, the client may pay for certain expenses directly. The client may prefer to do so when the client has negotiated a special rate or other arrangement with the supplier, such as a local hotel. If your client pays any costs directly, make sure you know what your company's internal travel policy says about how those costs should appear on your expense reports.

As you decide how to pay for your travel expenses, remember that most major credit cards have rewards programs that can qualify you for goods and services if you use the card frequently. The more dollars you charge on the card, the more rewards you receive. Travel is expensive and costs add up, so using a credit card for travel will likely contribute significantly to your qualification for rewards. If you use a company credit card, you need to find out whether the company's policy specifies that the reward points earned from using the card belong to the company or to you.

Bank credit cards (such as Visa and MasterCard) have two types of programs, and you can select a card in one or the other. Some of these cards have a tie-in to an airline, under which your frequent-flyer account with that airline will be credited for using the card (usually one mile for each dollar charged), regardless of what you charge. Other bank cards simply award points to the cardholder (usually one point for each dollar charged), and then have a schedule of rewards that can be "bought" with accumulated points. The rewards are typically both travel-related and nontravel-related goods and services. Other (nonbank) cards, such as American Express or Diners Club, have very flexible reward programs. You can have your points (usually one point per dollar charged) redeemed for a credit of miles to your frequent-flyer account on any airline (although usually at less than one mile for each point), for hotel rooms, or for a wide range of other travel and nontravel-related goods and services. In addition to hotel rooms and airline tickets, I have redeemed credit card reward points for tickets to sporting events and numerous other items. If you expect to be traveling a lot, be careful to pick a credit card that has a rewards program that best fits your preferences. Because you will almost certainly be using a credit card for business travel, take advantage of the opportunity to create a solid credit rating for yourself, especially if you are at the beginning of your career. Watch for your monthly bills and make sure they are paid promptly; avoid large unpaid balances. Doing so will not only benefit you in the short run by creating a good record with your credit card issuer, but will also help you in the future when you apply for such things as a home mortgage.

Expense Reporting

It's common sense: If you work for an organization where you'll be reimbursed for your travel expenses only after you've submitted an expense report, do yourself a favor and submit your reports on a timely basis. If you're a novice, familiarize yourself with the process and determine what timely submission means. You are only hurting yourself by being late. Also, make sure you don't forget anything—it's easy to do, and you're cheating yourself. For example, it's easy to forget to include any fees you pay an airline for itinerary changes. One way to help you stay on top of your expenses is to write down each day what you spent on that day. You can help yourself by using your credit card whenever possible and by keeping receipts, even for the smallest expenditure. Elizabeth, a software saleswoman, takes a preset amount of cash on each trip and, by using her notes, memory, and receipts, reconciles all her cash expenditures and remaining cash to ensure that she can account for every dollar.

It's worth repeating again: Expenses add up quickly, and you're responsible for payment, so stay on top of them. Most people wouldn't consider giving or loaning money to their employers, but that's what you're doing if you leave something off your expense reports or don't submit them promptly. If you're a veteran traveler, you may have built up a certain rapport over the years with your administrative assistant. Your administrative assistant may be able to complete your expense reports for you, thus ensuring that you stay on top of your expenses. Vicki brings an empty envelope with her at the beginning of each trip. She writes a note on each receipt and places all her receipts in the envelope. Upon her return, she gives the envelope to her administrative assistant, who uses the contents to complete Vicki's expense report.

Woman Road Warrior Checklist

___ Obtain and understand company travel and expense-reimbursement policies.

___ Understand differences in company travel and expense policies for international travel.

___ Establish a relationship with selected travel arrangement provider.

___ Enter travel agent, airline, and hotel phone numbers in your cell-phone speed dial.

___ Identify a "travel buddy."

___ Obtain travel credit card and understand all of its applicable rules.

___ Develop method of identifying and tracking reimbursable expenses.

___ File expense reports accurately and promptly.

CHAPTER 2

Air Travel with (Relative) Ease and Comfort

Since flying has long been one of the most significant aspects of the road warrior's life, you might think air travel would be simple and easy. *Not so.*

Airports are large and confusing; flight seating is uncomfortable; the food served, if any, is tolerable at best; and delays, which can affect your ability to achieve your business objectives (after all, we are talking about *business* travel), seem to occur frequently. Something as basic and unpredictable as the weather can seriously affect your ability to plan. Even people in the industry recognize the difficulties, challenges, and travails that are still a big part of air travel. Jennifer, a travel agent for more than 20 years, reminded me that choosing a flight remains notably difficult because the maze of ticket options and the rules are so inconsistent between airlines, and are even applied differently within an airline and to passengers at different airports. If you travel outside your home country, air travel becomes even more complex (see discussion in Chapter 7).

To make matters worse, air travel has become even more burdensome in the past few years. There are two primary reasons for this. The first is widespread financial weakness in the airline industry. Many airlines are bleeding money; several have been in bankruptcy or are teetering on the edge. In order to compensate and reduce their losses, many airlines are cutting costs and trying to increase revenue. Cost-cutting measures include decreases in service (for example, elimination of food service on many flights), reductions in personnel, and reductions in flight numbers (and thus availability). Attempts to increase revenues include such measures as increased ticket prices (or decreased ticket prices to increase volume), restrictive rule changes, and additional fees for itinerary changes.

The second main reason is concern for security. Since the events of September 11, 2001 and August 2006, airport security has tightened dramatically. Although the enhanced security has been implemented for travelers' protection, we pay a price of increased delay and frustration. Prior to these events, business travelers typically arrived at the airport with just enough time to check in, walk onto the plane, stow their bags, and take a seat before the plane departed from the gate. We've all played the game to see how close to takeoff we could arrive at the gate and still get on the plane. No business traveler wanted to spend any more time than was absolutely necessary either in the airport or on the plane before departure. Now, passengers are being advised to arrive at the airport at least an hour prior to departure for domestic flights and two hours prior to departure for international flights in order to pass through security. Being able to carry on your luggage is no longer a foregone conclusion. Gone is the relatively hassle-free process that used to characterize business travel.

So now you're probably asking yourself, "How can I *possibly* get through this process with any sanity, and how do I keep up with the rules?" Keep these key points in mind:

- Give yourself plenty of time to get through the airport to your flight, and pack extra patience.
- Always arm yourself with as much information as possible.
- Make sure you understand what is and isn't required, so you can be as efficient as possible.
- Don't hesitate to refuse to accept an answer that doesn't meet your needs.

- Remember that the rules are constantly changing, so it's a good idea to stay abreast of them.
- Check for last-minute security changes.
- Stay calm and courteous at all times. The process can be very confusing and frustrating, but you'll be much more successful if you do.
- Global travelers know that there is no consistent set of rules between airlines, airports, and countries.

WOMAN ROAD WARRIOR TIP:

Airline personnel respect a true road warrior— someone who is aware of her surroundings and who stays calm and respectful even under the worst of circumstances.

Frequent-flyer Programs

It seems as if everywhere you look these days, there are reward programs for frequent users of a particular product or service. The airlines pioneered this marketing approach through their frequent-flyer programs, and the extent to which these programs have been copied in nearly every consumer industry testifies to their success.

Each major airline has a frequent-flyer program that costs nothing to join. Such programs award a member a mileage point for each mile she flies on the airline; sometimes (on ticketed first-class flights, for example), the program will award the member a multiple of the actual miles flown. Miles can be redeemed for free tickets or upgrades or both; the "cost" in miles of a ticket or upgrade depends on the destination and class of travel. Each member has an account to which miles flown are credited and miles redeemed are charged; usually, a member receives a monthly statement of activity on her account, either by e-mail or regular mail, and she can check her account status online with the airline.

The popularity of the airlines' frequent-flyer programs has led to their expansion. Now, you can also earn miles by:

- flying on a different airline that has a tie-in agreement with your airline to recognize miles jointly;
- using a credit card that has a tie-in agreement with the airline, even to buy products or services that have nothing to do with travel;

- staying at certain hotels or using certain car-rental companies or other suppliers that, again, have a tie-in agreement with your airline.

In addition to the free tickets and upgrades for miles, each airline typically awards special program status to customers who fly a certain number of miles on that airline in a year. These must almost always be miles actually flown on the airline, not just mileage points collected from credit card charges or other tie-ins or flights on another airline. Most major airlines have three program status levels. United, for example, has Premier (25,000 miles in a year), Premier Executive (50,000 miles) and 1K (100,000 miles). You can also attain these status levels by flying a specified number of flight segments (a round trip is two segments) in a year. At United Airlines, you attain Premier by flying 30 paid segments in a year; Premier Executive, 60 paid segments in a year; and 1K, 100 paid segments in a year. If you're a new business traveler, you might think that you're not likely to fly 25,000 miles or 30 segments in a year. You'll be surprised, however, at how quickly the miles and segments add up if you travel for business. After all, 25,000 miles is only 4 or 5 round trips from one coast to the other, and 30 segments are only a little more than one round trip each month. If you travel abroad, the miles add up even more quickly.

Once you reach an airline program status level, a whole new world opens up to you. Each level has certain privileges that come with the status. A member with program status will earn priority seating in certain sections of the plane, early boarding privileges, and priority standby status. Some airlines provide separate check-in counters and security lines for program status members at some airports, which can greatly reduce your time spent maneuvering through the airport.

Most airlines will allow a member with program status to upgrade to a first-class seat (when available) for a modest cost, to fly in a special coach section (usually with more leg room), and—at times—to be given more flexibility when it comes to making changes. A passenger at any level can request an upgrade to first class, but if you have higher program status, you can request the upgrade earlier, and you are more likely to obtain it. For instance, American Airlines allows a Gold member to request an upgrade 24 hours before flight time; a Silver member, 48 hours; and a Platinum member, 72 hours. Since

WOMAN ROAD WARRIOR TIP:

If you are eligible for seat upgrades, you can and should auto-mate the process, either through your travel agent or directly with the airline, so your upgrade request is made automatically, and you don't have to be concerned about making sure to con-tact the airline on time.

each plane only has a limited number of first-class seats, you can see how your chances for an upgrade increase with your status.

Teresa, the chief information officer of a Fortune 500 company and a program status member with her regular airline, specifies her upgrades even further. The travel policy at Teresa's company requires that the employee pay for the cost of any upgrades. Teresa believes that an upgrade on any flight that is under two hours is not worth the additional cost. Her traveler's profile with her travel agent reflects this rule, and thus her name will not be put on the upgrade request list for a short flight. Once you attain program status, you too must decide which upgrades and other benefits you want to pay for.

These programs are designed to promote brand loyalty, and for the most part they've helped airlines meet that objective. Most business travelers will make all of their flights on the same airline, when possible, in order to accumulate miles and attain higher program status. They also may choose hotels and rental cars in order to increase their redeemable miles.

Staying with a single airline in order to collect miles does, however, limit flexibility when traveling, and it may result in higher costs. Furthermore, considering the financial problems of some airlines and the ever-present possibility of strikes and other service interruptions, you may pay a price for being loyal to one airline. Many of us veteran road warriors can remember the havoc created when our regular airline suffered a strike. The flight cancellations, long delays, and lack of communication that we encountered drove some of us to competitors and may have changed the way we look at airlines altogether. The consequences may be worse by far when "your" airline goes out of business. And always remember that airlines have the power to change the rules governing their frequent-flyer programs (and have done so from time to time), even to the extent of discontinuing the programs entirely.

First Class or Coach?

Most airplanes have two classes of seating for domestic travel—first class and coach (or economy). If cost were no object, everyone would prefer to fly first class. First class is simply more comfortable, and the service is far better than in coach. The seats are larger; the legroom is more plentiful; drinks, alcoholic and otherwise, are available at no cost and in virtually unlimited quantities; and food is served (free of charge) on far more flights than in coach. Of course, there's a cost to all this. A first-class ticket will probably cost 50 percent more than the cost of a full-fare coach ticket on the same flight, and 5 or 10 or even more times a discounted fare on that flight. In order to keep costs down, many discount airlines have done away with first-class seating altogether.

Overseas and some transcontinental flights will have a third class of seats, called business class. Business class will have similar services to first class, but the seats are a little smaller, they don't recline as far, and the legroom is a little less. Business class ticket prices are somewhat less than first class, but still much more than coach.

Some companies allow their employees to fly first class or business class under certain circumstances. Sometimes an employee above a certain management level can always fly first class; sometimes certain employees can fly in a class other than economy if the flight is, say, overseas or transcontinental. You definitely should find out if your company has any policy of this kind (especially if you are doing a lot of international traveling). Barbara, a chief financial officer, once worked for a small company where all the employees always flew first class, wherever they went. The company felt that the improvements in morale and productivity—including the greater ease of working on the flight in first class—made the additional cost worthwhile. Most of us aren't so lucky! But it certainly doesn't hurt to ask. If you do find yourself in first class for the first time, Judy, a veteran flight attendant, says that service begins as soon as a traveler enters the cabin section. The staff will hang up your coat and offer you a drink even before takeoff.

Most companies will allow you to travel first class or business class if you pay the difference between that class and coach. Assuming you don't want to do that, the best way to fly first class or business class is by upgrading.

As mentioned in the previous section, an airline will typically make seat upgrades available to those passengers who are members of its frequent-flyer program. Unfortunately, not all upgrades are free. Usually the airline will sell "upgrade certificates" to members of the frequent-flyer program, often only those who have attained a certain program status level, at a predetermined price. A typical certificate will allow you to upgrade to first class for a flight of a certain number of miles; if your flight is longer, you can upgrade if you use more than one certificate. On the other hand, depending on your status, the price of the ticket, and the generosity of the gate agent, you may be able to upgrade without using any certificates or, occasionally, even if you haven't attained the status that entitles you to buy them. Always ask if you can upgrade and at what cost, especially if you are on a major airline, paying full fare, or have upgrade certificates. If you can upgrade without using a certificate, so much the better! I have obtained upgrades in this manner traveling internationally, although it's typically more difficult than when traveling domestically. Like a lot of things when you're traveling, success depends on a number of elements coming together at once—and luck.

Some of the airlines run promotions from time to time that allow ticketed passengers to upgrade at the gate on a "seat-available" basis for a minimal charge. Occasionally, an airline may offer this opportunity to a passenger who has not attained a status level in the frequent-flyer program. Airlines use these kinds of offers to generate revenue as well as loyalty and goodwill. Upgrading on this basis is often worth the charge. If you are offered such an opportunity, be sure to consider whether the upgrade is worth the cost in light of the length of your flight.

Finally, from time to time, airlines may have special sales on first-class seats, perhaps even making them less expensive than coach on particular flights. When

WOMAN ROAD WARRIOR TIP:

The cost of an upgrade is typically a personal expense and will probably not be reimbursed by your company. Check your company's travel policy.

you make your reservation (especially if you use a website), check the flights to find out if you can obtain a special deal on a first-class fare. Of course, don't expect the airlines to have these sales very often.

Securing a Ticket

As described in Chapter 1, you generally have four options when it comes to purchasing an airplane ticket: an internal travel agent, an external travel agent, the Internet, or contacting the airline directly (solo). No matter how you buy your ticket, it is your responsibility to make sure you get what you want at the best possible price. You need to know the guidelines that airlines use to determine what you'll pay for your ticket.

Airline tickets are available for both full (undiscounted) and discounted fares. Airlines allot a number of seats per flight to different discounted fares; the rest of the seats are full fare. The farther in advance of your flight you buy your discounted ticket, the greater the discount you are likely to find. Therefore, the best way to guarantee that you'll get the lowest fare is through careful advance planning. The more time you have to plan your trip, the more travel options and deals you will have available. Remember that your company, like every company, is more conscious about travel costs than ever.

Of course, the nature of business travel is such that you don't always have the luxury of time to plan, but when you do, take advantage of it to save money. Here are some ways:

Purchase a discounted fare. The most heavily discounted fare for a flight is usually available until 21 days before departure; smaller discounts are available if the ticket is purchased more than 14 days before departure; and still smaller discounts are available if the ticket is purchased more than seven days before departure. If you are buying your ticket close to one of these dates, check to see if there is any price difference if you go from, say, a 7-day to a 14-day advance purchase. If the difference is significant and you have the flexibility, you may want to consider postponing your departure.

Discounted fares come with strict penalties for any changes to your flight itinerary (including cancellation). These rules mean that if you have to change your flight or decide not to go at all, you may have to pay a fee or even forfeit the ticket. Each airline and indeed each ticket may have different rules, so if you buy a discounted ticket, ask what happens if you need to change your plans. Remember that some travel websites will charge their own fees for changing a ticket, in addition to whatever fees the airline charges.

Stay over Saturday night. The airlines will sometimes offer you a discounted fare if there is a Saturday night between the date of departure and date of return. The airlines use these fares to entice non-business travelers. If you are making a last-minute reservation and have the flexibility to stay over a Saturday night, you may save some money. So it's worth checking into. Of course, in deciding whether to stay over, you need to consider the value of your time. You should also check your company's travel policy, which may provide that you will be reimbursed for your hotel room and incidentals if you save airfare by staying over Saturday night.

There may be other benefits to such a stay. Deborah, a senior vice president of sales for a computer software company, is an avid baseball fan. She routinely plans a Saturday night stay when she travels to any city that has a major-league team so she can go to a weekend game in that city's ballpark. By doing so, she satisfies her love of the game while saving her company some money.

Fly at off-peak hours. Cheaper seats may be available at off-peak hours. Off-peak is generally defined as the middle of the weekday (10:00 a.m.–3:00 p.m.), the middle of the workweek (Tuesday and Wednesday), after the evening rush-hour traffic, or on Sunday mornings. If you have some flexibility, traveling at these hours can save some money.

Do not fly direct. If you have the time and the patience, you may be able to save money by flying through an airline's hub city. A hub is a city in which an airline has a substantial presence (usually based on the number of gates it controls at the airport or the volume of flights it flies there) and therefore more flights and cheaper tickets. A list of hub cities for the major airlines is contained in the appendix.

If you want to save money this way, you fly into the hub city and change planes to get to your destination, instead of flying directly. A word of caution: Some travel sites do not have the flexibility to create itineraries of this type. Most travel sites assume you want the shortest, most direct route, so if you want to explore this option, check other sources or speak directly with your travel agent or the airline. Don't forget to consider the value of your time when you think about saving money this way.

If your itinerary calls for you to fly through a hub city and change planes, ask whether there is a direct flight to your final destination when you check in for the first leg of your flight. The airline may allow you to switch to the direct flight without charge. Bridget, an attorney, was traveling with her daughter to Phoenix from Chicago. In order to save money, she had bought tickets that required a plane change in Dallas. On the return trip, Bridget asked at the ticket counter if she could instead go on a direct flight so that she could be home earlier to be with her other children. The airline granted her request, and she and her daughter arrived home three hours earlier than originally scheduled.

Break the trip up into smaller increments. This option may save money if you are traveling to multiple cities during the same trip.

As an example, let's say you start from Chicago, your first stop is Boston, then you will be flying to San Francisco, and finally back to Chicago. Since flying from Boston to San Francisco can be very expensive, consider buying two round-trip tickets—one between Chicago and Boston and the other between Chicago and San Francisco. You will then have to stop in Chicago, probably changing planes, when you fly from Boston to San Francisco, but the cost of the two round trip tickets may be significantly less than the single ticket with multiple stops.

If you buy tickets in this manner, remember the tip from the preceding section. When you check in at the airport for the second (Boston to Chicago in this example) flight, where you will have to change planes at the destination, ask the gate agent if she would put you on a different, direct flight (Boston to San Francisco). If the airline has empty seats on the direct flight and if the agent is in a generous mood, your request may be granted. I for one have had successful experiences in such situations.

Fly from an alternative (usually smaller) airport. Smaller airports located in large cities (e.g., Chicago Midway as opposed to O'Hare) or in nearby cities (Providence as opposed to Boston) often provide better deals for the traveler. These airports once were home only to the second-tier airlines, but recently more of the larger airlines have begun to occupy gates at these smaller airports as well.

Often, the same airline will charge much less for a flight to the same destination from a smaller airport than from a larger, nearby airport. The smaller, lower-price airlines often operate from the smaller airports, and the larger airlines have to compete, so you can frequently find lower fares on both. The airline's cost of operations may also be less at a smaller airport. Also, because the airports are smaller, the entire process of maneuvering through security to the gate can be easier and quicker.

Of course, there are certainly some disadvantages in going through a smaller airport. Smaller airports generally have fewer flights, so if you miss your flight or your flight is canceled, you could be stuck. They also may be slower than the larger airports in responding to weather problems, and may receive less favorable treatment from air traffic control if bad weather affects arriving flights at your destination. Smaller airports also may not provide the amenities or food choices of their larger counterparts.

Check with the airline's website. Airlines are trying to promote their websites for ticket-buying purposes, and consequently an airline may offer an itinerary on its own website at a lower price than it offers directly over the phone.

If you're flying to Las Vegas, consider a tour package. Many "tour packages" are offered through travel agents for travelers to Las Vegas, and these usually include airfare and hotel accommodations at a price that is less than the total cost of both if purchased separately. Leslie, a colleague of mine, tried to obtain a hotel room in Las Vegas at the last minute during the Consumer Electronics Show and was told that all the hotels were full. Our travel agent found her a package tour at a very reasonable cost that included airfare and a room at a hotel she would have picked for herself.

> **WOMAN ROAD WARRIOR TIP:**
>
> Not all airline schedules are available on broad travel sites. You may need to use a particular airline's website to find its schedules and book flights.

Check the discount Internet sites. There are certain websites (the best known of which may be Priceline.com) that offer heavily discounted airfares. The catch is that the traveler has little or no choice as to flight times or even as to airline. By entering your destination city, days of travel, and a price maximum, the site will provide you with flights that fit your specifications. These sites impose heavy restrictions in making travel arrangements. These restrictions may include a requirement that you accept nondirect flights, may limit the days on which you can travel, and may require that you agree to travel at any time on the travel days you select. If you can accept whatever restrictions the site imposes and you are willing to take whichever carrier offers the price in your range, you may be able to save significant amounts by buying your ticket on one of these sites.

Jennifer, the travel agent, pointed out that the airlines are constantly changing the rules for discounted fares and frequently offer special deals of various kinds. When traffic is down, the rules are relaxed and prices reduced to encourage travel. When planes are getting full, the rules are tightened and prices are raised to increase revenue. For example, some airlines have begun offering discounted one-way fares (which by definition can't require a Saturday night stay-over) in order to increase traffic. Of course, an airline can terminate a program like this at any time.

If you're flying internationally, ask your travel agent about a consolidator. A consolidator is a company that will purchase a group of tickets directly from an airline at a heavily discounted price and sell them through travel agents. See discussion in Chapter 7.

Last-minute Air Travel

No matter how hard you try to plan, last-minute arrangements are the norm in the world of business travel. Unfortunately, last-minute arrangements equate to more expensive tickets, without a lot of alternatives. Airlines do, however, make some flights available at lower fares at the last minute on some websites (including their own). For example, American Airlines posts heavily discounted fares for certain destinations each Wednesday. The fares and destinations change each week.

When you need to buy a ticket at the last minute, you or your travel agent should check the Internet to see if cheaper fares are available.

Air-Travel Paperwork

Traditionally, all airline tickets were printed pieces of paper. Today, "paperless" electronic tickets (e-tickets) are the standard for domestic travel, and airlines now charge a processing fee for all paper tickets.

Substituting e-tickets for paper tickets reduces the processing costs for the airline, and charging a fee for a paper ticket simply allows the consumer who accepts the e-ticket to receive a benefit for doing so. For the most part, tickets for international flights are also "paperless," but in some countries paper tickets are still necessary. When you obtain an e-ticket, the airline or your travel agent will fax, e-mail, or mail you a written confirmation of your reservation in the form of an e-ticket receipt and itinerary. The itinerary will show the flights on which you have a reservation and will include your ticket number and your alpha-numeric record locator.

If you are traveling on an e-ticket, you should always have proof that you've purchased a ticket. That proof can be the printed itinerary that you received to confirm your reservation. You should also note your ticket number or your record locator or both in your calendar or PDA or in your e-mail system. The airline definitively identifies you and your reservation through the record locator and the ticket number, not your name. If there is no mistake, the airline can use your name to find your ticket number and record locator, but having that information ensures that your reservation will be honored. On one trip, Vicki purchased a ticket, and for some reason, the airline's system did not register her name properly. She proved that she had a reservation and had purchased a ticket by supplying the ticket number.

In addition, be sure that the name on your itinerary or ticket matches the name on your identification and on your frequent-flyer program membership card. You don't want to get to the airport only to notice that someone has misspelled your name, thus creating problems with security—not to mention the possible loss of miles in your frequent-flyer account.

Seat Assignments

If you're lucky enough to be in first or business class, you'll normally have only the choice of an aisle or window seat. An aisle seat is easier to get into and out of; a window seat has more light and maybe a view, and will best allow you to sleep undisturbed. If you sit in an aisle seat, someone in the window seat may be climbing over you to get out; if you sit in the window seat, you'll be that someone. Generally, though, you won't have to worry about comfort or legroom wherever you sit.

Since the majority of us take most of our plane trips in coach (economy), the remainder of the discussion that follows will focus on seating options in that section of the plane. There are a few choice seats in coach:

- **Economy plus.** Some airlines have created a separate "economy plus" section in coach; they generally offer these seats to customers who have attained a certain status in their frequent-flyer programs. These sections provide more legroom between rows than the rest of the coach cabin. If you are traveling internationally and do not have the ability to upgrade but can get a seat in this section, then by all means take it. You will appreciate having the extra legroom for all those hours.
- **Bulkhead row.** The bulkhead row is the very first row of the coach cabin, right behind the wall between coach and first class. This row does have extra legroom. On the other hand, because there is no row of seats in front of it, you won't be able to stow your carry-on luggage under the seat in front of you. It will need to go in the overhead bin during takeoff and landing and will be inaccessible to you during those times.
- **Exit rows.** The exit rows are those over the wings, beside the emergency exit door. These rows provide the greatest amount of legroom and are worth asking for. If you are fortunate enough to be offered a seat in one of those rows, grab it. Sometimes a seat in the exit row will not have a seat in front of it, so you will have to store your carry-on in the overhead bin during takeoff and landing. Also, passengers in the exit rows have certain responsibilities if an emergency arises. Sometimes an airline will assign the exit-row seats in advance only to passengers with higher program status, or it will not assign them in advance at all. It never hurts to ask for an exit-row seat when you get to the gate, even if you have a different preassigned seat.

Andrea, a veteran flight attendant for a major airline, tells me that you might want to avoid sitting near the galley (kitchen) or bathrooms, especially if you want to sleep, as there is always a lot of traffic going through these areas. You will feel the impact of sitting in these locations even more during long international flights when you are trying to sleep.

Most seating rows in coach contain either five or six seats—either three on each side of a center aisle (such as in the Boeing 737 and 757 or Airbus A319 or A320) or two on one side and three on the other (such as in the McDonnell Douglas DC 9-30, 40, or 50). Some larger planes (such as Airbus A300, Boeing 767 and 777, or McDonnell Douglas DC 10) have rows of seven, eight, or nine seats—two aisles, with three or five seats in the center between the aisles and two on the outside of each aisle. And some smaller planes (such as Canadair Regional Jet 700 or CRJ) have two seats on each side of a center aisle. The website SeatGuru.com includes detailed seat layouts for all plane types by airline. You can also find airplane seat layouts on airline websites and on the websites maintained by the aircraft manufacturers (such as Boeing and Airbus). SeatGuru will also give you online advice regarding the desirability (or lack thereof) of any particular seat on the plane.

The relative benefits of the aisle and window seats are the same in coach as in first class. But in almost every row in coach there are also the dreaded middle seats, generally perceived as the least comfortable seats in each row. As Shawn, a customer representative for a major airline reminded me, 33 percent of coach seats on most airplanes are middle seats, so it's inevitable that you'll be sitting in one of them at some time. When that happens, try to make yourself a little more comfortable by putting your carry-on luggage in the overhead bin above your seat instead of under the seat in front of you, to give yourself a little more legroom. And not all middle seats are created equal—the middle seats in economy plus, the exit rows, and the bulkhead rows have the advantages described above.

Seat preference is an individual choice and one that may change over time. When I first started traveling, I preferred an aisle seat because I wanted to be the first one off the airplane. Now, I prefer the window; I like the natural light and looking out the window and getting into my seat and not moving (unless, of course, it's a very long flight). Other travelers have other reasons for preferring certain seats:

- Janet won't sit in the first three rows of any airplane. She has found that the people who board the airplane first tend to store their luggage in the overhead bins closest to the door, and she likes to have her luggage by her seat. Thus, she has found that she's more likely to find space in the overhead bin near her seat if she sits farther back in the plane. Janet also prefers the extra legroom in economy plus and will voluntarily sit in the middle seat in economy plus (but not in the first three rows) instead of an aisle or window farther back.

- Melinda, a chief marketing officer for an advertising company, prefers an aisle seat in the front of the plane. Melinda is claustrophobic, but her job demands that she travel on airplanes. She somewhat compensates for this condition by trying to get off the plane as quickly as possible.
- Teresa's preference is a window seat. Experience has taught her the hard way that yes, just as the flight attendants remind you before every flight, the overhead bins *can* open unexpectedly during flight, especially in turbulence, and things can drop on your head.

On most airlines, you can request and obtain a seat assignment at the time you buy your ticket. If you can, do it. Recently, however, some of the large airlines have begun issuing advance seat assignments only to members of their frequent-flyer programs, often only to those passengers who have attained a higher status level. Not all airlines follow this rule; check while making your reservation. But you can almost always get an advance seat assignment if you have attained a higher status level and will have more opportunity to change to a more desirable seat at the airport ticket counter or at the gate.

A few additional tips to keep in mind:

- Seats in the last row of a Boeing 737 do not recline.
- Seats in the exit rows on certain wide-body planes (i.e., Boeing 757, 737-200 or Airbus 319) typically have only two seats instead of the standard three, which means there is no middle seat.
- The noisiest part of the plane is in the rear, near the engines.
- The row of seats over the wings, even if it is not an exit row, almost always has a little more legroom. It is also in the most balanced part of the plane and, if you are in that row, you are less likely to feel turbulence.

As with all air travel, the earlier you book your flight, the more seat choices you will have.

Southwest Airlines does not preassign any seats on its flights; rather, seats are assigned on a first-come, first-served basis. Southwest will issue you a boarding card with a letter (A, B, or C) when you check in for your flight on the Southwest website, at the airport electronic kiosk before you

> **WOMAN ROAD WARRIOR TIP:**
>
> Some airlines do not assign seats for up to 30 percent of the ticketed passengers on their flights. However, higher status members of their frequent-flyer programs typically get seat assignments.

enter through security, or at the airport check-in counter. Each passenger holding a boarding card with a particular letter boards the plane with the rest of the group holding cards with that letter. The earlier you check in, the better chance you'll get the coveted A card and the chance to board first. You can sit in any seat that is empty when you get on the plane. The earlier you obtain your card, the earlier you board the plane and thus the more seat choices you will have.

Getting a seat assignment is not the end. There are a number of other things you need to know about seat assignments:

Seats are forfeited 30 minutes prior to departure for domestic flights. If you have not checked in for your flight and received your boarding pass at least 30 minutes prior to scheduled departure (though this is the most common deadline, each airline has its own—some shorter, some longer—check to make sure you know the deadline for your flight), the airline may take away your assigned seat even if you are holding a ticket. Since the events of September 11, 2001, this rule is being strictly enforced. If you show up late for your flight and have forfeited your seat, your name will go to the bottom of the standby list, which means that you will get a seat only if one is available when everyone ahead of you on the list receives a seat. If there aren't enough seats for everyone, you won't be allowed on the plane.

This rule is enforced regardless of your program status with the airline. Therefore, don't assume that just because you have a higher program status you'll get special treatment if you're late. If you are late and your seat has been forfeited, you may go to the top of the priority list for open seats for the next flight out, but the airline won't hold your seat indefinitely. If you know you will be tight on time, check in for the flight on the airline's website before you leave for the airport if you can. If you don't check in online and you are late to the airport, try to check in at an electronic kiosk immediately to help yourself avoid seat forfeiture.

If you are not on the plane when the gate agent issues the final boarding call, your seat may be forfeited, even if you have checked in on time and have been issued a boarding pass. The airlines reserve the right to give your seat away to a standby passenger if you are not on the plane when the final boarding call is issued. Even if the plane isn't full, the doors may be closed, and the flight may leave without you.

If availability allows, you can always change your seat assignment. A request to change your seat assignment can continue until you are on the plane. If you want to change seats, continue checking with the gate agent regardless of the first answer you are given. Remember that passengers who have not checked in 30 minutes prior to departure will lose their seats, which are then reassigned. Although priority goes to those on the standby list, additional seats are often left open. Therefore, keep checking. Even after you're aboard and the doors have been closed, you can still switch your seat if space allows.

Having a reservation for a particular flight does not necessarily guarantee you a seat. I know of at least two airline practices involving seat assignments that create stress. First, flights are routinely overbooked, which means that tickets are sold to more passengers than can fit on the plane. Depending on the time of day, the airlines anticipate that between 2 and 10 percent of the ticket holders for a particular flight will not show up. If their calculations are correct, the passengers who do show up will fill, but not overfill, the plane. At the same time, as noted above, the airlines will hold back up to 30 percent of the seats and will not assign them to ticket holders in advance.

Sometimes the number of no-shows is less than expected, and more passengers show up than the plane can hold. For example, during school spring-break periods, flights to warmer destinations such as Florida and Arizona do not necessarily experience the typical number of no-shows. Although the airlines ask for volunteers to surrender their seats under these circumstances, you could be bumped from your flight even though you have a ticket for it if not enough people volunteer. If you don't get a seat on your reserved flight, the airline will put you on the next available flight, on standby if the flight has no seats but ahead of any other standby passengers for that flight. Thus, having a preassigned seat is very desirable so you can be sure of getting on the flight for which you have bought your ticket.

If you do not receive a seat assignment when you make your reservation, keep calling the airline (or have your travel agent call) to ask for a seat assignment. If you do not have luck with the reservation agent on the phone, ask to speak to a supervisor. If you have not received a seat assignment 24 hours before departure, you must wait until you arrive at the airport. If you have not been assigned a seat before you show up at the airport, you will be assigned one of the unassigned seats (if any) when you check in or at the gate. Passengers without preassigned seats generally receive seat assignments in the order in which they check in for the flight. If you do not have a preassigned seat, get to the airport and check in as early as you can, and if you do not receive a seat assignment upon check-in, go directly to the gate. You will be less likely to be bumped from your flight and more likely to have a wider range of seat choices.

> **WOMAN ROAD WARRIOR TIP:**
>
> Monday-morning flights are typically filled with business travelers. The airlines also have their most senior personnel working the morning shift. Morning travel allows you to work with the most senior staff and gives you further flexibility and choices if you do not get on your original flight.

Navigating the Airport

Attention to airport security has increased tremendously since the events of September 11, 2001 and August 2006. Gone are the days of easy and unlimited access to airline terminals. Now, only ticketed passengers who have checked in for their flights are allowed past the security checkpoint in the terminal. Someone who comes with you to the airport will not be able to accompany you to the gate or to any place beyond the security checkpoint—which generally includes most airport retail shops and restaurants.

Passengers face longer lines at baggage check-in (whether it's curbside or airline terminal check-in), at the security checkpoints leading into the gates, and at the gates themselves before boarding. Unfortunately, there is no formula for making this process easier. The waiting time, and sometimes even some of the procedures, are inconsistent between airports.

You might think that the larger airports, with more traffic, would have longer delays, but the smaller airports have limited space and therefore only a certain number of security bays, so delays are sometimes longer than at bigger airports. The time of day also has a direct impact on how quickly traffic flows. Peak times (and longer lines) are early morning and early evening. One thing you can count on: As soon as you have it figured out, the process will change. If you fly often with one airline through one airport, you may be able to predict how long it will take you to get to the gate, but you still cannot be too cautious about allowing yourself enough time.

> **WOMAN ROAD WARRIOR TIP:**
>
> The security lines at a smaller airport may be longer than you expect.

CHECKING IN

Most people check their bags, if they check them, when they check in for their flight and obtain their boarding pass (the piece of paper which allows you through security and, if you have obtained an assigned seat, onto the plane). You should be aware, however, that in certain circumstances, some airlines have established a deadline for checking luggage that is farther in advance of flight time than the deadline for simply checking in for your flight. For example, in certain airports some airlines require that you check your luggage 45 minutes before flight time, even though you may be allowed to obtain your boarding pass up to 30 minutes before flight time. If you don't check your luggage on time, you may not be allowed on the flight. Thus, if you think you might be cutting it close, try to pack so you can carry all your luggage on the plane. In any event, you should check with the airline regarding the applicable deadlines.

If you are holding a reservation and a ticket for your flight, you can check in, check your bags, and get your boarding pass in one of the four following ways:

Airline website. Most airlines now allow you to check in for your domestic flight and get your boarding pass over the Internet up to 24 hours before your flight if you are a member of their frequent-flyer program. If you use this service, you simply go to the airline's website, enter the relevant information, and print out your own boarding pass. Then, when you arrive at the airport, you go directly to security (assuming you do not have luggage to check). If you checked in using the airline's website and are now planning to check luggage, go to the kiosk located at the ticket counter where you can go to print luggage tags and have the luggage processed by airline personnel. If you are going to use this type of service, be sure to arrive at the airport well before the luggage cutoff time, which is usually about 45 minutes prior to departure. Betty, a seasoned traveler, got caught in traffic coming out of New York City on her way to Kennedy Airport and was stuck in a long line to check her luggage and print off the luggage tag; she missed the deadline to check her luggage and thus missed her flight.

Check-in kiosk. Nearly all airlines now have automated check-in kiosks for passengers traveling on e-tickets. Most such kiosks are located near or at the ticket counters (some kiosks for passengers checking bags and others for passengers with no checked bags), while others are located elsewhere in the airport. To use these kiosks, you insert a credit card, your frequent-flyer card or any card with a magnetic strip that identifies you to begin the process. Follow the prompts to access your reservation record and print out a boarding pass, which will confirm your seat assignment if you have one and which may assign you a seat if you don't. Kiosks adjacent to the ticket counter will print out a tag for any luggage you want to check. The tag is printed behind the ticket counter, where an airline agent should be standing. The agent will attach the tag to your luggage and take it or direct you to take it to be x-rayed (and possibly searched) and loaded on the plane.

The check-in kiosk allows you to check in for your flight and obtain your boarding pass, generally without standing in line, and may be especially valuable if you're running late and are close to the 30-minute deadline to keep your preassigned seat (especially if you don't need to check any luggage). Remember that some e-ticket kiosks are next to the ticket counters, but the lines at the kiosks should be much shorter than the lines at the ticket counters.

Curbside check-in. If you use curbside check-in, you normally get out of the vehicle that brought you to the airport and check your bags with a skycap at the curb in front of the terminal from which your flight is departing. You need to show the skycap your paper ticket, or your itinerary receipt if you hold an e-ticket, or—if you checked in online—your boarding pass, and your personal identification. Curbside is generally quicker than the ticket counter check-in, and the lines are usually shorter. Passengers are now charged $2 per bag to use curbside check-in. If you use this service, don't forget to tip the skycap. He supplements his income with tips.

Most airlines now also allow you to check in for your flight and obtain your boarding pass when you check your luggage with the curbside skycap, if you haven't already gotten your boarding pass online. If you're flying on an airline that won't allow you to do this, you can still check your bags with the skycap at the curb, but will then need to check in separately for the flight and obtain a boarding pass at a check-in kiosk or at the ticket counter before proceeding through security to the departure gate.

Ticket counter. If you use the airline's ticket counter in the airport, you can check your bags and check in for your flight and obtain your boarding pass at the same time. Unless you're traveling on a paper ticket, the airline agent at the counter will normally need only your personal identification in order to complete this process. Since a number of different ticket transactions (to purchase a ticket or change a ticket, as well as check-in) can be completed at the ticket counter, the

WOMAN ROAD WARRIOR TIP:

If you are checking your bags and have an itinerary that requires you to change airlines, find out if you will have to retrieve your bags from the first airline during your layover and recheck them with the second airline. Airlines will exchange luggage with other airlines only if they have a reciprocal baggage-handling agreement, and not every airline has such an agreement with every other airline. Find out in advance; don't be surprised when you get to the airport.

lines tend to be longer, and the entire process can take more time than the curbside or kiosk options. If you find a long line at the counter, consider using a check-in kiosk, or even going back outside to curb-side check-in. A number of airlines have a special line for passengers traveling in first class or for those members of their frequent-flyer program that have attained a higher status. These lines tend to be shorter and move faster.

If you are flying outside the United States, different rules apply. For international flights (which for U.S. passengers now include trips to Canada, Mexico, and the Caribbean) flight check-in requires a trip to the ticket counter, where you will need to show your travel documents (passport and/or visa) and will obtain your boarding pass before you proceed through security.

LUGGAGE: TO CHECK OR NOT TO CHECK

Prior to the events of September 11, 2001, checking your luggage on a typical business flight would be the exception, not the rule; you would carry everything onto the plane if you could. Nobody liked to wait at baggage claim for her luggage and take the risk that the airline would abuse it or lose it. Most people, myself included, still prefer to carry on luggage when it is practical. Now, however, because of the rules regarding how much and what you can carry on, it may make more sense to check your luggage. On the other hand, a requirement that you check your luggage for your flight earlier than you need to obtain your boarding pass may be an incentive to carry on all your luggage.

You are only allowed to carry two bags onto the plane. Before the events of September 11, 2001, this rule was widely ignored; now it is rigidly enforced. A purse is considered a carry-on item—which means that if you have a briefcase, a purse, and a suitcase, you are over the limit. Of course, you can put your purse inside another bag, but only if you have room without making your other bag bulge too much to be carried on. According to Shawn, this is a Federal Aviation Admin-istration rule, and airlines can be assessed a fee for not enforcing it.

Even if you pack lightly to avoid checking your luggage, you still must be sure that you do not have anything that can go on the plane only if it's checked and not carried on. Since August 2006, the list of restricted items that you can't carry on has grown enormously, and all checked luggage is still being x-rayed and subject to search. See

Chapter 6 for a more in-depth description of what you can and cannot carry on, and what you should do to be sure your bags are ready to be searched.

A luggage tag is produced for each checked bag. The tag shows the destination, flight number, and passenger's name. Whoever is checking your luggage should attach part of the tag to the bag (it usually wraps around the handle) and attach the other part (the receipt portion, with matching information) to your ticket. Be sure you keep the receipt portion in case you need it to claim your luggage at your destination or trace it if it is lost.

WOMAN ROAD WARRIOR TIP:

If you are checking your luggage, put a copy of your itinerary in each checked bag. If the baggage tag comes off (as occasionally happens amidst the handling of millions of suitcases), the airline will find your itinerary when it opens the bag in order to try to figure out what to do with it, and it can then send the bag along to you.

When you check your baggage, make sure that the destination city listed on the tag is really your destination. Lorrin, an owner of a women's clothing shop, was on a flight headed for Boston, her final destination, with a stop in Hartford. She looked at the luggage tags that the agent had attached and found that the bags were headed only for Hartford, and not for Boston. Fortunately, she caught the mistake before the bags disappeared from sight.

When you are traveling internationally, you will find it more difficult to avoid checking your luggage. International trips are usually longer than domestic, so you might need more clothing than will fit in a carry-on bag. See Chapter 7 for a discussion of this subject.

IDENTIFICATION

Before boarding a plane, anyone over 18 years of age will be required to show picture identification several times: at curbside or the front counter, if you go to either; at the terminal security checkpoint; and (sometimes) just before you board the plane, as you present your boarding pass. The most commonly used pieces of identification are driver's licenses, passports, and state identification cards. Whichever you prefer to use, your picture identification must meet the following criteria:

- it has been issued by a government agency;
- it includes a picture of you;
- it hasn't expired and won't during your trip;
- it should identify you by the same name as the name on your ticket (security personnel are becoming more rigorous about checking this); and
- it should be signed. If your identification is not signed, you may be asked to sign it and also to provide additional identification.

Because you show your identification so many times throughout the airport, be sure you keep it in the same place after each showing, so you know exactly where to reach for it the next time you're asked for it. It's always awkward and time-consuming when you have to fumble around to produce it, especially if you have to set down an armful of carry-on bags to hunt for it while other travelers wait behind you. Consider using something like the A-Way Ticket Tote (www.awaytravelgear.com) to hold your ticket and identification.

It's also not a bad idea to carry two different forms of identification with you—perhaps a driver's license and a passport. If you lose or misplace one, you'll still have the other. Lorrin obtained a state identification card, which is different from a driver's license, to use only for air-travel identification. That way, if she loses or forgets the state identification, she will still have her driver's license. And don't forget that a valid driver's license is necessary to rent a car. You don't want to arrive at the car rental counter to find that you dropped your driver's license on the floor of some distant airport. If you are carrying your passport, always keep a photocopy back at home in case you lose it while you are traveling. See the discussion in Chapter 7 about passports and what to do if you lose yours.

SECURITY

In order to get into the passenger terminal, everyone has to pass through the security checkpoint. At certain times of the year and certain times of the day these lines can be quite long and frustrating.

Give yourself plenty of time to get through them. It is not uncommon for a number of international flights to be scheduled to leave almost simultaneously, making the queue at security quite long.

If you are late to the airport and find that you may miss your flight because of the length of the security line, go to the front of the line and explain your situation to the attendant. He or she may let you pass through without waiting at the end of the line. Don't wait until it's too late, hoping that the line will move fast enough. Remember, though, that this approach isn't foolproof, especially for international flights. Many of the people at the end of the line may be trying to make the same flight you are, or other flights leaving at about the same time.

WOMAN ROAD WARRIOR TIP:

Certain airports will have a separate security line for those travelers who have reached a higher status in the airline's frequent-flyer program and for first-class passengers flying on domestic and some international flights. These lines tend to be shorter than the average airport security line.

Anything and everything is subject to search when you go through the security checkpoint. These security searches require, at a minimum, having your carry-on bags x-rayed on the conveyor, and being required to walk through a metal detector. It may also require having your bags hand-searched by one guard while you stand with your arms and legs extended as another guard passes a metal-detecting wand over the outside of your body (including head and feet), and possibly even pats you down. More thorough searches have become increasingly common since the events of September 11, 2001.

Certain security procedures apply to everyone, and by now, most regular air travelers are very familiar with the post-9/11 security-checkpoint rituals. Before you walk through the metal detector, you must place all of your luggage and your coat on the conveyor belt to go through the x-ray machine. You must also empty your pockets of all metal objects and place the contents in one of the plastic containers provided in order for these to be run on the conveyor belt through the x-ray machine. I often take off any belt with a metal buckle. Your laptop computer, if you're carrying one, must be removed from its case and placed in a separate plastic container to go through the x-ray machine as well. You must also remove your shoes and place them on the conveyor belt or in a plastic bin for x-ray. Most women I know cringe at the idea of walking barefoot on the airport floor. Currently, you can wear socks through security but I always manage to step into something wet and I'm afraid I'll slip and fall. I wear A-Way Travel Treads (www.awaytravelgear.com), which are washable travel socks with a nonslip waterproof sole (just what every woman road warrior needs).

I always put my purse and laptop on the belt last, so I can watch them until they pass through the metal detector and will be waiting for them when they emerge from the x-ray machine. I have heard of too many instances of items being stolen off the x-ray machine belt while someone's back is turned. Andrea, a flight attendant, takes her coat and shoes off before going through security. She places her sweater or coat over her purse—she wants to make it as difficult as possible for someone to take off with any of her items.

Since August 2006, the Transportation Security Administration (TSA) has required that liquids and gels (excluding prescription medicines and baby formula and milk) in carry-on luggage must be in containers of no more than 3 ounces each, all of which must fit into a single one-quart zip-top bag. You must remove this zip-top bag from your carry-on luggage and allow it to pass separately on the conveyor through the x-ray machine. If you are traveling internationally, you should check on the security procedures for the country or countries of your destination to make sure you can comply. You don't want to miss your flight because something you absolutely need at your destination has to be in your checked luggage,

> **WOMAN ROAD WARRIOR TIP:**
>
> You are within your rights to say that you do not wish to take off your shoes or walk through the metal detector for health or other reasons. If that is the case, you will be subjected to a hand search, and your carry-on bags will also be hand searched.

and you made it all the way to the front of a long security line before you found out.

Once you get through the metal detector, security may request that you turn on your computer and perhaps your cell phone or other electronic device before you are allowed to proceed, to demonstrate that these are actually working machines.

If you are one of the "lucky" ones who set off the metal detector or are just randomly picked for further search, you should try to get your wallet or purse to ensure that it will not be lifted off the x-ray belt when nobody is looking. Ask the security guard to allow you to retrieve these items before continuing, or ask him/her to do it for you.

Always be patient and follow orders. Additional searches may be trying on the nerves and uncomfortable—there's nothing pleasant about a stranger going through your belongings and waving a wand over your body—but they are harmless.

The Airline Lounge

The airline lounge is the one facility that can make your navigation of the airport a little easier and your stay a little more comfortable. Most of the major airlines maintain a private club or lounge at each major airport they serve. United has its Red Carpet Club; American has its Admirals Club; Delta has its Crown Room Club; and so on. Unlike the frequent-flyer rewards program, club membership is not free; the airline charges an annual fee, although a rewards-program

WOMAN ROAD WARRIOR TIP:

If you work for an organization that has a formal travel and entertainment policy, check to see if the policy allows the cost of the club to be a reimbursable expense. If not, but you are a senior member of the organization, check to see if you can obtain an exception. If your company will not reimburse you, but you are a member anyway, do yourself a favor: If you see your boss or a senior member of your company waiting at the gate when you are at the airport, ask her if she wants to join you in the lounge. Club rules typically allow a member to bring up to two guests.

member who has earned higher status may receive her membership at a discount. You can join a club by simply walking in and paying the annual fee with a credit card, by applying online, or by completing the application you can find in the airline magazine on your flight or on the airline's website. The fees are not cheap—generally they run around $400-500 per year—but I have always found it to be worth the cost. A list of the major airline club lounges and their locations is in the appendix.

These lounges provide comfortable furniture with telephones, workstations (usually with Internet or wireless connections), meeting rooms, fax machines, and similar equipment. They also furnish drinks, light snacks, and hors d'oeuvres. If you want to relax, you can watch television or read the newspaper (various papers are provided free). You can make changes to your itinerary or seat assignment at a counter in the lounge.

If you are a frequent traveler with a particular airline and are typically traveling through major airports, membership may be worth the cost. The usefulness of these memberships has only increased since the events of September 11, 2001, because travelers are now required to arrive at the airport so far in advance of their flights. The more time you spend waiting to board your plane, the more attractive waiting in the lounge will be. Janet thinks of her membership as sort of an insurance policy. She never knows when she'll be stranded at an airport because of bad weather or other flight delays that may affect many passengers, and she would rather sit in an airport lounge than try to find a seat at a gate in a crowded airport. If you do not travel enough to justify the yearly membership fee, most airline lounges now offer a daily rate. A discussion of lounges for the international traveler can be found in Chapter 7.

WOMAN ROAD WARRIOR TIP:

Some airlines have special lounges for those veteran travelers who are at the highest program status of an airline's award program (such as United's 1K or American's Platinum). These special lounges are very similar to the regular airport lounges but are less crowded and provide even more attentive service.

You may need to present photo identification along with your membership card in order to enter most airport club lounges. The airlines have found (surprise!) that membership cards have been passed around to relatives and friends of the members.

Boarding

Once you have passed through security, there are several ways you can spend your time, depending on how long you have before your flight departs.

If you are about to get on a long flight, you might walk around the concourse. If you don't like your seat assignment and want to try to change it, or if you don't have a seat assignment, you should probably go to the gate as soon as possible, check in, and then take your walk.

Because you often don't know how much time you will have at the airport, you might consider having some snack food, such as dried fruit, protein bars, or—my favorite—chocolate bars in your purse or carry-on bag for emergencies. Some airports have added amenities beyond the security gate because of the time passengers now need to spend in the airport before boarding, so if you have extra time, you might want to explore some of these. These amenities can be rather elaborate, such as health clubs, spas, and other recreational facilities. If you expect to spend significant time in the airport, you might check in advance to see what is available and plan accordingly. Our website (www.womanroadwarrior.com) contains a list of amenities for businesswomen at major airports.

WOMAN ROAD WARRIOR TIP:

Fight dehydration: bring something to drink with you on the airplane. One major airline suggests that its flight attendants drink one liter of water for every hour of flying. Water is just as important for passengers.

If you don't have any bottled water to take with you onto the plane, you should buy some. You may want to make some other purchases and take care of other needs (such as food or something to read). Remember that the new TSA rules will not allow you to carry bottled water or other drinks through security, so you will probably want to buy some after you pass through. The longer the flight, the more water you need. Hold on to your receipts; there have been times (especially for international travelers) when the gate agent has asked to see the receipts for purchases of drinks to verify that they were purchased after passing through security before the passenger carrying them could board the plane.

Generally, it is best to be at the gate, boarding pass in hand, when the attendant announces that boarding will begin. Most airlines divide the passengers into boarding groups, with each passenger's boarding pass showing the group to which she has been assigned. The gate attendant announces when each group is permitted to board the airplane.

Many travelers do not like to get on the plane early, preferring to sit in the waiting area until the last possible moment. I recommend, however, that you board the plane as soon as you can, especially if you have any carry-on luggage. Remember that all carry-on luggage must be either stowed in the overhead bin or under the seat in front of you. Only the smallest of suitcases will fit under an airplane seat, and therefore most carry-on bags must go in the overhead bin. Most passengers have at least one carry-on bag to store in the overhead bin, and generally there is not enough space to hold everyone's bag. Bin space becomes even scarcer during winter—when everyone is stowing a heavy coat—and during the holiday season—when many passengers are carrying gifts.

If all the overhead bins are full when you try to stow your belongings, your bag will be taken by the onboard flight attendant and checked as if you had checked it at curbside, and you will wait for it at your destination. The sooner you board the plane, the less likely it is that the overhead bin will be full when you want to put your bag in it.

WOMAN ROAD WARRIOR TIP:

Travelers who have achieved a higher frequent-flyer program status typically may board the plane with the first boarding group, regardless of where their assigned seats may be. Take advantage of this privilege, especially when the flight is crowded and overhead-bin space is at a premium.

When you move toward the entrance to the plane, take out your boarding pass. You will need to present your boarding pass to the gate agent before you board the plane. More and more airports only require that you show your personal identification at the security checkpoint and not at the gate, but be prepared with your identification in case your situation is different.

After you present the boarding pass, the agent will normally tear it and give you back the stub or put the boarding pass through a reader and then give it back to you. If you are a member of the airline's frequent-flyer program, keep the boarding pass or the stub so you can check your monthly statement of miles flown or your account online and be sure you receive credit for this flight. If the airline makes a mistake and does not record the credit for the miles, the boarding pass or stub can help you correct the error. The stub may also be part of the documentation you need for expense reimbursement. Or it can double as a bookmark if you need one!

Once you walk on the plane, stow your carry-on luggage, take your seat, and fasten your seatbelt. If you have a lot of things to stow, get out of the aisle first and then put your items away. Flight attendants say that they can always spot an experienced traveler by how efficient she is during the boarding process. Passengers who block the aisle while they get out of their coats, arrange their seats, and stow their carry-ons can be a frustration to everyone else waiting to board.

If your luggage has wheels, turn the luggage so the wheels go in first and are to the back of the overhead bin. More items will fit in the bin if the wheels are turned in this direction. Pamela, a seasoned woman road warrior I know, recently learned this trick from a fellow passenger. She was surprised that there were still tricks for her to learn after all these years of traveling!

Remember that you cannot use your cell phone during flight, and different airlines have different rules about when in the flight process (at the gate only, on the ground only, etc.) you can use your cell phone. If you need to make a call, do so early

> **WOMAN ROAD WARRIOR TIP:**
>
> Each airplane model is different. Therefore, when you get on the plane, look around and figure out where the exits nearest your seat are located.

so you can complete it before the flight attendant announces that cell phones must be turned off.

Even before you sit down, take note of where the exits are on the plane, and make sure you know what's where. Especially if you're unfamiliar with the particular plane you're on, pay close attention to the flight attendant's safety announcement. Since the events of September 11, 2001, it has become even more important to know your exit strategy. It takes a matter of seconds and in the unlikely event that something happens, it could save your life.

Flight Comfort

Airplane flights are by nature uncomfortable. Passengers sit in narrow, firm seats; have little or no elbow or legroom; breathe recycled, dry air; and for much of their flight, are strapped into their chairs.

There are some things you can do to make your flight as comfortable for yourself as possible. For example, grab at least one pillow out of the overhead bin when you board the flight, to use as a head pillow or to place in the small of your back for additional support or to place under your feet to relieve pressure. Joanne, a flight attendant with a major airline, brings her own small pillow with her when she travels so that she will be sure to have one, no matter how crowded the flight; she also likes having something comfortable and familiar of her own while she's traveling. Also, take one of the blankets in case you get cold (it is generally not regarded as proper etiquette to remove the blanket from the sleeping person in the seat next to you). Domestic flights (unlike international flights) do not have a blanket and pillow for each passenger. Be sure to bring any additional personal items with you onboard that will make the flight more comfortable.

I have found that these steps somewhat compensate for the uncomfortable nature of airplane seats. Remember, however, that your definition of being comfortable may be very different from the airline's. The airline primarily wishes to complete the flight safely, as it should, and will not worry about your comfort as much as you will.

Every road warrior has experienced the discomfort that occurs when the person in the seat in front of her reclines his or her seat as far as possible. When that happens, you feel almost as if that person has laid his or her head in your lap. You can show your sophistication as a traveler by being sure you recline your seat only partially, or better yet not at all, and not causing discomfort to the person behind you. Unfortunately, you'll benefit only when the person in front of you is as sophisticated and courteous as you are.

WHAT TO WEAR

Business attire has changed enough over the years so that one can look professional and be comfortable at the same time. Take the time to choose carefully the type of clothing and shoes you'll be wearing on the flight. For better or worse, travelers—especially women—are treated better and more deferentially if they are dressed well.

Vicki always dresses in business attire when she travels. She has found that she is treated with more respect, and she says that she wants to be sure she's ready for anything that happens. For example, if her checked luggage is lost, she can wear her travel clothes to a business meeting the next day. Danielle, an attorney with the U.S. Attorney's office, always wears at least business casual when traveling. She finds that if you dress for first class, you're more likely to end up there. Also, you just never know when you'll run into someone you wouldn't want to see if you're not well dressed.

Still, be sure that dressing well doesn't come at the cost of being uncomfortable. Travel often produces strange situations where the wrong clothing affects your comfort. Teresa was once on a plane that required an emergency landing and then an evacuation. Everyone had to slide down the emergency-exit slide. Teresa was wearing a skirt and found that it wasn't the most practical clothing to have on as she slid down the emergency slide. That was hardly a predictable outcome of her flight, but since that day, Teresa has sworn to wear a pantsuit on every flight! Ever wonder why many flight attendants wear pantsuits?

I have found that during air travel, my body reacts to the changes in altitude by retaining water. If I eat or drink anything with too much salt or sugar, I retain even more. When your body retains water, it tends to expand. Therefore, clothing that expands easily is by far the most comfortable on an airplane. Try to wear loose-fitting clothing with elastic waists.

Pick your shoes carefully. My back is paying for all of my years spent walking through airports in heels, carrying a briefcase slung over one shoulder and a hanging bag over the other. Now, I won't wear anything but low-heeled shoes or flats in airports and on airplanes.

Not only do they help your back, but these shoes are also easier to slip on and off as you go through the security checkpoint. Low, flat shoes that cover the foot are better than sandals. In the unlikely event that you need to evacuate the plane, they are safer, easier to keep on, and provide better protection.

If you like to take off your shoes during flight, Judy suggests that you bring A-Way Travel Treads to put on your feet. They keep your feet warm and also allow you to walk around the plane comfortably without touching the sometimes icky cabin floor. She especially emphasizes not walking in the bathroom in bare feet.

I'm not sure who regulates the temperature on the planes, but it's a constant source of aggravation for me. I am one of those travelers who is always cold on airplanes, no matter what time of the year it is. My solution has been to bring a wrap with me whenever I travel. This keeps me warm, and I also find it comforting to have a soft, warm piece of my own clothing wrapped around me. I also use the airplane blanket (if I can find one) on my lap if I need additional layers to keep warm (especially for my feet). Consider wearing layers of clothing. Remember that it's easier to remove layers if you get warm than to add them—especially when you don't have them—if you get cold.

AIRPLANE AIR

Think about it: You're in an enclosed space with at least 100 of your closest friends, and you're all breathing the same recycled air. The changes in altitude, the dry air, and whatever your neighbor might be carrying can have a direct impact on your comfort and your health. There are, however, a few things you can do to minimize these effects.

Cabin air is both stale and dry. The airlines try to freshen it by pumping oxygen into the cabin to replenish what we take out as we breathe, but doing so alleviates the staleness problem only somewhat and does little to combat the dryness. Within my first two years of traveling, my face started to peel because of the dryness caused by spending so much time in cabin air. I quickly learned that if my face was going to survive, I had to take some precautions. I learned to do the following:

- Drink plenty of water (I cannot stress this point enough).
- Wear minimal makeup while in the air (especially foundation).

- Use a water mist, which can be found at the drugstore, and spray it on your face before departure and midway through the flight.
- If you wear contact lenses, bring (and use) wetting solution.
- Apply a light moisturizer if your face feels dry during the flight (a heavier one may be needed during winter months).
- Apply an undereye cream. Andrea, a flight attendant, uses this technique all the time.
- Use lip balm early and often. Some lipsticks contain aloe, which can keep your lips moist. If you use a lipstick that does not contain aloe, apply lip balm on top of your lipstick.

Nearly everyone has experienced the ear clogging that occurs during altitude changes, especially on takeoff and landing, as a result of the changes in cabin pressure. This clogging can become painful, especially if you are traveling with a cold or sinus congestion. I have seen grown men and women flying with a cold brought to tears by air-pressure discomfort (I have great sympathy for those babies who are crying while the plane is landing). In fact, if you have a cold or other respiratory infection, you might even consider postponing your flight; it is possible for your eardrums to burst under such circumstances. Here are a few ways to help alleviate this pressure:

- Try the traditional methods—yawning, swallowing, or chewing gum.
- EarPlanes—a product that can be purchased in any drug store or at the airport. I have tried this product, and it seems to have some benefit.
- On descent, pinch your nose closed and exhale into your nose until you feel the pressure equalize.
- Keep a bottle of saline nasal spray with you and use it right before takeoff; it moistens nasal passages and helps to open passages between the ears and nasal cavities. Continue to use it for longer flights. If you are carrying the bottle through security, be sure it contains less than three ounces of liquid and fits in your one-quart zip-top bag.
- Take an over-the-counter decongestant at least half an hour before the plane takes off; some travelers find that starting use of a decongestant a few days before a flight provides even better results.

- Place hot towels over your ears when the pressure starts to build. Ask the flight attendant to place towels in a cup and pour hot water over them to dampen them. You don't want the towels to be soaking wet, because they could burn you. If you can't remember all of this, just tell the flight attendant you are traveling with a cold, and nine times out of ten they'll know to bring you the towels. Don't remove the towels until the flight has either leveled off or is on the ground.

As a precaution, it's a good idea to get up and walk around the plane or do some exercises every two hours or so if you are on a long flight. You can find simple onboard exercises on our website (www. womanroadwarrior.com) and on some airline websites. If you are on a long flight, you may want to get up and move around. Remaining stationary for extended periods of time could be harmful to your health. Much has been written lately about deep vein thrombosis (DVT), a rare blood-clotting condition associated with prolonged immobility. Some airline websites also have information about this disease.

WHAT TO EAT AND DRINK

Prior to the events of September 11, 2001, passengers expected that some type of food would be served on all but the shortest flights. Some of us would plan our meal schedules around the flight. Now, to save money (and also to minimize the threat of using the utensils as weapons), the food service offered in coach has been drastically reduced. Generally, food service in coach is offered only on international flights; on domestic flights, some airlines offer box lunches or snack boxes for purchase, but no meals are available for free. Except on the shortest flights, airlines continue to offer drink service, and with the drinks typically comes a little bag of "munchies," such as pretzels, but those snacks are generally not very filling and are usually very salty.

Especially on longer flights, if you don't want to buy the box lunch or snack box or if the airline doesn't offer it, you can get pretty hungry—even more so if your flight is delayed. Consider doing the following:

- Contact the airline directly to see if anything is being served in-flight. If you don't have time to check, then assume that no food will be provided and plan accordingly.

- Bring something with you from home to eat on the plane (make sure it doesn't contain liquids, which you can't take through security).
- Buy something in the airport to eat on board. The good news is that there are a number of vendors that sell tasty and nourishing food in most airline terminals. As the airlines have decreased the food they serve, the food selection at the larger airports has become wider, and the quality of the food has risen over the years. Just make sure to use plastic utensils, and avoid bringing any plastic knives on board.
- If your flight does include food service, most major airlines will serve you a special meal if you order it in advance. A special meal can be anything different from the standard offering or it can meet any dietary requirements, such as low carbohydrate, kosher, or vegetarian. I have ordered a number of special meals over the years and have been pleasantly surprised by the quality and quantity of the food. Indeed, I have found the special meals to be almost always more to my taste than the standard offer-ings. You must contact the airline directly to order a special meal, and your request typically needs to be in the airline's system at least 72 hours prior to flight departure. If you use a travel agent who keeps your traveler's profile, make sure the profile notes that you wish to order food this way, and it will be done automatically.

I'll say it again: *Drink plenty of water.* Drinking water is a great way to ward off dehydration, water retention, and that bloated feeling that can occur on an airplane. Water also helps keep your skin from drying out and helps keep it looking healthier.

Normally, the flight attendants will make at least one trip through the coach section to offer a drink to everyone. The small glass of water served is not much. Furthermore, storage space on the plane is limited. You should not rely on the airline to offer you an unlimited amount of bottled water. Do yourself a favor and buy bottled water before you board the plane. If you don't have time, or if you forget, you can ring the service bell and ask the flight attendant for more water if you need it. Don't sit and suffer.

If water is not for you, you can obtain something else to drink on the plane. If you prefer carbonated drinks, try ordering sugar-free, since sugar is loaded with calories and can foster water retention. If you are looking for something sweet, try a can of juice. If you are cold, try coffee or tea. Coffee is usually available in regular and decaffeinated. The tea served is sometimes prebrewed black (caffeinated) tea. Since I like green tea, I never leave home without a stash of tea bags, and on the plane I ask for a cup of hot water.

Of course, there is always alcohol to drink. Alcohol can be purchased in the main cabin. As Jody points out, the airplane is not a bar, and thus, you can't necessarily obtain your favorite label. Alcohol can also cause dehydration. But I suppose that if you drink enough, you may not care! Alcoholic drinks, beer, and wine all must be purchased from flight attendants, while other drinks are free. If you wish to buy alcohol on a flight, make sure you have the cash on hand that you'll need to pay for it. One flight attendant told me that the overall effects of one drink in the air are the same as the effects of two drinks on the ground—so consume your alcohol carefully on the plane.

All of these rules and ideas regarding food and drink are less applicable when you're flying first class. First-class passengers are generally offered food, typically a full meal, on longer flights. I usually find the food reasonably good. First-class passengers are also offered unlimited drinks, alcoholic and otherwise, so you probably don't need to bring bottled water if you are traveling in first class.

ENTERTAINING YOURSELF

Business travel on an airplane has at least one major benefit: You know that for the duration of your flight, you will be sitting in your seat, uninterrupted by phone calls, visitors, and just about anything else. Thus, for most woman road warriors, it's a great time to work—perhaps to prepare for the meeting that awaits you at your destination or, on your return, to organize what you learned during your business trip. Just be careful that your seat neighbor can't see what you're reading or your computer screen if you're dealing with anything of a sensitive nature. Similarly, if you're traveling with a colleague and using the time to talk about business, always assume that someone sitting nearby is listening to what you're saying.

For the same reason, a flight is also a great time to catch up on reading or correspondence. I always have a stack of unread periodicals lying around at my office or home, and air travel gives me time to make a dent in the stack. Unfortunately, the periodicals are often very heavy, so I like to scan them and tear out what I want to read to take with me on a flight. Then I throw the material in the trash after I have read it, usually before landing. Be sure, though, that you don't leave anything with any address labels or other material in the garbage that could facilitate identity theft.

Sometimes I use flight time to catch up on other business reading or the latest good book that someone has recommended to me. Lorrin listens to audiobooks or music on her iPod.

THE UNWANTED CONVERSATIONALIST

I've never understood why, in all my years of traveling, I've never sat next to someone who had movie-star looks and charm, and flirted with me for the whole trip. I've never even sat next to someone who was reasonably cute, and all my woman road warrior friends tell me they haven't, either. (In the interest of full disclosure, though, I have to say that my husband tells me that he never sat next to a good-looking woman on an airplane—at least, until he started traveling with me!)

Instead, especially when we're tired and most want to be left alone, we often find ourselves next to someone who just wants to talk until we land. Of course, that person may be your mother's long-lost college roommate—or a potential business contact—so you don't want to be totally rude. But what to do if you just want a little quiet and privacy?

You can try reading a book or doing a crossword puzzle, although you may find that your neighbor wants to read over your shoulder or "help" you with the puzzle. Perhaps the best solution is to put on a set of headphones—even if you're not listening to anything. Another possibility is to lean back, put on your sunglasses (even if it's the middle of the night), close your eyes, and try to sleep. You may want to try turning on your laptop and doing something (other than playing games—that is seen as interruptible) on your machine, at least as long as your neighbor doesn't pry. Unfortunately, occasionally nothing works, and you just have to grin and bear it.

Vicki always tries to carry an air of "leave me alone" when she travels. She has found that if someone starts to talk to her, she'll pick up something to read and perhaps nod to a few comments, but she makes no eye contact and gives no verbal or body-language clues that she is interested in what they have to say. If this approach doesn't work, she'll lean back and close her eyes.

Tipping

Tipping at the airport is pretty simple: you need to do very little of it. You should tip the skycap who takes your luggage at the curb if you use curbside check-in, in addition to paying the standard $2 per-bag charge; an appropriate tip is one or two dollars per bag. If you use the help of a baggage handler at the destination to take your bags from the baggage claim to your taxi or limousine, you should tip that person a similar amount. These individuals rely on tips as part of their income. Otherwise, you do not need to tip airline and airport employees.

Of course, if you go to a full-service restaurant or a coffee shop, or get a manicure at the airport, you should tip in the same way you would tip if the establishment were located at a place other than the airport.

Dealing With the Unexpected

Even the best-laid plans can and do go astray. Changes can occur because your business trip was cancelled or rescheduled, you missed your flight, the weather caused flight delays or other changes, or there was a problem with the airline. Although you will find any of these occurrences frustrating and unnerving, you should be prepared by assuming they will be the norm rather than the exception. The key: *Expect* delays and changes, and celebrate when everything goes according to plan.

Here are some of the common reasons why your flight arrangements and

WOMAN ROAD WARRIOR TIP:

When you are dealing with airline personnel, always be pleasant, respectful, and appreciative. I have always regretted the results on those occasions (fortunately few) when I have not followed my own advice in this regard. Airline personnel actually have a great deal of discretion in many areas and, like everyone, respond much more favorably to someone who treats them well.

flights don't go as planned and some general ways to deal with these situations.

International flights pose some different and more difficult problems, and Chapter 7 contains a more detailed discussion of dealing with the unexpected for the international traveler. Remember that the rules regarding fares and airline policies, both domestic and international, are constantly changing, and you need to keep up with them to be sure you make the correct decisions.

Your business trip was cancelled or rescheduled. If you have an undiscounted, unrestricted ticket, contact the carrier through your travel agent or directly to cancel or rebook the flight. If you booked your ticket through the airline's website, you will need to work directly with the airline. If you booked the ticket through a travel site, you will need to contact that site directly. You can try, if you prefer, to call the airline directly, but the airline may simply refer you back to the travel site. Either way, since the fare is unrestricted, the airline should impose no charge for processing the change. The travel website may charge a processing fee.

If you have a discounted fare, you will normally pay a fee if you make a change to your itinerary. In general, the airlines take a very hard line on collecting this fee.

In any event, you must notify the airline of any changes, either directly or through the travel site, when you have a discounted fare. If you do not notify the airline that you won't be on the flight before the originally scheduled departure time, you may not be able to reschedule at all and may forfeit any unused portion of the ticket. If you do notify the airline in time, you will typically have one year to reuse the ticket for a different flight. The airline will normally charge you a change fee, and, if you booked the flight through a travel site, the site may also charge a change fee.

Understand, though, that airline personnel have discretion regarding collection of the change fee and will waive it under appropriate circumstances. Danielle made a reservation for one flight from Chicago to Phoenix with a restricted fare, with the return flight on an unrestricted fare on a different airline. When her first flight was delayed, she bought a ticket on a third airline and used that ticket for her flight to Phoenix. For her return flight to Chicago, she decided that she could use the airline that she had been scheduled to use for the trip to Phoenix, and that airline allowed her to use the original Chicago-Phoenix ticket for her return flight, without adding a change fee. She received a full refund from the second airline for the original return ticket from Phoenix to Chicago.

The change fee is not necessarily the only amount you pay if you reschedule your trip or change destinations. When you reschedule, the airline will recalculate your fare for the new ticket as if you had never bought the first ticket and, if the fare for the new ticket is higher than what you paid originally, you will be charged the difference.

For example, if you reschedule your flight 10 days before the new flight departs, the airline will determine the new fare, based probably on a 7-day advance purchase. If your original fare was based on a 21-day advance purchase, the new ticket will almost surely be more costly, and you will have to pay the difference, in addition to the change fee. If you buy your new ticket less than seven days before your flight departs, chances are you will pay a full, undiscounted fare, less what you paid for the old ticket, plus the change fee. If you booked your flight through a travel site, you may be charged an additional fee.

Thus, changing your itinerary can be expensive. You should be especially aware of this expense if you are going to multiple destinations on the same trip. Business may require a change to a later flight to one destination, which may have a chain-reaction effect, requiring changes to other flights and resulting in substantial expense. Under these circumstances, you should consider buying a somewhat more expensive ticket that allows more flexibility in making changes.

There are times when emergencies (for example, illness, death in the family) occur that prevent you from making a trip. In these circumstances, your best course is to contact the airline directly and ask to speak to a supervisor. It has been my experience that a supervisor is in a better position to help you work through extraordinary circumstances and might be more flexible.

For travelers who have obtained a higher frequent-flyer program status with an airline, these rules may not be strictly enforced.

You missed your flight. Almost every woman road warrior has missed a flight at one time or another. Your major concern will be getting to your destination as quickly as possible for that meeting or whatever takes you there.

If you're holding a full-fare ticket (undiscounted), you should simply make a reservation on the next flight to your destination. You can use your internal or external travel agent or call the airline directly. Get a seat assignment if you can. When you get to the airport, you should be able to use curbside check-in or a check-in kiosk or just go to the front ticket counter to check your luggage (you will only be able to check your luggage if you have an assigned seat) and obtain your boarding pass. Remember that if you do not have a seat assignment on your new flight, you are subject to the usual risks of showing up for any flight without a seat assignment and should go immediately to the gate when you get to the airport.

The process is much more complex and possibly expensive if you're traveling on a discounted fare. The cost depends on whether you are willing to take your chances by going standby on a later flight on the same day or whether you want a reservation (and either an assigned seat or a better chance of obtaining one) on a later flight on the same day or on another day.

If you are willing to go standby on the same day, the airline should charge you nothing. If there is not another flight to your destination on the same day, and if you go to the airport ticket counter on the same day to make arrangements, the airline has the discretion to allow you to go standby on the first flight on the next day on the same basis. Generally, the airline's policy is consistent from customer to customer at any particular time, but changes with passenger loads and revenue needs.

If you elect to go standby, you should go to the ticket counter, where you will receive a document that will refer to the later flight and will allow you to pass through the security checkpoint. You can check your luggage, which will be tagged for standby and will be loaded on the plane if you get on the flight. The obvious possibility of an error under these circumstances should encourage you to carry your luggage onto the plane if at all possible. The airlines will not send your luggage to your destination unless you are on the flight.

If you want a reservation and a seat assignment or if you change the day of your flight (unless the airline allows you to go standby the next day because you missed the last flight to your destination on the day of departure), the rules may be more complex. For the initial leg of your flight (what the industry calls the "outbound"), the airline will recompute your fare and charge you the difference, as described above, plus the change fee. Since your departure was delayed because you missed your flight, not because you postponed your trip, the recomputation is likely to result in your paying a fare based on no advance purchase, meaning full fare or something close to it.

For the return flight (what the industry calls the "inbound"), the airline will charge you only the ticket-change fee. If you want to make a reservation, you can go to the ticket counter and change your ticket (and pay the additional charges), as well as check your luggage and obtain your boarding pass, or change your ticket over the telephone, as you would if you were purchasing a new ticket.

Remember: If you are on a discounted fare, *you must reschedule before the scheduled departure time for your flight, whether inbound or outbound, or you risk forfeiting the unused portion of your ticket.* Although these rules are generally applicable, they can vary among airlines and can be enforced or waived by airline personnel.

Your flight doesn't depart on time. Few things in life or in business are more irritating than flight delays. You can encounter delays before you board the plane—you'll typically find out about delays when you check the flight schedules on the video monitors in the airport—and still others after you're on the plane. You should start checking on flight status by calling the airline or looking at the airline's website before you leave for the airport, although you still need to be checked in (online or at the airport) 30 minutes before the originally scheduled departure time in order to keep your seat assignment. You should also ask about flight delays when you check in at the airport or when you arrive at the gate. Sometimes airline personnel aren't completely forthcoming when it comes to discussing or predicting potential delays; watch them for nonverbal cues—grimaces, hesitations, and avoidance of eye contact—which may suggest that the video monitor information may be somewhat optimistic.

When you learn of a flight delay, you can just live with it or you can look for alternatives. Both the length of the predicted delay and your schedule should determine your course of action. Of course, everyone has had the experience of seeing a scheduled flight's departure postponed in ever-lengthening increments. Thus, if your schedule is tight, you might want to assume that the delay will be longer than the airline first tells you. You may be able to better gauge how long a delay you can expect by calling the airline and asking for information on the inbound flight that will become your flight. If that flight is delayed for mechanical or weather reasons, you may have an idea regarding how long you will actually be delayed.

Every so often fate works in your favor, and you will learn of the delay when you check in at the front kiosk before you pass through security. If that happens, the system will ask you whether you want to go on an earlier flight. If there are open seats on the earlier flight and you punch "yes," the system will switch you to that flight. If there are no seats on the flight, you will be put on the standby list. In that case, you should go directly to the gate and wait for your name to clear the list.

If you decide to look for alternatives, you should first find out when the next flight to your destination is departing. Depending on the reason for your flight's delay, the next flight may depart first. Therefore, you may wish to go over to the gate for that flight and register on the standby list. You can only be on one standby list at a time. Airlines have become more stringent in enforcing this rule.

If there isn't such an obvious alternative, you should look for something less obvious. For example, there may be another airport somewhere near your destination or a flight on another airline (especially if you're on a full-fare ticket) or some alternative means of getting to your destination. If you encounter any type of delay, use whatever resources you have available to find out what is going on. You may try chatting up the gate agent, or you may even need to call the airline on the telephone with your questions; other alternatives are to call your travel agent, or go online if you have a wireless device.

Unless you're indifferent to the delay, don't be passive; look for alternatives. On one trip, I was scheduled to fly to one of the Washington-area airports when my flight was delayed for mechanical reasons. Even though the video monitor said otherwise, the delay looked like a long one. The next flight to that airport looked fairly full. Instead of taking my chances and going standby on one of those flights, I went to the airline's lounge and, with the help of the agent there, I found a less-full flight to one of the other airports in that area and arrived fairly close to the original schedule.

The most frustrating kinds of flight delays occur after you're on the plane. These can be created by mechanical problems, weather, air traffic at the departure or destination airport, or some other cause. Unfortunately, there isn't much you can do to change plans once you are physically on the plane. If you know how long the delay is going to be, you can use your cell phone, a phone on board, or your wireless e-mail device (such as a Blackberry) to communicate with someone about the changes. This is especially important if you are going to a meeting or someone is waiting for you on the other end.

If you expect to be late, you should also call the hotel, if you have a reservation, and tell the front desk that you will be late, so there will be no question of your intent to stay there. Lorrin once failed to call her hotel when her flight was delayed and found herself without a hotel room when she arrived after midnight, even though she had prepaid for a guaranteed room even in case of a late arrival. The hotel was full, and the staff had assumed that she was a no-show.

Whatever the cause of the delay, and whether it arises before or after you board the plane, you can be sure that airline personnel will be much more concerned about getting your flight underway as soon as possible than about providing you information about the problem or its consequences. Don't rely on just the information routinely furnished you. I was sitting on a plane recently when the pilot announced that there would be a delay and that he would continue to report the flight status as it became available. I immediately called my travel agent, who told me that the airline's computer listed the flight as cancelled. She was able to reserve me a seat on the next flight to my destination, and when the pilot finally announced that the flight was cancelled, I was already covered.

Be aware that flight status can and does change at a moment's notice. If you are not at the gate when a change occurs, you run the risk that the plane might take off without you. Airlines will post a new departure time or gate due to a mechanical or weather-related problem with little advance notice; their objective is to get the flight out as close to schedule as possible. If a weather delay occurs, the airline is constantly monitoring the situation, and as soon as clearance is granted, the flight will depart, regardless of where you may be and regardless of what time they have told you the flight would leave. The airline will make an announcement of such a change, but if you happen to miss it for whatever reason, you could be left behind.

If you're traveling with another person, use the buddy system. Keep one person at the gate, preferably with a cell phone, so you can communicate if anything should change.

If you're traveling alone, stay at or near the gate for all but the shortest time periods. I know of several instances where people sitting on a plane were told that the flight was going to be delayed and that they could leave the plane and wait in the terminal until the rescheduled departure time. They left the plane and went for some food, but when they came back at the rescheduled departure time, they found that the plane had left without them—and with their luggage, no less! Don't be left at the gate because you aren't paying close enough attention.

You may be able to alleviate the consequences of a possible flight delay with planning. Especially during seasons where weather delays are common (for example, midwinter in the upper Midwest), try to go on an early morning flight. The airplane probably came in the night before, so you will not be delayed by waiting for the plane to arrive if the weather is bad. Otherwise, if you are traveling on a day when the weather looks threatening, or if you hear reports of bad weather at your destination, go to the airport early if you can and try to go on an earlier flight. Once weather delays start, they usually compound throughout the day, making the delays for the later flights even longer.

Also, you should check on hotel availability early once you realize that weather delays are possible; if flights are canceled, many passengers will be looking for rooms. At the minimum, you should be talking with your travel agent (assuming you are using one), who can monitor the situation for you. The sign of a really good travel agent is one who takes the initiative to contact you with changes as they unfold.

Your flight is cancelled. Barring something that affects an airline as a whole (such as labor problems or terrorism), flights can be cancelled for one of two reasons: mechanical or weather. If the flight is cancelled due to the weather, the airline will put you on another flight, which might not be on the same day. If your flight is cancelled for mechanical reasons, the airline is obligated to get you on the next available flight. In this circumstance, you may want to consider changing airlines.

As soon as you become aware that your flight is cancelled, get on the phone and contact either your travel agent or the airline and request that they reserve you a seat on the next flight. If your flight is cancelled for weather reasons, realize that the later flights that day may be as well, and thus your travel agent or the airline may only be able to get you a seat on a flight the next day. After you make that call, go to customer service, the airline lounge (if you're a member), and/

or the gate. At any of these locations, you'll be reissued a boarding pass for the flight you requested. If you choose not to make that phone call, but only go to customer service, the lounge, or the gate, you run the risk of waiting in line only to find that the next flight is already full and that you'll be delayed even longer. You should also ask for meal vouchers, which should be given to you if your flight is cancelled for mechanical reasons and may also be given to you if the flight is cancelled because of the weather.

> **WOMAN ROAD WARRIOR TIP:**
>
> As soon as you learn your flight is cancelled, for whatever reason, contact your travel agent or the airline to find out what your options are and, if possible, to make a reservation on an alternative flight. Also check on the availability of hotel rooms in case you are stranded for another day.

If the next available flight does not have enough seats to accommodate everyone, as is typically the case when a flight is cancelled, some passengers will go standby, and people low on the standby list may be bumped to a much later flight. The order of priority on the standby list, as usual, is generally first come, first serve, so you will have a better chance of getting on the next flight if you move quickly and go where the line may be short, such as the airline lounge. Again, however, having a special status with the frequent-flyer program can be a big help in getting you moved toward the top of the list.

Persistence in looking for alternatives can often save you a lot of time. On one occasion, I had a reservation on a flight scheduled to depart from Phoenix at noon. When I arrived at the gate, I found that the flight was delayed and was rescheduled to depart at 2:00 p.m. I noticed that the airline had another flight to my destination that was scheduled to depart at 1:00 p.m., so I went to the gate for that flight hoping to be added to the standby list. When I arrived at that gate, I found that the 1:00 p.m. flight was cancelled for mechanical reasons. Within the next hour, the airline "uncancelled" the 1:00 p.m. flight by using the plane that was to have been used for my original noon flight! The airline then delayed and rescheduled the noon flight to depart at 5:00 p.m., five hours late—the airline was waiting for another plane to be flown in from San Francisco to be used for the noon flight. While standing in line to see about getting on the now uncancelled but delayed 1:00 flight, I called the airline and reserved a seat on a flight to my destination scheduled for a 3:00 departure. In the end, I flew out on the 3:00 flight and arrived at my destination before either of the two earlier flights.

If you have not left for the airport when you find out your flight has been canceled for weather-related reasons, and the weather conditions indicate that most flights will be canceled, stay at home or wherever else you are at least until you talk to an airline representative and find out what your choices are. If you go to the airport, you will find yourself sleeping on the floor, eating food out of the vending machines (assuming they haven't run out of food), and stuck with thousands of your closest friends. If you don't go to the airport, you will eventually reach an airline representative (yes, it might take a day or so if many flights have been canceled) and the airline will get you on a plane (most likely without a penalty).

Your flight is oversold. As described earlier, the airlines routinely sell more tickets than they have seats on a flight, anticipating that 2 to 10 percent of the ticket holders will not show up for the flight. Of course, there are situations where there are fewer no-shows, and more people will show up with tickets than there are seats on the plane.

When this occurs, the airlines start looking for volunteers to take other flights and often offer incentives to induce people to do so. Typically, these incentives are dollar credits applicable to future flights on the same airline. If the traveler will be unable to be accommodated on a flight on the same day, she may also be offered coupons applicable to the cost of a hotel room and food. I have known a few business travelers who have accepted these offers, although most do not have the scheduling flexibility to do so. Your company may have policies regarding this situation. Such policies can tell you whether any of the incentives offered by the airline are yours or the company's and describe circumstances under which you are permitted or required to change your plans.

If you have checked your luggage, you will not be eligible to accept the airline's offer to go on a later flight, because you and your luggage must travel on the same flight. If you are eligible, still be careful before you accept the airline's offer. Deborah was flying home for the weekend and innocently offered to give up her seat so that a young married couple could go on the flight together. The gate attendant told her that she could have a seat on the next flight. After the flight had fully boarded, she was told that the airline had made a mistake—she would have to go standby on the next flight. She finally got home two days later. She discovered—too late, of course—that the airlines were packed with school spring-break traffic and all the flights were full.

If you don't want to change your plans *and* you have a seat assignment, as long as you are at the gate on time and board the plane on time, an oversold flight shouldn't affect you. If you do not have a seat assignment, your name will go on a list, and customers without seat assignments will generally be given the unassigned, surrendered, or forfeited seats in the order in which they have checked in. If there is no seat for you, the airline will put you on the next available flight. I've found (maybe it's my imagination) that sometimes it can be helpful to stand around the counter at the gate and talk to the gate agent. And, as always, it also helps to have special status under the frequent-flyer program.

You are stranded. You may find yourself in a situation where you are stranded—you're away from home and can't get to where you're going (either home or some other final destination) by airplane. For instance, a number of people were stranded in different cities for days after the events of September 11, 2001. Weather can also close airports and can keep travelers stranded, such as during hurricane season in the Southeast. If you can't get out of town by plane, look for alternative transportation. This alternative could be in the form of a train, bus or car. Contact your travel agent (if you're working with one) or your organization's human resources department in order to come up with alternatives.

The news was full of stories about how resourceful travelers became when the airlines stopped flying after the events of September 11, 2001. For example, many people rented cars to get back home and shared them with others who happened to be in the same area at the time but lived in their home city. See Chapter 5, regarding alternative ways to travel, for some additional ideas.

If you are able to wait, find a hotel room and settle in until whatever is going on passes. If you decide on this course of action, do it quickly, because if you're stranded the odds are you're not alone. As previously stated, there are only a limited number of hotel rooms available in any given area, so be aggressive and make plans quickly. These arrangements can always be cancelled if the situation changes suddenly. As always, your travel agent can be very helpful in dealing with such situations.

Your luggage has been lost. Although luggage does not get lost very often, it does happen, and you need to be prepared for it to happen. If you are certain all the bags from your flight have been unloaded and yours have not yet appeared, talk to an airport representative immediately. There are usually skycaps or baggage handlers in the baggage claim area. Let them know that your bag did not arrive on the carousel and show them your luggage tag receipt. Request that they contact airport personnel on the tarmac in order to recheck the plane for any luggage left onboard. If you wait too long, you run the risk that the plane will take off again before anyone can check. On one flight, I asked an attendant in the baggage area to check the plane when it was obvious that all the bags (but mine) had been unloaded. The plane had not taken off again, and in fact my luggage was still onboard.

If your luggage has not been found onboard, you should go immediately to the airline's baggage-service office in the baggage-claim area. Since large airlines store and track all checked luggage electronically, the baggage claim agent can check the computer and track where your luggage should be. You then fill out a lost-luggage claim form, which identifies the flight you were on, a description of your luggage (see Chapter 6), and your name and contact information. If you are at a destination where you will be for only a few days, be sure to provide another address in case your luggage is found after you have departed.

If your luggage has not shown up, one of three things has occurred: It is on a later flight, it was sent to the wrong place, or it is lost. Your luggage should show up in the computer tracking system if it is on a later flight or was sent to the wrong place. If either is the case, the airline must deliver the luggage to you once it arrives at the proper destination.

Sometimes, luggage appears lost because the tag put on the bag at the departure airport somehow tore off, and the bag ends up in the lost and found at the destination airport. Vicki had the experience of going to an airport lost and found and claiming a bag of hers that had arrived at the proper destination but with all identification torn off.

If you're not so lucky, and your luggage truly is lost, you need to file a claim for reimbursement. A claim must include a description of your luggage (in this instance a photograph—that's what cell phones are for—is truly worth a thousand words...or a thousand dollars!) and an inventory and valuation of the contents. If you have a very expensive piece of luggage, keep the receipt to prove its value. The airline will reimburse you for the loss, but you will almost certainly receive less than the cost of replacing the items. Filing a claim with your personal insurance carrier may help supplement the difference.

As a business traveler, your more immediate concern than reimbursement will probably be replacing what you need to accomplish the business purposes of your trip. Unfortunately, there is no easy way to replace lost items. If you've carried your medicine and valuables onboard with you (again, see Chapter 6) and maybe a few important clothing items, you may be able to go for a day or two without replacements.

The airline will give you a toiletry kit that can replace certain items, but that will usually make only a small dent in the problem. You may be able to get some items sent from home. If not, you may want to work with the concierge at your hotel; he or she may be able to obtain replacements for some items without your having to go shopping yourself. If that fails, it's time to find a mall.

If you have no clothing suitable for business use and no way to obtain some, your last resort may be to ask the hotel for a hotel uniform. A hotel uniform is usually a pantsuit, and hotels have been known to loan them to guests in emergencies.

Woman Road Warrior Checklist

Securing a reservation

___ Be sure the name on the reservation matches the name on your identification (including your passport and visa) and frequent-flyer card.

___ Exhaust all avenues for securing a ticket.

___ Check to see if a bargain first-class fare is available.

___ Obtain seat assignment.

___ Request upgrade, if applicable.

___ Request special meal, if applicable.

___ Register for frequent-flyer program and ensure miles are recorded.

___ Record ticket number and/or record locator in calendar.

Don't leave home without...

___ Your itinerary.

___ Personal identification, passport, visa (if necessary), and your special state identification card (if any).

___ Luggage (remember baggage limitations).

___ Putting a copy of your itinerary in any luggage you plan to check.

___ Personal essentials in carry-on.

___ Knowing the latest carry-on restrictions.

___ Your travel agent's phone number in your cell phone speed dial.

Navigating the airport

___ Be sure tag on checked luggage accurately reflects destination.

___ Obtain boarding pass at least 30 minutes before scheduled departure for domestic flights and one hour before scheduled departure for international flights.

___ Look for special lines for elite travelers with certain airlines.

___ Be sure carry-on contains only permitted items.

___ Purchase water, food, and/or reading material (liquids only after going through security—don't forget to save your receipts).

___ Have boarding pass and identification easily accessible at all times.

___ Board your flight as soon as you are permitted.

The flight

___ Stow carry-on luggage overhead, wheels in first.

___ Obtain pillow and/or blanket.

___ Turn off cell phone.

___ Note plane exits.

___ Drink plenty of water.

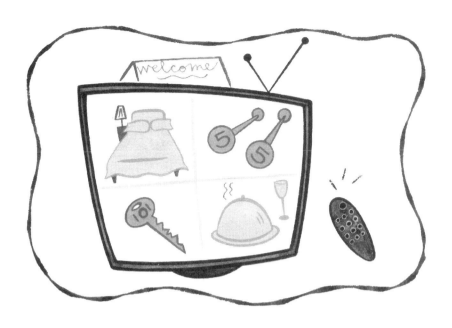

CHAPTER 3:

Hotels—Your Home Away from Home

Choosing a hotel presents you with even more options than choosing a flight. After all, there are only a limited number of airlines, all of which offer pretty much the same services. On the other hand, in any city there is almost always a huge variety of hotels from which to choose, each of which offers different services, is in a different location, and has different features that may add to or detract from your comfort. In 2005, there were more than 47,000 hotel properties in the United States, according to the American Hotel and Lodging Association. It can be very difficult to find out which hotel is best for you in which circumstances, and which are best at meeting the particular needs of women travelers. I hope what follows will help you sort out the bewildering quantity of available options and considerations and help you learn how to make good decisions for you, for your budget, for your schedule, and for your company.

When you travel for business, it's inevitable that you will sometimes have to stay away from home overnight. Thus, hotels become a fact of your professional life. Sometimes it's a night or two—maybe you have to spend a short time at a client's office, but the distance or business or transportation schedules will not allow a day trip—and other times it may be weeks, or even months, such as for a lengthy consulting engagement.

Since you may be spending a lot of time in your hotel, you should be sure it works as well as possible for you given your budget. I can tell you from personal experience that staying in a hotel that is either un-comfortable or that fails to treat you well can ruin your outlook while you're away—and also make your trip far less productive.

Much of the discussion below applies to both domestic and inter-national travel, but the great variety of hotels in other countries and the language and cultural differences raise somewhat different issues for hotels and hotel selection in other countries. See Chapter 7 for a more thorough discussion.

Choosing a Hotel

Here are the main things you need to consider to narrow your search quickly:

- Check your company's travel policy first. It might require that you stay at a particular hotel or at a hotel in a particular chain, such as Wyndham, Hyatt, Marriott, or Westin. In the travel industry, people sometimes refer to a hotel that is a member of a hotel chain as carrying that chain's "flag."
- Even if your company does not have a travel policy that con-strains your lodging options, it may still have negotiated a cor-porate rate with a particular hotel or chain. Find out from your internal travel agent or your manager. It may be impossible for you to match that rate at a hotel of comparable quality without the benefit of such a discount.
- If you are traveling at a client's expense, you should also ask if the client has any expectations about your lodging. The client company may expect you to stay at a particular hotel or chain at which it's negotiated its own corporate rate, which you may be able to use. Asking about this will earn you goodwill with the client, and the answer may save the client money—which can only make the client happy (or, at least, less unhappy).

- If neither the company nor the client has any requirements or expectations, then you should ask your colleagues, client, or friends for recommendations. Don't forget to talk to someone in any office of your company in your destination city.
- Consult hotel publications or guidebooks, either in hard copy or online. Many travel guidebooks (including publications such as *Zagat*) list hotels in specific cities. Unfortunately, this research could take a lot of your time.
- Contact your external travel agent (if you are using one).
- Consult the Internet—general travel sites have a tremendous amount of information, and there are also plenty of dedicated lodging sites, such as Hotels.com.
- Pick a hotel in the destination city that is part of the same chain as a hotel that you've found comfortable in some other city.

Assuming you have a choice of where to stay, although cost may be important in determining which hotel you choose, you also may want to consider the following:

LOCATION

In many cases, your decision about where to stay will be based on finding something near the location of some meeting or the client. If that's not the case, here are a few things to consider:

- *Will you have access to a car?* If the hotel you choose is far from where you will conduct business, you may have to take on the additional expense of renting a car.
- *Are you most concerned about convenience?* You may not want a long commute back to the hotel from where you're conducting your business. Although hotels located outside the center of town are typically less expensive, the savings may not be worth the time and inconvenience.
- *Will you be entertaining in the evening?* If so, then you may not want to be driving a long way to your hotel after a late night elsewhere.
- *What's the timing of your business commitments?* Do you have a number of meetings staggered throughout the day? If so, you may want the flexibility to go back to the hotel between

meetings. Staying somewhere that isn't easily accessible could require a lot of back-and-forth travel.

HOTELS VS. MOTELS

Hotels and motels, despite the similarity in names, differ significantly in prices and service levels. Motels are designed to accommodate those traveling primarily by car, and typically a guest can access her room directly from the parking lot (usually a surface lot, not a garage), without going through a lobby. Motels, unlike hotels, are generally not located in central cities. Hotels normally require the guest to pass through a lobby in order to go to her room from the entrance. Hotels offer more services than motels, such as on-site full-service restaurants, room service, bellman services, concierges, and health club facilities. Hotels are usually more expensive than motels.

I always prefer to stay in a hotel if I can. I prefer the higher level of service, find it much easier to stay in a place where I can eat in the hotel, and find room service very useful. I am not comfortable with the level of security when someone can have direct access from outside the building to the door to my room. Most business travel will take you to locations with a number of lodging options. However, in some less-populous cities and towns, your only choice may be a motel.

Most of this chapter focuses on hotels, rather than motels, since, like most business travelers, you will be more likely to want to stay in a hotel if one is available because of the better service, greater security, and more convenient location. Much of the discussion in this chapter, though, is applicable to motels as well.

HEALTH CLUB

Is exercise important to you? If so, do you care whether your hotel has facilities on the premises?

Health-club amenities differ greatly from one hotel to another. If you are unfamiliar with a hotel and you expect to use its health club, ask specific questions in order to determine whether the facilities will meet your expectations. You don't need to be dressed for a workout early in the morning, expecting a session on Nautilus equipment, only to find that the hotel has just a bike and a treadmill. Also, an offsite health club, while perhaps offering a wider range of facilities than one onsite, may be much less convenient.

Also, make sure to ask whether the hotel charges guests for use of the health club; it's often one of those things that show up on your bill when you're not expecting it.

IN-ROOM REFRIGERATOR

For some women, an in-room refrigerator may not only be desirable, but also necessary. For instance, if you are a mother who is breast-feeding and traveling without your baby, you may find storing milk while traveling to be a huge logistical challenge. Unless you are traveling with an ice chest or are shipping milk home every day, you may want an in-room refrigerator. You may also have special dietary or medical needs that require ready access to a refrigerator.

OTHER SERVICES AND AMENITIES

If there are other services or amenities that could be important to you in deciding on a hotel, ask about them before you make a reservation. For instance, if you plan to work extensively in your hotel, you may want to ask about the availability of computers, printers, fax machines, copiers, Internet access, and wireless capabilities. Many hotels have business centers with this type of equipment and service. By now, most hotels offer in-room high-speed Internet access, either wireless or cabled, for those traveling with a laptop. Some hotels will impose an extra charge for Internet access, and others will not. Some hotels will offer free wireless Internet in the lobby and hotel common areas, but not in the rooms, and some of those may advertise "free" Internet access; if free in-room Internet access is important to you, ask specifically about its availability.

Some hotels are located in complexes with movie theaters and shopping, which can offer some attractive diversions when you are not at work. Others have recreational facilities, such as golf courses. Still others might have special spa facilities or hair or nail salons onsite. You may want to stay at a hotel with a highly regarded restaurant—or a restaurant that gives special treatment to women eating alone. If staying in a hotel with such a restaurant is important to you and you find yourself lacking the relevant information, you can try asking someone (such as a fellow traveler) who might be a reliable source, or you can delve a little deeper using the usual resources, such as guidebooks or the Internet.

CANCELLATION POLICY

How flexible is the hotel if you have to change your plans? True road warriors know that their plans can change on a moment's notice and that they need hotels that can adapt to their need for flexibility.

You will want to ensure that you won't lose your room if you arrive at a late hour (an arrangement called "late arrival"). You will have to guarantee (usually with a credit card) payment for the room if you don't show up and haven't cancelled your reservation in accordance with the hotel's cancellation policy. Many hotels will allow you to cancel your reservation as late as 6:00 p.m. the day of arrival, but others have different requirements. If you do not cancel your reservation before the time specified by the cancellation policy, you will be charged for at least one night's stay.

If you make your reservation through a travel site, pay particular attention to the site's own cancellation policy, which may differ from that of the hotel. Some sites do not allow cancellation, and even those that do may charge a cancellation or change fee.

If your plans change at the last minute and you are unable to cancel your reservation in accordance with the hotel's cancellation policy, contact the front-desk manager and explain the situation. The hotel may be willing to make an exception to its policy. Note, however, that if you make your reservation through a website other than the hotel's, especially a site that offers heavily discounted rates on hotel rooms, the hotel may be less willing to make any exception.

ROOM TYPE

Hotels offer a variety of different room types. Each has cost and amenity implications, so you need to decide what you're willing to pay for. Most hotels offer the following room types, each of which may have different in-room amenities that will vary among hotels:

- *Standard rooms.* Standard rooms are the basic, no-frills rooms that include a bed, bath, and usually a desk and an easy chair. You may typically choose a room with either a king or queen bed, or with two double or (occasionally) twin beds. Not all hotels offer all bed types.
- *Deluxe rooms.* The definition of a deluxe room can vary widely from hotel to hotel, and there can even be different types of deluxe rooms in the same hotel. A deluxe room typically

includes (in addition to the basic bed, bath, and desk) a seating area with a couch or similar furniture and possibly a larger bath than a standard room. Choices of bed types are usually the same as for standard rooms.

- *Suites.* A suite typically includes a bedroom and bath, furnished much the same as a standard room, and a separate sitting room with a couch, chairs, and probably a television. Of course, some hotels may have a few much larger (and much more expensive) suites. The extra space in a suite may be particularly attractive if you will be in the hotel for a long stay.

Remember also that hotels will designate certain rooms, and even certain floors, as smoking and nonsmoking. If you have a preference, be sure to be specific when you make your reservation.

CONCIERGE/CLUB FLOOR

Many hotels offer a separate concierge (or club) floor or floors. A room on the concierge floor will come with a higher level of service and amenities than the same type of room on a different floor, but of course this will likely entail a higher cost.

Usually the concierge floor will offer guests complimentary breakfast in the morning and complimentary hors d'oeuvres in the early evening; a lounge with comfortable furniture, television, and newspapers, as well as coffee, tea, and other drinks; and a concierge who serves only guests who are staying on that floor (for more on concierges, see "Making the Concierge Your Friend," below).

Laura, an investment banker who occasionally travels with her husband on business, told me that they always stay on the concierge floor and find that the money they save by not paying for breakfast more than pays for the higher cost of the room.

Access to concierge floors typically requires a special key made available only to guests staying on that floor; this policy provides greater privacy and security. Many hotel chains have reward programs that make access to a concierge floor one of the program's rewards (when higher status levels are reached).

Reserving a Room

You generally have four ways to make a hotel reservation: through an internal travel agent, an external travel agent, a travel website, or by contacting the hotel directly. No matter how you make your reservation, though, you need a basic understanding of how hotels price their rooms, because the way you reserve your room may cost or save you money. Hotels generally have two types of rates: undiscounted (sometimes called "rack") and discounted. If you become involved directly in negotiating your rate, showing your knowledge by using this terminology may be of some help in the process.

If your company has discounted or corporate rates with a particular hotel chain, then it's probably a foregone conclusion that you'll stay at a hotel in that chain and pay your company's discounted or corporate rate. In this case, how you make your reservation will not affect either your choice of rooms or their price. But if this is not the case and if you are using a travel agent (internal or external), then you should let the agent start the process of negotiating your rate for you. You can always tell your agent that the rate the hotel quotes is too high and to negotiate a lower one. If you are not satisfied with the rate ultimately offered by the travel agent, then you should negotiate and make the reservation yourself.

> **WOMAN ROAD WARRIOR TIP:**
>
> Hotels charge different rates on different days. Typically, the weekday rate is Monday through Thursday, and the weekend rate Friday through Sunday.

If you are not using a travel agent, or if your travel agent can't get you an acceptable rate, you can call the hotel directly, once you pick one, or use the Internet. I generally have had the best luck calling my preferred hotel directly, rather than using travel sites. On the other hand, some other road warriors prefer the Internet for price comparison to start, and often for making their reservation.

If you make a reservation by telephone, you can call the hotel directly or, if it's part of a chain, call the chain's toll-free number to make a reservation at any one of its hotels. I strongly prefer to call the specific hotel directly, whether or not it's part of a chain. I find that I get better service.

Once you find out whether a room is available, you can begin to discuss prices. Begin by pricing a standard room; you may ultimately

> **WOMAN ROAD WARRIOR TIP:**
>
> Many of the major trade organizations and other membership groups have negotiated discounted rates for their members, and you will be surprised how likely it is that you are a member of such a group. The American Bar Association, American Medical Association and American Automobile Association are just three of the groups whose members can get discounted rates at many hotels.

be able to persuade the hotel to give you a deluxe room or suite at no or minimal extra charge. Next, always ask whether any corporate rates, specials, or discounts are available to you.

Be persistent. If you know that a better rate is being advertised on the Internet or is offered by a competing hotel, tell the reservation agent. If you are not satisfied with the rate offered and think it could be lower, ask to speak to a supervisor or the manager. They have authority to agree to better deals.

Why this focus on negotiating your rate? Because hotels have significant flexibility—much more than airlines—when it comes to charging different rates to different customers and have far fewer rules to apply in determining prices. Angela, a vice president of marketing for a large hotel company, told me that most major hotel chains categorize their business customers based on the projected "lifetime value of the guest." Based on the guest's demographic profile and other data the guest provides, the hotel computes the revenue that the guest can be expected to generate for the hotel over a period of years. The hotel will be more generous in its dealings with customers whose "lifetime value" is expected to be high. If you know you plan to be staying frequently with the hotel chain, and even more so if you can commit to doing so, make that known to the hotel so the hotel can take your plans into account in its dealings with you. Under the proper circumstances, you may be able to negotiate your rate very effectively.

If you make your hotel reservation over the telephone, make sure the hotel gives you a confirmation number before you hang up. This number identifies you to the hotel. Like an airline's record locator, a hotel reservation confirmation number—and not the customer's name—is used to track an individual hotel reservation. You should also receive a written record of your confirmation, with your confirmation number, by e-mail, fax, or standard-mail delivery shortly after you make your reservation. Be sure you take this information with you so you have it when you check in at the hotel.

Similarly, if you cancel your hotel reservation, make sure that you are given a cancellation number and that you retain it for your records. There have been occasions when I was charged for a room even though I had cancelled the reservation in accordance with the hotel's cancellation policy. I was able to dispute the charge successfully only because I had recorded the cancellation number.

You can use the Internet as an alternative to making your reservation over the telephone. Even if you prefer (like I do) to make your reservation by telephone rather than using the Internet, the travel or hotel websites can be very useful for price comparison.

If you decide to use the Internet to reserve a hotel room, you can go to:

- the hotel's or hotel chain's own website;
- a large travel website such as Orbitz, Expedia, or Travelocity;
- a website that strictly offers hotel choices and reservation service at many hotels (e.g., Hotels.com);
- a website that offers heavily discounted rates but with very limited flexibility, such as Priceline.com.

If you go to the website for a particular hotel or hotel chain, you will probably be able to specify your preference as to room type, smoking preference, and other features that may be important to you. If you go to a broader website (probably because you are looking for a variety of hotel choices), the range of preferences you can designate will be more limited. The website will probably give you choices based only on the desired location of your hotel, your check-in and check-out dates, number of rooms, and number of guests. If you are using a website that presents you a number of hotel choices in response to a query about a particular city, you will probably be able to be more specific about the part of town in which you wish to stay. Depending on the site, you may also be able to narrow your search even further, but you will probably not be able to be as selective as on a hotel's or hotel chain's own website. If you use a website such as Priceline.com, which offers heavily discounted rates, your choices will be limited even further. You will probably be required to accept any room in a hotel in your destination city that will meet your pricing criteria (and perhaps a qualitative standard).

WOMAN ROAD WARRIOR TIP:

If you secure a room though a website that doesn't allow you to make choices that may be important to you (for example, room amenities or smoking preference), contact the hotel directly once you receive your confirmation and request what you want. If you use a discount-driven website such as Priceline.com, though, the hotel may be reluctant to do much for you.

Hotel Reward Programs

Like the airlines, hotel chains have their own reward programs, which cost nothing to join. Where an airline uses miles as its measure, a hotel chain uses room nights. Like the airlines, the hotels have status levels within their program, under which members who stay in the chain's rooms a certain number of nights in a year attain a level that gives them certain benefits.

Regardless of status levels, accumulated room nights may be redeemed for free stays in the chain's hotels or for room upgrades. Then, depending on the particular chain's program, members who have attained a higher status level may obtain:

- Room upgrades at little or no cost, depending on availability.
- Access to concierge or business level floors for no additional cost.
- Guaranteed availability of a room in any hotel in the chain, even if the hotel is full. To take advantage of this guarantee, a member normally has to make her reservation a certain period (which may be as little as 48 hours) in advance.
- Members-only lines for check-in and check-out.
- Early check-in and late check-out without charge.

You may prefer to stay at a hotel where you are a member of the program. Being a known, loyal customer at a hotel always has its advantages. Less obviously, most hotel chains use the same layout at many of their different hotels, which makes it easier for you to know what room to request. On the other hand, brand loyalty may result in your staying at a more expensive hotel, which may bother your company or your client.

Some hotel chains also have tie-in programs with one or more airlines. Under these programs, instead of getting room nights at the hotel chain's reward program when you stay in one of the chain's hotels, you are awarded miles in the airline's frequent-flyer program. This choice would be attractive when you are not likely to stay a large number of nights in the chain's hotels and thus not likely to attain the higher status entitling you to the expanded benefits. If you elect this alternative, be sure to have your airline frequent-flyer number when you check in at the hotel.

Room Request: How to Get the One You Want!

When I check into a hotel, I typically change rooms about half the time, often after I've already been given the key and gone to the room. I'm not alone. Sophie, an advertising executive, often goes to the desk, asks for room keys, and "goes shopping" by looking at a number of rooms before she accepts a room assignment. If you don't want to spend the time to shop, there are a few questions you can ask at check-in that may help to facilitate this process:

- Is the room type what you reserved? In other words, is the room assigned consistent with your expressed smoking preference, bed-type preference, and anything else you have specified? If not, insist that the hotel make a change. If the desk tells you that what you reserved is not available, ask for an upgraded room. If all else fails, talk to the manager. After all, the hotel made a commitment to you; you're only insisting that the commitment be honored.

- If you are going to be working in your room, check to be sure that Internet and electrical outlets are easily accessible. I've frequently found myself in a hotel room working in an uncomfortable position because of the poor outlet location.

- Even if the room is consistent with your reservation, you might ask if an upgraded room (deluxe or suite, club or concierge level) is available (at no or minimal additional charge). On occasion, if an upgraded room or suite is available, a hotel will honor this request. If you don't ask, they won't tell you. If you are not a member of a hotel's rewards program, the hotel may also put you on the concierge or club level in order to induce you to become a member. If you stay or plan to stay frequently at the same hotel, make a point of getting to know the front-desk personnel. Once they get to know you, they may be more willing to honor this request.

- This may sound insignificant, but it's something you should think about: If you're traveling with a male colleague, try to be assigned a room on a different floor from his. Janet, a human resources professional, says that you can easily be the target of malicious gossip that can harm your career, no matter how innocent the facts. Just as you don't want a reputation as the "room service" person, you don't want an undeserved reputation because you picked a hotel room unwisely. By the way, for much the same reason, if you need to meet with a colleague (especially a male colleague) after hours, try to use a restaurant or hotel meeting room. Hotel meeting rooms are usually empty after hours, and the front desk will usually allow you to use one if you need more privacy than you can find in a restaurant.

The biggest consideration in picking a hotel room? Location! When I do change rooms, it's usually because after I've seen the room I've been assigned, I find it's in a bad location. Take it from me: Room location may not sound like a big deal, but after one night of interrupted sleep, it becomes *huge*. After all, this room is where you're going to be spending a lot of time while you are away from home. Not only do you want it livable, but you want to ensure that you can get the maximum amount of comfort and security. Therefore, things to consider—or avoid—include the following:

- I stay off the first floor whenever possible. This floor can be noisier than other floors. The first floor is also a security risk because people from the lobby have easier access to wander through the halls unnoticed. On one trip, I had my jewelry stolen from my hotel room, which was on the first floor near the pool. I am convinced that someone who was watching the room just came in through the front door when I went out to the pool. Another floor would not have provided a place for a thief to watch my room without being noticed.

- Stay away from rooms close to the dining rooms, bars, or any other form of entertainment. Rooms located above, below, or next to these areas tend to be loud. These establishments open early and close late and have a lot of foot and voice traffic, not to mention the aroma of food.
- Don't accept a room near the health club or pool—while the proximity can be convenient, it can also be noisy. Some health clubs and pools are open 24 hours a day. The last thing you need is to hear the clanging of weights all night long, not to mention the foot traffic and voices in the hall.
- Avoid rooms that are next to the elevators, ice machines, service elevators, and stairwells. These areas have more noisy foot traffic, and an intruder can more easily slip in and out unnoticed. You want to make it very difficult for anyone to get to you or your possessions.
- If you have allergy problems, like I do, try to avoid staying in a room that has been sprayed with deodorizer. I once had an allergic reaction to the room deodorizer at a very fine luxury hotel.
- Sometimes even the best hotels have rooms where the water pressure is not as strong as you want. Large hotels have water heaters in several locations, and water pressure will be the strongest on the floor or floors nearby.
- Stay away from rooms in an otherwise vacant wing or building of a hotel. Danielle checked into a resort hotel that included several separate buildings and arrived at her room at night. Although everything looked and felt fine, she was awakened in the middle of the night when someone tried to get into her room. It turned out that the night watchman needed to use a bathroom and just happened to pick her room for that purpose. He even had a key! The night watchman informed Danielle that hers was the only room being occupied in that

building within the resort. Although no harm came to her, she demanded to be moved immediately and left the hotel the next day.

> **WOMAN ROAD WARRIOR TIP:**
>
> When you check in at the hotel, the desk clerk will tell you which room has been assigned to you. What he won't tell you is that you can change your room assignment if you don't like it. You can always get a room change as long as a room you prefer is available.

- You can exit the hotel more quickly if you are on a lower floor. Thus, a lower floor may be safer in the event of fire or other casualty. A lower floor, however, may have a less attractive view, and concierge/club floors are typically the highest floors.

After reading all of this, you are probably wondering if there are any rooms that are acceptable. The answer is yes: These rooms are typically somewhere in the middle of a floor above the first floor and on a part of the floor away from the facilities mentioned above.

Hotel Comfort: Getting a Good Night's Sleep

It may sound self-evident, but, unlike your home, probably the most important use you make of a hotel room is for sleeping. If something about the hotel prevents you from sleeping well, then the hotel room isn't serving its purpose. And sleeping well in a hotel isn't always easy under the best of circumstances. After all, you're in a strange environment, unaccustomed to the room layout, the bed, the pillows, and the lighting. A hotel room can present all kinds of environmental disturbances. Although with experience you'll get used to dealing with these conditions, there are things you can do to make it easier. What are some of the tricks?

ROOM ALARM CLOCK

It sounds so obvious, but when you first get to your room, check the clock in the room, if there is one, to be sure it shows the correct time and that the alarm is off. I can tell you that I have forgotten this advice and have been unceremoniously awakened by an alarm long before I was ready. That certainly won't help anyone get a good night's sleep!

LACK OF HUMIDITY

Hotel room air can be very dry, which can affect your skin and sinuses. A few suggestions to combat dryness:

- Keep the window open if you can, consistent with your security needs. Fresh air may make the room more comfortable.
- Limit the heat; if possible, make the room a little cool. Too much heat always makes the air drier.
- Bring a humidifier with you. Some manufacturers produce small portable humidifiers that do not take up a lot of luggage space and can add much-needed moisture.
- Request a humidifier from the hotel. Some hotels keep a supply of portable humidifiers for their guests.
- Run the hot water in the shower with the bathroom door open. Although you probably shouldn't run the shower all night long, you can add humidity while you're first trying to get to sleep if you run the shower just before you turn in.
- Place a few glasses of water on top of the room heater or radiator. Doing so will add moisture to the air if a flat floor unit distributes the heat.
- Use a saline nasal spray and water mist. The saline nasal spray will keep your air passages moist. The water mist is for your face or any other body part that needs additional moisture.

NOISE

Unfortunately, hotels can be noisy. There are people coming and going all night, and the walls between the rooms are not always the thickest; noise from another room or the hall can often be heard. I've even been awakened by someone snoring in the next room! If you are sensitive to noise, try the following:

- Use earplugs.
- Keep the TV or radio on to provide white noise. It doesn't have to be at full volume.
- Use some other type of device for drowning out hotel noise,

such as the fan on the air conditioning unit or a portable humidifier.

- If noise is coming from an adjacent or nearby room, complain to the front desk; if that doesn't work, ask to change rooms.

LIGHT

Sometimes the curtains that cover the windows do not close properly, or the light from the hall comes in under the door. You can prop a chair or table against the curtains to keep them closed. Stuff a towel in front of the door to block out the light from the hall. Eye masks also come in handy in situations like this. Masks not only block out light, but certain kinds can provide soothing comfort to your eyes and face.

PILLOWS AND LINENS

Some hotels use feather pillows. Although these pillows are very comfortable, you may be allergic to feathers and thus require a foam pillow. Some travelers with allergy problems bring their own pillows. If you think that a pillow is too bulky to carry, you can ask the front desk or housekeeping for an acceptable pillow. Similarly, if you tend to get cold and need extra blankets or you need other linens, go ahead and ask for them.

Don't be shy about pursuing what you need to be comfortable. There are a number of distractions and disturbances that can occur while you're in a hotel room. It's up to you to be creative and do whatever it takes to get a good night's sleep and stay healthy. Do not be embarrassed about asking for things. Remember: You are the one footing the bill, and you are entitled to your rest and comfort.

Keeping Yourself and Your Possessions Safe

Today, most hotels use magnetic keycard systems to control access to their rooms; you insert your keycard into the lock to open the room door. A few hotels still use metal keys to open conventional locks on the room doors. When the desk clerk assigns your room, he should advise you of your room number by showing you the packet that holds the keycard or by telling you the room number in a voice that only you can hear. Ideally, other than you and the hotel personnel, the only person who should know your room number is someone you tell. Don't be embarrassed to ask for a new room if the desk clerk announces your room number in too loud a voice. You never know who is listening.

Before you go to your room for the first time, you will probably be asked if you want assistance with your luggage. You should seriously consider accepting this offer—not because you can't handle your luggage or because it's a nice perk to have someone else carry it, but because someone else will be with you when you enter the room. Not only is there safety in numbers, but it's great to have a buffer between you and an uninvited intruder.

If you are alone when you enter the room, prop the door open with your suitcase (keep your identification with you, in case you need to leave quickly)—then check the closet, under the bed, and in the shower for anything amiss before settling in. Also check the phone lines and make sure they are working. On one trip, I arrived in a room very late one night to find that the phone in the room didn't work. That's not a good situation to be in if you need to contact someone in an emergency.

If there is someone in the room who shouldn't be there, get out of the room as fast as you can. Since you haven't settled in yet, it's your choice whether you leave your luggage in order to get away quickly. The number one priority is *your safety*; if anything is going to slow you down, forget it and go back later (preferably with hotel security or the police).

Most hotels do a pretty good job of keeping their rooms clean, and I generally don't take special precautions or do any supplementary cleaning when I first get to a hotel room. On the other hand, my friend Andrea, the flight attendant, doesn't have as much confidence as I do in hotel housekeeping. When she first gets to her room,

WOMAN ROAD WARRIOR TIP:

Suppose you've arrived at the room, everything has been in order, but there is still something that feels wrong, or you're uncomfortable. Request a change! Too often we accept what is given to us because we are tired, we don't want the hassle, or we think that it's going to get better. More often than not, our first impressions prove to be right.

she wipes the room telephone, the television remote control, and the toilet seat with an antiseptic wipe she brings with her. She also wears A-Way Travel Treads when she walks around the hotel room and, when she lies on the bed, she makes sure not to lie on the bedspread. While most hotels change their bed linens daily, they don't clean the bedspread as often.

After you've settled in your room, here are a few things that can help ensure that you and your belongings stay safe:

- **Avoid getting in an elevator if you are uncomfortable.** If you look into the elevator and see someone or something in there that makes you uncomfortable, don't get on. Don't be embarrassed. The old saying that there is safety in numbers also applies to elevators. Danielle will not get into an elevator with only one other person if she is uncomfortable for whatever reason. Similarly, if you arrive at your floor and don't feel comfortable getting out of the elevator, then just don't. If you feel you must give some explanation, simply pretend you forgot something.

- **Don't sign your entire name and room number to items like dining room checks and health club registrations, which can be easily picked up and viewed by the wrong person.** You never know who is watching. If you leave this information around, anyone can look at it and identify your room. Sophie was eating alone at a hotel dining room when a stranger asked her if he could buy her a drink. She declined and he left without incident. Sophie finished her meal and signed the bill with her room number. A half hour later he was banging on her door and screaming obscenities! If you do have to sign the restaurant bill and include your room number, hand it directly to your server or hostess; don't just leave it on your table.

- **Ask room service to call you when your delivery leaves the kitchen.** You should never open your hotel room door to an uninvited stranger. If room service notifies you when your food leaves the kitchen, you can expect the delivery. Although you still have to be sure that the knock on your door is really from room service, you have much less concern that you're allowing someone you shouldn't into your room. You can also make sure you're dressed to receive the delivery; every traveler can remember the time or times she has been interrupted or has had to run around the room to put on something decent while room service is waiting outside the door. Actually, I discovered on one trip that a call before room service delivery has been standard practice at all Wyndham hotels for some time. Maybe at some point all the hotels will adopt this practice, but, until then, I will always ask my hotel for such a call.

- **When preordering breakfast, do not identify yourself as a female alone.** Hotels today often allow you to order breakfast from room service by filling out a form the night before and leaving it on the doorknob of your room. Although these hotels have made it convenient to order breakfast in the morning, they've also compromised security. The form you leave on the doorknob often asks for your name and the number of people being served. If you fill in that information, the form identifies you as a woman alone, and you don't know who will see it. One woman I know of had ordered breakfast by leaving the completed form on her door. She opened the door the next morning to a stranger who identified himself as room service and then assaulted her. Only fill in your initials or your last name or leave the name blank on the form. You may also want to inflate the number of people being served. The worst that will happen is that you'll have silverware and/or coffee or tea service for two.

- **Stand at the door while room service is being delivered.** Even when you're expecting a room service delivery, you still need to be careful. When I'm traveling alone, I always stand at or near the door, leaving the door open, when the server brings in the cart or tray. I sign the bill when the server is on his way out the door or out in the hall after delivery.

- **Minimize the trips to your room by maintenance and other hotel personnel.** Even beyond room service, you may need visits to your room from hotel personnel—hotel maintenance, deliveries, and other types of assistance. When you're traveling alone, minimize these visits, especially at night. If something in your room needs to be fixed, try to have that work done the next day, when you're not in the room. If the problem really needs to be repaired immediately, consider whether you want to change rooms rather than be bothered by maintenance personnel.

* **When leaving the hotel room, especially at night, turn on the TV or radio.** Most intruders want to enter and leave undetected. Noise indicates occupancy and an uninvited person could be deterred by the noise of the TV or radio.
* **Consider having hotel security dead bolt your room lock from the outside when you leave.** Some hotels have room locks that can be dead-bolted from the outside. Some particularly security-conscious travelers have hotel security dead bolt the lock from the outside when they leave their rooms. You may want to consider this option if your hotel offers it. If you do, you will need hotel security to reopen the lock when you return, which may be inconvenient, but means that you won't be alone when you return to your room.
* **Don't hang the "service please" sign on the door when you leave your room.** You're simply telling anyone who cares that the room is empty. Maid service will still take care of your room, and you can always call housekeeping or the front desk and ask for maid service before you leave the room.
* **Keep secondary locks bolted whenever you're in the room, regardless of time of day.** You never know who may walk into your room. One night, I did not bolt the secondary locks, and someone had a keycard to my room and just walked in. The front desk had inadvertently assigned the same room to the two of us. Luckily, it was all very innocent, but it certainly made a lasting impression.
* **Keep windows and patio doors locked.** Ashley, a flight attendant, was in a hotel in Las Vegas one night and didn't follow this rule. She awakened to find an intruder coming into her room through the patio door. She was able to chase the intruder out the door and contact security without harm, but now she doesn't forget to lock these doors.
* **Don't assume the door is locked when you leave the room just because the door closes.** Janet once left her hotel room and watched the door close. When she came back to the room, though, she found that the door had not closed fully and the

latch had not shut. Fortunately, no one else discovered that she had essentially left her room door open before she returned. Take a second when you leave the hotel room to verify that indeed the door has closed and is locked.

- **Know where the floor exits are.** If you want to be safe, be prepared. You'll only care where the floor exits are in the middle of an emergency, when it will be too late to find out for the first time. After the events of September 11, 2001, it is more important than ever to have an exit plan. Most hotels have floor plans showing the emergency exits in the rooms or in the printed in-room materials. If you didn't notice the exit signs when you walked to your room, go back and find them. You may want to count the number of doors between your room and the exit so you can find the exit if for some reason your vision is blocked (for example, by smoke) when you try to find your way off the floor. In an emergency, you'll be glad you took the time.

- **Keep your identification easily accessible.** In an emergency, every second counts. I like to keep my purse, jewelry, flashlight, and room key either on the nightstand or by the front door. This way, I know where things are and can find them quickly if I need them in an emergency. You need to identify what is important to you. Do not try to bring everything with you when leaving the room in an emergency. The last thing you need is to be carrying a lot of items while trying to maneuver down a flight of stairs.

- **Leave a note in your room when you leave.** A major airline recommends to its flight attendants to leave a note when they're going out, an excellent practice for any business traveler. Leave the note in your room or, better yet, slip it under the door of a colleague's room, if you're traveling with one. The note should state what time you left, where you're going, and what you were wearing. You may also want to advise the front desk or doorman. At a time that so many travelers have cell phones, you might think this precaution excessive. However, you never know when your cell phone's battery may run out, or someone may take the phone.

- **Always carry identification.** Regardless of where you are going or how long you'll be gone, always carry some type of identification. It confirms what you tell people yourself if you need help and may get you quicker assistance if for some reason you can't speak or be understood.

- **Store your valuables (including passport) in the room or hotel safe.** Most hotels provide either a safe in the room or one at the front desk where you can store your valuables. In-room safes are secured using a password or code that belongs to you. If you are concerned that you might forget your valuables and leave them behind, put a single shoe in the safe. When you pack or dress for departure and find only one shoe of the pair, you'll remember that the other is in the safe with your valuables. Although the in-room safes are pretty secure, valuables stored in these safes are typically not covered by the hotel's insurance. Your personal insurance might cover a loss, but you would have to file a claim with your own carrier. The best way to avoid an uninsured hotel loss is either to keep all your valuables in your possession or to use the hotel safe located at the front desk. The hotel may charge a fee for using the safe at the front desk. Of course, the safest way to avoid a loss of your valuables in your hotel is not to have them with you. Emily, an executive recruiter, always leaves her jewelry and other valuables—even her wedding ring—at home when she's on the road.

- **Request that all deliveries be made to the front desk.** When you're traveling on business, you may be receiving courier packages, messenger deliveries, and other similar items at the hotel. You may buy something and direct the store to deliver it to the hotel. Under extreme circumstances, you may even order food from outside the hotel and have it delivered. When you are making the request for delivery, *never* give out your room number. Give the front desk this simple rule: all deliveries must be screened at the desk; no one may deliver anything directly to your room. When the front desk calls you to tell you someone has a delivery for you, you can decide whether to have it delivered to your room or to go to the desk and pick it up yourself.

- **Never open your room door for someone you don't know and aren't expecting.** I've said this more than once, but it bears repeating: Never open the door to your room for someone you don't know and aren't expecting. One major airline even includes this rule in its employee handbook for, among others, flight attendants and pilots. If someone asks you to violate this rule, just say no. If someone shows up unexpectedly, you can send the person to the concierge or front desk.

- **Request that the hotel not give out your room number to anyone.** You should never really need to make this request, but every so often someone makes a mistake. The front desk and the hotel operator are the only people between you and the outside. Hotel personnel need to be extra careful in protecting your privacy, especially if you're traveling alone. The only other person who should know your hotel room number is someone you tell. Make sure you protect yourself.
- **If you find that someone is trying to enter your room that shouldn't be, try not to panic.** Again, the hotel may have inadvertently assigned the same room to two guests, and the person who is trying to enter your room may be doing so totally innocently and may be just as surprised as you. If the situation seems more serious, make sure that the secondary locks are secure, and contact the hotel operator, security, or the front desk immediately. If you feel you are not getting the cooperation required, call the police. If there is a problem with the phone lines, use your cell phone if you have one. Do not hang up the phone until the situation has been rectified.

Changing Hotels

On some occasions, you may find yourself in a hotel that makes you uncomfortable for whatever reason—maybe even something you can't identify or articulate—and you want to move to a different hotel. If you made your reservation through a travel agent or on your own, and not over the Internet, you should have more flexibility in changing hotels. If you made the reservation through a travel site and prepaid for the room, however, your options will probably be more limited.

You may feel uncomfortable in a hotel for any one of a number of reasons, such as:

- The location is much farther away from where you need to be for business.
- The hotel doesn't have appropriate security in the lobby. Emily was once standing in a hotel lobby waiting for some colleagues. A stranger walked into the lobby from the street, came up to

her, and asked her for money; when she said no, he walked out another door. There was no bellman or other security personnel in the hotel lobby to escort the man to the street. Needless to say, this experience didn't raise her comfort level, and she went to another hotel.

- The hotel doesn't have adequate room locks.
- You must walk down a long, dimly lit hallway to get to your room.

During a trip to upstate New York, I once checked in at a hotel in a large city late at night after a long day of work. Although the hotel was advertised as being a member of a major chain, when I arrived it was clear that the hotel had lost its flag. Even though my intuition told me to leave, at first I just didn't want to deal with the hassle. But finding my room was like working a maze through long, dark corridors. When I finally opened the room door, the room was dark, and then I found that the bathroom wasn't clean. Then, when I picked up the phone to complain, I found that it didn't work. I felt *very* uncomfortable with the entire situation. I went back to the front desk immediately and told the clerk I was leaving and expected that my room charge would not show up on my credit card statement. No one tried to persuade me to stay, and no charge ever appeared. Using the yellow pages in the room that I left, I had found a hotel with a recognized name, which I contacted using my cell phone. I was able to spend the night there.

But I can also say that I haven't always followed my own advice and, on more than one occasion, ended up putting a chair in front of the hotel-room door, suffering a very fitful night's sleep and leaving the next day. Now, I just follow my instincts from the beginning and move if that's what they tell me. The inconvenience is more tolerable than the lost sleep and the anxiety.

My experience is that most hotels will respect your feelings and will allow you to relocate without charge, rather than engage in a lengthy debate with you. If you get some initial resistance, ask to speak to the manager. If that doesn't work, you may have to leave the hotel anyway and fight with the hotel through your credit card company or by writing to the hotel's owner or senior management or, if the hotel is a member of a chain, to the hotel company. In general, though, if you have the slightest concern about your safety in a hotel, change hotels, even though it may cost you something; your safety is more important than any amount of money.

Make the Concierge Your Best Friend

Traveling to a place for the first time can be confusing and frustrating. Once you arrive, you may want or need the following:

- some advice as to how to explore the city;
- a good place to have dinner or go to the movies;
- hard-to-get tickets to that play or sporting event;
- guidance on the best way to arrange a site for a meeting or other event;
- the location of the nearest copy shop, fax machine, or ATM;
- a recommendation of a tailor to repair or alter some clothing;
- a place to get a haircut or massage or to get your nails done.

The solution: Ask the hotel concierge. The concierge is one of the best-kept secrets of the hotel industry. Most major hotels have a concierge whose responsibility is to be of service to guests. Let the concierge be your guide.

Nancy, a concierge in a hotel in a major city, says that it's her goal to simplify your life if you're a guest in her hotel. She thinks of herself as the gatekeeper to everything you might want to do. The concierge is trying to build credibility in your eyes, but also has a short time in which to achieve this. Concierges are busy; the time they can spend with you is limited. Do yourself a favor and try to communicate your needs to the concierge as precisely as possible. Concierges who know their area and have experience with the restaurants, stores, theaters, and other venues or neighborhoods are worth their weight in gold. Don't forget that a concierge who makes a reservation or gives a suggestion has a vested interest in making sure you're happy.

With the assistance of a concierge, I have been able to get into restaurants that were full and secure tickets to events that were sold out. I have consulted a concierge for recommendations on solutions to the most mundane, yet immediate, problems that have arisen during my business travels. On one trip, I found that the suit I had brought for an important customer meeting needed alterations. The hotel concierge sent me to a tailor who fitted the suit and finished the alterations while I had lunch in a nearby restaurant.

I cannot say enough about the benefits of concierge assistance. I frequently contact the hotel concierge before my arrival and start asking for help. I have found concierges to be helpful beyond my expectations, and I would find it difficult to conduct business or navigate a new city without one. After years of travel, I am on a first-name basis with concierges at hotels in many cities across the country. Obviously, the personal relationships and resulting personalized service are added benefits of just asking for their help. If you find that you are staying in a hotel without concierge service, inquire at the front desk for directions and recommendations.

Although I discuss hotel tipping in general in a separate section, concierge service is so specialized and so valuable that I think tipping for the concierge warrants separate treatment. Concierges, like all hotel personnel, live off their tips. There are fewer "rules" regarding when and how much to tip the concierge than for other hotel personnel. In general, though, if the concierge performed a service, I suggest a generous tip. A good relationship with the concierge can be invaluable, and your generosity can only help cement that relationship. If the concierge makes a routine dinner reservation or checks on the status of my air travel, I will give a $2-$5 tip. On the other hand, if the concierge obtains a reservation at a full restaurant or tickets to a sold out performance or event, I will sometimes tip $20 or even higher. Remember that a concierge may have pulled a personal favor in order to get you that ticket or reservation.

The concierge service becomes even more important when you travel globally. See the discussion of hotel concierges abroad in Chapter 7.

Hidden or Not-so-hidden Costs

Hotels are becoming very creative in generating additional revenue. Being aware of hotel charges can help avoid major surprises at checkout. A few common hidden or not-so-hidden additional costs might include:

- **Parking.** Your hotel may offer valet parking or garage or surface lot self-parking. Parking charges are sometimes added directly to your bill, so inquire as to the hotel's rules upon check-in.
  - Valet parking is especially handy if you are out late at night

or if you just do not wish to be responsible for self-parking in a lot or garage that may or may not present security concerns. If you do use valet parking, call the valet service before you leave the room and ask that your car be brought to the hotel entrance. You will minimize or eliminate the time you spend in the lobby waiting for your car. Normally, if your hotel offers valet parking, you will be charged a daily rate and will not be charged extra for taking your car into and out of the garage during the day.

- Some hotels located in major cities will also have a self-park garage located next to the hotel and will charge you to park your car there if you'd rather not use the valet. Other hotels, typically in areas of lesser population density, will offer only a self-parking garage. Some hotels will charge for garage self-parking, and others will not. In some cases, the hotel will charge the same for the self-parking as for the valet, making it more likely that you will want to use the valet. On the other hand, some hotels that have self-parking will charge you every time you go out of the garage, so if you are in and out of a garage several times a day, the cost could easily equal or exceed a higher cost for valet. Some hotels offer surface parking on all sides of the hotel. If you arrive at the hotel late at night, you don't need to prove that you are fearless by driving around to the back of the hotel and walking through the parking lot alone.

- **Telephone.** It seems that each hotel has a different policy regarding the use of the hotel phone. The in-room guide to hotel services found in most hotels will tell you the charges for the hotel phone; sometimes, the charges are posted on the phone itself. Normally, you will be charged for any local and long-distance calls that you dial direct. For long-distance calls, you will pay the charge imposed by the telephone company (whichever long-distance company the hotel uses) and usually a charge imposed by the hotel. Historically, toll-free, collect, calling card, and credit card calls were free to hotel guests. Recently, however, especially as the long-distance carriers have established their own toll-free numbers for long-distance calling, many hotels have begun to impose a charge for those toll-free calls. If you are using a telephone calling card or a toll-free number to access your office, these charges can add up, although direct dialing from the room is still more expensive. Since cell phone service has become so economical, you may find you'll save by using your cell phone instead of the hotel phone if reception is adequate.

- **Business services and Internet access.** Hotels often have business centers with computers, fax machines, printers, and similar equipment. In addition, some of this equipment may be available in your room. Most hotel rooms now have direct high-speed Internet connections for your laptop. Also, the hotel's front desk will often transmit or receive faxes for you. Of course, these services almost always cost money. You can charge business-center services directly to your room or to your credit card. You will probably incur a charge for faxes transmitted or received at the front desk. Internet access from your room may involve a daily charge or may be included with the room. These services can get very expensive very quickly and are usually added to the room bill.

> **WOMAN ROAD WARRIOR TIP:**
>
> You may need to access either your company's e-mail system or network from your hotel room. But you many not want to pay the charge for the hotel's high-speed Internet service, or you may be at a hotel that doesn't offer that service. If so, check if you can get access using a local dial-up access number in the area code of your hotel. Typically, these calls within the hotel's area code are local calls with a very modest, or sometimes no, charge.

- **The minibar.** Many people find the drinks and snacks in their room's minibar almost irresistible. But the convenience of using minibars to get food or drink 24 hours a day, without leaving your room or waiting for delivery, comes at a premium cost. Your hotel, of course, hopes you will get the urge at some point to raid the minibar. If you want to eliminate all temptation, leave the minibar key with the desk clerk when you check in. Don't forget that you're free to bring food or beverages into your room. I like to drink bottled water, so I buy several bottles before I get to the hotel and bring them to the room with me. If you don't have time to stop to buy water, it's still cheaper to order the largest available bottle of water from room service than it is to take the bottled water from the minibar. Many hotel gift shops and newsstands also sell bottled water at a price lower than the minibar. Many hotels now equip the minibar with a sensor that recognizes when you open the door and take something out and charge you accordingly, without noticing if you put it back. For example, if you buy something that you want to store in the minibar refrigerator and remove an item to do so but then put it back, you could nevertheless be charged as if you had consumed it. Check your bill when you check out of the hotel.

- **Service costs.** Some large hotels and resorts now charge a daily fee (sometimes called a "resort fee") for support staff (i.e., housekeeping, bellmen). This charge is added to your bill. If the hotel imposes this charge, you don't need to tip any of the hotel staff. It's a good idea to check when you make a reservation, especially at a resort-type hotel, if the hotel imposes this kind of a charge.

- **Early checkout.** Often a traveler will reserve a room at a hotel for several days but have to leave the hotel before she has stayed that entire period. Some hotels impose a charge on guests who check out prior to their scheduled date, although I have not seen this charge as much recently. Given the uncertainty of business travel, I find this charge absurd and do not hesitate to voice my opinion. On occasion, I've been able to persuade the hotel to waive it. If you have reached an elite status in a hotel chain's reward program, the hotel will typically waive this kind of charge for you.

- **Health club.** Some hotels charge for use of their onsite health clubs. Other hotels only charge for use of an offsite club. Still other hotels charge for neither. If you plan to use the health club, you should ask about the hotel's policy when you make your reservation. This is another one of those charges that can sneak up on you, so plan accordingly.

Ask as many questions as occur to you about the hotel's policies regarding extra charges before you make your reservation—or at least before the cancellation deadline. Being aware of these costs can save you some frustrations and surprises upon checkout.

If you do not agree with a charge, take the time to dispute it and get it resolved prior to leaving the hotel. Remember that everything is negotiable. Talk to the desk agent, and if you don't get a satisfactory resolution, talk to the manager. If a charge shows up on your credit card that you dispute or do not understand, contact your credit card company immediately and explain the situation. In my experience, most credit card companies will work with you to resolve these issues. For best results, communicate with your credit card company immediately, before the credit card company makes payment to the hotel. Otherwise, you run a greater risk of being liable for the charge.

Tipping

Staying at a hotel normally means lots of tipping. As Suzanne, a hotel manager, reminded me, most hotel employees make a large part of their living through tips. Therefore, hotel employees expect tips, and you will generally be better off if you meet those expectations. Of course, you should not feel obligated to tip anyone who provides less than adequate service, but tipping is part of the culture of staying in a hotel.

Some general rules for hotel tipping:

- **Doorman.** Tip the doorman $1 or $2 if he assists you with your luggage and one dollar if he hails a taxi for you. Otherwise, no tip is expected.
- **Bellman.** Tip the bellman who escorts you to your room or who picks up luggage from your room when you depart. The amount should be $2-$5, depending on (1) whether he brings your luggage to your room, (2) how many bags you have, and (3) whether he performs other services, such as bringing you ice. You may also take into account the city and the nature of the hotel in determining the amount.

- **Delivery to room.** If the bellman delivers a package to your room or housekeeping brings you a towel or pillow, give one or two dollars to the person who does so.
- **Room service.** Most hotels add a gratuity or service charge to the room service bill that you receive with your meal. If so, you do not need to add anything further, although I usually give $1 or $2 extra to the person who brings the meal. If no gratuity or service charge has been added, then you should add a 15 to 20 percent tip.
- **Maid service.** Because the maid typically works in your room when you are absent, housekeeping staff is easy to overlook, but a little gratuity can go a long way. I tip at the end of my stay and leave the money on the desk or in an envelope marked for housekeeping. I usually leave $1 to $3 per night, depending on the city and the hotel. Sophie typically leaves all her change on the desk each night and lets it remain there at the end of her stay as a tip for housekeeping.
- **Valet-parking attendant.** I usually give a dollar to the valet parking attendant who brings my car whenever I take it out.

If you have received particularly good service from someone at a hotel, you should also consider writing or otherwise contacting the hotel manager in order to praise that person. In addition to being a nice gesture, such a note or phone call can be helpful to someone's career.

Dealing With the Unexpected

As always, you'll find yourself in situations that will require you to troubleshoot and improvise. Here's how to handle some typical difficulties:

The hotel does not have your reservation. Sometimes you may have a reservation at a hotel, but your name does not appear on the reservation list for that day. If this occurs, supply the front-desk agent with the confirmation number. Hotels keep track of reservations by number and not by guest name. I have shown up at hotels that did not have a reservation in my name, but found the reservation when I supplied the number. On the one occasion that I did not have the number, I would have had to find another place to stay, except that the hotel happened to have available rooms anyway. If the hotel has no rooms and you have no number, you may be out of luck.

The hotel has your reservation, but does not have any rooms. Hotels can and do intentionally oversell rooms for a night, just as airlines can oversell seats. Sometimes a hotel may be oversold because some people who had been scheduled to check out simply stayed. When your hotel is oversold, it is particularly critical to have a confirmation number verifying that you have a reservation at the hotel for that night. Of course, it always seems that your hotel is oversold only

> **WOMAN ROAD WARRIOR TIP:**
>
> Be sure to remain calm and professional in any travel situation, but especially when you are dealing with someone regarding something that has gone wrong. Don't allow yourself to be dismissed as "just another hysterical female."

after you've had a long day of travel and meetings and when it is very late. Remain calm. You'll get nowhere if you start yelling at the desk personnel.

You should know that it is not uncommon for hotels to hold rooms for special situations, such as the surprise arrival of a celebrity, so first ask about the availability of any of these rooms. If that doesn't work, ask to speak directly with the manager. Although desk agents will want to be helpful, they do not have the authority required in a situation like this. Remember: your main objective is to secure a hotel room as quickly as possible and without any additional cost to you or your company. Whatever you do, don't move away from the front desk. The last thing management wants is a scene, and if you stay put, they will feel additional pressure to resolve the situation.

The manager may suggest that you go to a different hotel. Be sure that the other hotel is of at least comparable quality and location, and get a confirmation number or some guarantee of a reservation. Also, be sure to verify that the alternative will be no more costly than the rate specified in your reservation. If you do not have transportation, ask how you are getting to the new hotel and be sure that you are not expected to pay. Before leaving the first hotel, make sure you have the name and phone number of the manager and desk agent there, as well as the name, address, phone number, contact person, and confirmation number for the place you're going. The last thing you want is to show up at the other hotel and be told they can't accommodate you.

The best bargaining position you have is when you're physically standing with the manager at the front desk of the hotel that made the original error. Don't depart until you are satisfied that everything has been resolved.

Although checking into a hotel and finding out you have no room is not pleasant, it can have its bright side. On one trip, I had a reservation with a corporate rate at a decent but hardly luxurious hotel in a major city. When I arrived, I learned that the hotel had no rooms available. After a lengthy discussion with the manager at the front desk, he agreed to move me to a far more expensive room in a luxury hotel a short distance away. The accommodations were much better, and I paid not a dime more.

Check-in and checkout times. There are times when you want to check into a hotel earlier than the standard check-in time or extend your time later than the standard checkout time. Check-in time at most hotels is 3:00 p.m. If you arrive early, inquire at the front desk if the room is ready. Checkout time is typically between 11:00 a.m. and noon. If you need additional time, contact the front desk.

Hotels will generally accommodate late checkout requests. Sometimes hotels will charge for late checkouts, the amount varying with the lateness. I have found that if I ask the desk agent for a late checkout, the clerk will warn me if I will incur a charge. On the other hand, others I know have been surprised when they see their room bill and been told that the in-room guide to hotel services specifies these charges.

Being an elite member of a hotel's reward program comes in handy when dealing with this type of request. Hotels typically accommodate elite members by allowing early check-in and late checkout without charge.

Room is noisy or otherwise unacceptable. As discussed earlier, if your room is not acceptable, insist that you be moved. You can make this request at any time, even in the middle of the night. Once, during my first night in a hotel, I was constantly disturbed by people knocking on my room door. I discovered that my room number had been erroneously posted as the hospitality suite for a company that was holding meetings at the hotel. I telephoned the front desk at about 11:00 p.m. and was moved to a different room.

Your room is vandalized. Few things are more upsetting than to walk into your hotel room and realize that someone other than you or the maid has been there. Should this occur, immediately leave the room and contact security; let security personnel determine whether the intruder has left the room. If you are staying in a hotel room with an electronic card key, the front desk should be able to run a computer program to determine who has had access to your room. You should then formally report the theft to the hotel and the police. Try to make a complete list of what is missing or damaged. Ask for a copy of the police report (you may need it later for insurance purposes). If your wallet has been taken, you will need to alert your credit card companies to the theft. Also contact your home office and report the theft; your company may have to file a claim with its insurance company.

Service or anything else is not satisfactory. Many different things can and do go wrong at hotels, far too many to list and probably too many to think of. You may find:

- hot water shortages;
- heating or air conditioning doesn't work properly;
- something else in the room doesn't work;
- room service meals don't show up when promised.

Hotels are always dealing with situations like this, and they are as responsive as they can be. After all, they need to keep their guests comfortable in order to stay in business. Hotel general managers like to hear from guests with both positive and negative feedback. You'll never get any satisfaction if you keep a hotel's shortcomings to yourself, and you won't help the hotel do a better job in the future. Talking to the manager may help future guests of the hotel (possibly including *you*) enjoy their experiences.

I was on a trip to one city and stayed at one of its most famous hotels, a nationally renowned institution. Unbeknownst to me, the

> **WOMAN ROAD WARRIOR TIP:**
>
> If something isn't or wasn't right, express your dissatisfaction. Follow this rule even if the circumstances are really unusual.

president was staying at the same hotel at the same time, and noisy, flag-burning demonstrators surrounded it. The resulting confusion and security mess made it impossible for me to park my car in the hotel garage, and at one point, even to get anywhere near the hotel. I intentionally stopped my car in the middle of the street near the hotel and was engulfed by a crowd of policemen. Ultimately, I was directed to a different garage, farther away from the hotel, and was escorted back to the hotel by an officer. When I told the hotel manager that I would never have stayed in the hotel had I known what I was about to face, my bill was reduced substantially. I got a further reduction when I disputed the charge with my credit card company.

Sophie had a similar experience when her "doggie bag" filled with chocolates from an expensive New York restaurant disappeared after being checked with the bellman. When she suggested that she should not be charged for her room, not only was the room charge removed from her bill, but she received a free breakfast and a certificate for a free stay in the future.

Long-term Stays

Business travel does not always consist just of a series of brief trips to different places. You may be assigned to a project or job that can last from days to weeks to years. During this time, you may be away from home much or all the work week and only return home (if at all) on weekends.

If you will be away from home for a project or job that lasts longer than a month, you should consider living elsewhere than in a hotel. If you are traveling to the same city week in and week out, you would probably prefer to stay in a place where (1) you don't have to pack and unpack every week, (2) you can leave your work-related clothing behind, and (3) you don't have to check in and out every week. In addition, the cost of paying a daily hotel rate over a long period can become very high. In this situation, you have essentially two alternatives: a corporate apartment or a long-term-stay arrangement with a hotel.

Corporate Apartment Living

Corporate apartments are available in most major cities and are much cheaper than hotels. Some companies have their own corporate apartments in various cities, and their employees stay there when they are in one of those cities on a long project. If you need to find your own corporate apartment, there are a few nationally known brands, such as Oakwood Corporate Housing or Marriott ExecuStay. I recommend working with a nationally known agency that can guide you or your company in your efforts.

A corporate apartment will typically be a studio (efficiency) or one-bedroom, fully furnished with a small kitchen and kitchenware. Some type of maid service is usually offered, with the price depending on the level of service. Usually, you must rent the apartment for at least a month, with a lower rate for longer leases.

If you are finding your own corporate apartment, take the time, if you can, to look at the unit or a comparable unit in the same building. Here are some items to consider:

- Is there adequate building security? Find out whether there is 24-hour attended security, a buzzer system, some combination of those, or something else. You are probably going to be living in a city where you are a stranger, so be sure you are satisfied.
- What are the parking alternatives? If you're in a city long enough to have a corporate apartment, it's likely that you will also have a rental car. Typically, apartment buildings provide parking, but again focusing on security, consider the following:
  - Is parking outdoors? Is it covered?
  - How is the area secured?
  - How far is the parking from the building entrance?
  - Is the area well lit?
- What kind of physical locks are on your unit? How secure is it? You may want to request that the locks be changed before you move in. I like to have a new set of locks and keys that no one has used before.
- Are the hallways or entryways well lit? Pay attention to how many outside fixtures there are and how well the place is maintained. Burned-out light bulbs in the halls or unsecured outside doors indicate something about the upkeep of the building.
- How much noise will you hear from adjacent units? It's difficult to find the answer to this question when you look at an apartment, but find out what you can. Get some assurances, if possible. You don't want to be awakened in the middle of the

night because of the noise coming from your neighbor. You won't be able to change apartments as easily as you can hotel rooms.

- Are pets allowed? If you will be away for an extended period of time and want to bring your pet with you, make sure your living arrangements will accommodate him or her.
- What types of housekeeping arrangements are available?
- What types of amenities does the building have, and what other amenities are nearby? You may prefer a building with a health club, cleaner, grocery, or convenience store. You may want to be in a neighborhood where restaurants and other amenities are within walking distance.

Traveling between home and work cities is much easier when you live in a corporate apartment. You can leave work clothes behind and travel with minimal luggage. When the time comes to move out, you can bring your things back over a few weeks. Alternatively, you can bring an extra piece of luggage for the last trip home or pack your things in a box and ship them home.

Over the years, I have had some great corporate apartments in cities across the country. I have found that I can really get to know a city better when not living in a hotel. Having a corporate apartment also allows you to cook for yourself and have the types of foods you like to eat.

Long-term Hotel Stay

If a corporate apartment is not an option, but you find yourself in the same city for an extended period of time, try to make an arrangement with your hotel, both to save money and enhance convenience. Ask the following:

- Will the hotel offer a reduced rate if you rent a room for a long period of time, such as a month? The rate needs to be low enough that you will save over the regular hotel rate, even though you are paying for those weekend nights when you are not there.
- Will the hotel offer a further discounted rate for a longer-term commitment?
- If the hotel will not make a long-term commitment financially

attractive, can you store luggage there while you are not occupying a room?

Although most guests in a hotel stay for only a few nights, most large hotels will have the flexibility to enter into an agreement with a reduced rate for a longer commitment. The hotel is guaranteed an occupied room for a defined period of time, which means guaranteed revenue. When negotiating this type of an agreement, make sure you are talking to someone in management who has the authority to speak for the hotel. Otherwise, you may think you have a deal, but will need to wait to get it approved or start over with someone else. If such an arrangement is or might become important to you, limit your hotel choices to one that will offer it.

Woman Road Warrior Checklist

__ Explore all options to get best rates and availability.

__ Determine what your needs are, let them be known, and don't compromise.

__ Reserve late arrival, if needed.

__ Obtain, note, and keep at hand your confirmation number.

__ If arriving later than planned, call front desk and confirm your plan to show up.

__ Be sure appropriate credits are recorded to frequent-flyer/reward programs.

__ Change assigned room until you are satisfied.

__ Upon entering room, check security and maintenance: no one in room, phone works, clock set to correct time and alarm off, etc.

__ Don't let your room number be announced or written and viewed.

__ Don't make it obvious that you are alone in your room or that it is empty.

__ Leave a note in the hotel room when you leave with your time of departure and destination.

__ Contact the hotel general manager if you are not satisfied.

__ Make the concierge your best friend.

__ Consider a corporate apartment for a long stay.

CHAPTER 4

Renting a Car

Once you arrive at your destination, you still need to get around. Unless your trip is by car, you need to decide how to go from the airport, train station, or other terminus to your hotel or business destination. You also may not find it practical to walk or take taxis everywhere you need to go in your destination city.

Although a rented car is perhaps the most common kind of local transportation, you should not assume that you'll need one. A car does provide flexibility, but it may be more costly than the alternatives. Remember, you will be paying the car rental charges, gasoline, and the cost of parking at your hotel and wherever else your business takes you. You also will be driving in a place that may be totally unfamiliar to you; you will have to contend with traffic and other unpredictable variables; and you will have to figure out where to park and then walk from the parking space to your destination. Car rental may be more cost and hassle than it's worth. Obviously, you need to take into account the distances involved in getting from place to place and what alternatives are available to you—taxi, limousine, or mass transit—and their costs.

I rent a car the majority of times I travel on business, at least domestically, but my choice is usually city-specific: For example, I always rent a car in Atlanta or Los Angeles, never in New York or Boston, and rarely in San Francisco. I almost always rent a car when I travel to a smaller city or town.

Reserving a Car

Choosing a car-rental company is more like choosing an airline than a hotel. There are a limited number of car-rental companies; they all provide similar services, and they all operate pretty much nationwide and make reservations centrally. Hertz, Avis, and National, the largest players in the car rental market, are the companies that probably focus most on the business traveler, but there are a number of other choices, as well.

Some car-rental companies have a tie-in with one or more airlines, so that renting a car earns the renter miles in an airline's frequent-flyer program. If you are a member of an airline's frequent-flyer program, you may want to rent from a company with such a tie-in with your airline. Be sure to tell the car-rental company the airline program to which you want your miles credited. The car-rental company may charge a fee to credit miles to your frequent-flyer account.

You can reserve a rental car through your internal or external travel agency, through a travel website, or on your own, either through the car-rental company's website or over the phone. Your company or your client or customer may have negotiated rates with a specific car-rental company, which also may apply to you. Generally, individuals under 21 years of age cannot rent a car, except in New York, where anyone over 18 can rent a car. Drivers under 25 generally pay a surcharge— as much as $25 per day. If the renter's company has a corporate agreement with the car-rental company, this charge will ordinarily be waived.

Normally, you or your travel agent can make a reservation through the company's toll-free number. If you are unsuccessful, which happens occasionally, try to contact a local agency office directly. In one instance, I called a car-rental company's toll-free number and was told that no cars were available at the airport location of my destination. I called a local office of the company at a hotel near the airport and had no difficulty reserving a vehicle. Today, very few reservations are made locally; most car reservations are made using the toll-free number or the Internet, which could explain why you can sometimes have more luck at the local agency. Often a car-rental company will hold back some cars during a convention and leave them unreserved, while the company will tell you that none are available. If you request a rental for one week or longer, however, you have a better chance that the car-rental company will rent you one of the "held-back" cars. You can tell the desk agent that your plans have changed when you pick up the car or call the company after you've left the lot. Remember that your daily rate may increase when you change from the long rental commitment to a shorter one, but the company should not charge you a higher rate than it would have quoted you had you specified the shorter period from the start.

The Car-rental Process

Most business travelers pick up and drop off their rental car at the airport. Most car-rental companies also have downtown locations, however, so you can make arrangements when you make your reservation to pick up your car there if you prefer. If you pick up your car at the airport, you will either ride a van supplied by the car-rental company or, in a few cities, by the airport, to a remote lot or will walk to a garage or lot near the terminal to pick up your car. Many travelers prefer, where possible, to rent from a company that keeps its vehicles within walking distance of the terminal. Most large airports, however, require all the rental companies to keep their cars in remote lots.

Almost every car-rental company provides express check-in and checkout services for members of the club program sponsored by that company. For example, Hertz has its #1 Club, and National has its Emerald Club. As in the airline and hotel industries, these programs can be a real plus for the business traveler. Some companies charge a fee for membership, usually about $50 per year, which will often be waived if your company has a corporate account with the car-rental company; other companies make membership free for anyone. To join, in addition to paying any fee, you typically fill out a questionnaire and tell the company the kind of car you prefer, the insurance you want to buy (if any), and the airline frequent-flyer program to which any miles you earn should be credited. You also include your driver's-license number and the number of the credit card you want to use for renting from this company.

If you join a club program, you can normally bypass the car-rental agency's counter at the airport and go directly to the car. The rental contract will be in the vehicle, already completed with the preferences you listed in your original questionnaire. If you can't bypass the counter at the airport or wherever you pick up the car, there will usually be a separate line for program members. If you are not a member of the program, then you go to the agency's desk at the airport to complete the car rental agreement and then head for the vehicle.

When you rent a car, you must have a valid driver's license and a credit card. Even if you make a cash prepayment or your company prepays, you must give the car-rental company a credit card to cover any unexpected charges or damage to the car.

> **WOMAN ROAD WARRIOR TIP:**
>
> Check your driver's license, especially if you're traveling near your birthday, to be sure it doesn't expire during your trip. If it does, the car-rental company won't let you take the vehicle.

In some states, such as Illinois, the officer issuing you a traffic ticket will take your license when he gives you the ticket; the state will only return it to you when your case is resolved. Your ticket acts as your license in the interim. The car-rental company may or may not rent you a vehicle if you are using a ticket as your license. If you are driving on a ticket, make sure to ask the car-rental company whether you will be allowed to pick up the car before you arrive to take possession of it.

There are a number of different choices you need to make when you rent a car, either when you make your reservation or when you sign the rental agreement:

Car type. Rental cars come in a number of different sizes and shapes, with a different rate charged for each category. Some rental car options include:

- subcompact (two-door automobile that can accommodate up to four passengers);
- compact (two- or four-door automobile that can accommodate four or five passengers);
- intermediate (two- or four-door automobile that can accommodate up to five passengers);
- full-size (four-door automobile that can accommodate up to five passengers);
- premium (four-door automobile that can accommodate up to six passengers);
- luxury (four-door automobile that can accommodate up to six passengers);
- sport utility (four-door vehicle that can accommodate up to five passengers);
- minivan (four-door van that can accommodate up to seven passengers);
- convertible (two-door automobile with retractable roof that can accommodate up to four passengers).

You should designate the type of car you want when you make your reservation. Ask your travel agent or the car-rental company to advise you if you're not sure which car is best for you.

Smoking versus nonsmoking vehicle. Like hotel rooms, rental cars today are generally designated smoking or nonsmoking. If you care, specify which you want when you make your reservation. On occasion, I have reserved a nonsmoking car and been assigned a car in which someone has clearly been smoking. Each time, I have requested, and been given, a different car.

Rate. Car rental rates are generally quoted on a per-day or per-week basis. The rate you pay depends on a number of factors. The larger or more exotic the car, the higher the rate will probably be.

As with hotels, many companies receive the benefit of discounted corporate rates, and members of affiliation groups like the American Bar Association or American Medical Association may also benefit from reduced rates. Be sure to find out if any of these rates are available to you, and have the discount number or name of the association with you. You may also be charged a lower rate if you reserve the car for a longer period of time or rent the car over a weekend or other nonpeak period.

Rates can also vary geographically; you're likely to pay more for a car in New York than in Peoria. Different car-rental companies may charge different rates at different times for basically the same car, so it often pays to shop around. Also, the company with the lowest rate on one trip may not have the lowest rate on the next trip.

Long-term rental. If you plan to be in the destination city on a project or assignment that will keep you there for a longer time, ask about a long-term rental, even if you plan to commute home on weekends. The cost of a long-term rental may be relatively low, and you will not have to return the car when you go home and re-rent it when you come back. Technically, a car-rental company cannot rent a vehicle to you for longer than 31 days, so you will need to sign a monthly rental addendum, which, in effect, automatically creates a new rental agreement at the end of the month when the previous rental agreement expires. If your company has a corporate account with the car-rental company, the long-term rate will already have been negotiated. If parking costs permit, you may want to park the car at the airport when you go home for the weekend to provide easy transportation to your hotel or corporate apartment when you come back.

Mileage charge. In addition to a daily or weekly rate, the car-rental company may impose a charge for each mile you drive. Find out when you make your reservation whether your rate plan includes such a charge; normally, if you are picking up and dropping off your car at the same place, you won't pay a mileage charge. Depending on how much you drive, this charge can add up quickly, so if you are comparison shopping, be realistic about how much driving you will actually be doing.

One-way rental. You may want to pick your rental car up in one location and drop it off in another. Doing so comes with a cost, called a "drop-off fee," which may be surprisingly high. Sometimes, you will be charged mileage instead of the drop-off fee. If your company has negotiated an agreement with a rental company, sometimes the agreement will provide that there will be no charge for a one-way rental. If you are not covered by such an agreement, you can always ask the company to waive the fee and any mileage charge.

Insurance. There are four types of insurance that can be purchased from a car-rental company:

- *Loss damage waiver* (LDW) insures what would otherwise be the renter's responsibility for any loss or damage to the car. If the rental car is lost or damaged, the loss damage waiver provides insurance coverage.
- *Liability insurance supplement* (LIS) provides coverage to the renter or to an authorized operator of the vehicle for any claims by third parties arising from the operation of the car.
- *Personal accident insurance* (PAI) covers accidental death and medical expense benefits for the renter and her passengers. It covers the renter 24 hours a day while in and out of the rental vehicle, and covers passengers while they enter, occupy, or exit the rental vehicle. PAI pays in addition to any other insurance available.
- *Personal effects coverage* (PEC) covers loss or damage to most types of personal effects, such as luggage, cameras, skis, etc. PEC protects the personal effects of the renter and those of her family members who live with her and are traveling with her, 24 hours a day, during the rental period. This coverage is usually included in the PAI coverage on most rental agreements.

The cost of this insurance is charged on a daily basis and can become very expensive. You are not obligated to take the car-rental company's insurance, but you will need to make sure you are covered, especially for liability to third parties. If your employer has a corporate account with the car-rental company, insurance may automatically be included when you rent your car. If not, try to obtain insurance through a source other than the car-rental company. If you own a car, check your personal car-insurance policy: most provide some kind of coverage to the insured when driving a rental car. Some homeowners' insurance policies also provide car-rental liability insurance. Some credit and charge cards also automatically provide coverage if you use the card to rent the car; you need to be careful about relying on these policies, though, because some of them provide only secondary coverage, meaning that any other policies that provide primary coverage (which could include your own auto or homeowners' policy) would be the first source of recovery. Your employer may also carry its own insurance for employees' car rentals. Some renters buy the expensive rental company's insurance so that a claim does not affect the rates on their own automobile or homeowners' policies.

Bottom line: Have proper insurance, or buy the coverage the rental agency offers. Otherwise, you could be personally liable for any damages to the automobile, and possibly for liability to third parties as well. Be especially careful if you combine business with pleasure on a trip. For example, if you rent a car to use for business but you stay for the weekend and continue to use the car, insurance coverage provided through a corporate policy may not be effective when you're not driving on business.

Concession fee recovery. In some locations, the government imposes a fee or tax on the car-rental charges, called a "concession recoupment fee." This fee is usually a fixed percentage of the total rental charges. Although all the rental companies at a particular location will have to collect this fee, you may want to take it into account when you decide whether to rent a car at all.

Fuel option. Car-rental companies give you two options regarding the gasoline that you use while driving the car. You must make your choice when you pick up the car:

- You can agree to return the car with a full tank of gas; if you don't, the car-rental company will refill the car and charge you for the fuel at a rate two to three times what you'll pay if you refill it yourself.
- You can prepay for a full tank of gasoline at a much lower rate, close to what you would pay at a service station. Upon return, you will be charged only for that tank of gasoline, and you need to buy fuel only to keep the tank from becoming empty. If you prepay and don't drive very much, though, you will be paying for gasoline you don't use.

Obviously, if you are thinking strictly of cost, you should never prepay and should always return the car with a full tank of gasoline that you buy from a station near the place you return the car. The prepayment option simply gives you a way of minimizing the consequences of being too rushed to stop at a service station when you are ready to return the car. If you know you won't have time (or just don't want) to refill the car before you return it, prepayment will be cheaper than a car-rental company refill if you use more than about half a tank. Of course, if you elect the prepayment option, you should return the car with as little fuel as possible.

Global positioning system (GPS). GPS is a satellite-based navigation system that will help direct you to your destination while you are driving. Most car-rental companies now offer GPS devices in their vehicles if you are willing to pay an additional daily fee.

There are alternatives, of course: Each company will supply you a map of the area, and the desk staff will direct you at least out of the airport and to your hotel or other location. You can also find your way by using whatever other alternative you would use if you were driving your own car without a GPS system.

Additional drivers. Any person who will be driving the rental car must be listed on the rental agreement. Your insurance coverage may be jeopardized if you allow an unauthorized person to drive. Usually the car-rental company imposes a charge for adding an authorized driver. This charge will normally be waived for a renter who is covered by a corporate account and always for a renter who is a member of the car-rental company's club when the additional driver is her spouse.

Before you leave the car-rental location with the vehicle, double-check the following:

- Is the rate correct? Verify that the daily rate and any agreed-upon discounts are listed in the rental agreement. Some rental agreements list only the undiscounted daily rate in dollars and then include a code that specifies any discount to be applied to the normal rate for the particular renter. If you are entitled to a discount and the rate in the agreement is not what you expected, look for the code and ask what it means.
- Check the back seat and trunk before you put your luggage in the car, especially if the car is in a remote part of the rental lot or garage. You don't want to find anyone or anything in the wrong place.
- Do the car keys open the car doors? Jody, a training specialist, once drove her car out of the lot without checking; when she stopped for breakfast and locked the car, she couldn't get back in. She contacted the car-rental company and was able to

obtain a proper key for the door, but wasted a lot of time doing so.

- Is the gas tank full? If not, notify the attendant, who will either fill the tank up or note the deficiency on the rental agreement. If the car does not have a full tank of gas, refill the tank only up to the original level when you return it. If you elected to prepay for the gasoline, do not leave the lot without a full tank of gas.
- Is there any visible damage to the outside of the car? If so, be sure it is noted on the rental agreement. If the damage is not noted on the rental agreement, there is no proof that it did not occur while you had the car, and you could be charged for it. If the damage is serious, ask for another car. You don't need to risk a breakdown.
- Is the car size what you reserved? Sometimes, a car-rental company will upgrade your vehicle to the next larger size for no additional cost. Although an upgrade usually means a larger, more comfortable car, you are not obligated to accept it. In any event, be sure that you will not be charged for the upgrade.

Remember, you must note any deficiencies before you take the car from the lot. Therefore, do yourself a favor and take the few minutes you need to check the car—and the contract. Doing so could save you a lot of time and aggravation in the long run.

When you return the vehicle to the rental agency, the employee who accepts the car will normally print out a receipt. Check the receipt carefully to be sure you have been charged the proper rate and mileage, that the fuel option you selected is correct, and, in general, that the charges are consistent with the rental agreement and your understanding. When you return the car, you're likely to feel rushed to make your airplane flight (especially if you need to ride in the car-rental company's van to the terminal), but take the few seconds required to examine the receipt closely. Errors do occur, and (surprise!) they rarely seem to favor the customer.

Tipping

Tipping practices for car rentals are pretty simple—generally, you don't. Obviously, you can reward someone for superior service, but car-rental company employees do not expect tips. If someone does perform particularly well, you may want to write the company or the manager of the office with your compliment. Such a letter can help someone's career and may be appreciated even more than financial generosity.

Although the process of renting a car abroad is much the same as at home, there are a few differences, which are discussed in more detail in Chapter 7 (The Global Traveler).

Dealing with the Unexpected

When you're traveling, you're always dealing with the unexpected. Here are a few ways to handle some of those situations involving rental cars:

Mechanical breakdown. You should deal with a mechanical breakdown involving a rental car in much the same fashion as a breakdown involving your own car. That said, the car-rental company should take charge of its vehicle, towing it (if necessary) to a repair shop and making sure it's repaired. If necessary, the company should supply you with a replacement vehicle. You should immediately call the car-rental company's emergency number, which you will find on the folder that contains your rental agreement or on the agreement itself. Be sure to make a note of the name of the car-rental company representatives with whom you speak and what they told you.

If your car breaks down, your paramount concern should be your safety. If you feel you are in an unsafe neighborhood, make sure you tell the car-rental company. If the car will run, drive it some place where you feel safe. If not, wait inside with the doors locked, or call the police or maybe even a taxi to pick you up. If you will not be with the vehicle when the person sent by the car-rental company arrives, be sure to tell the company.

It may seem obvious, but you should be sure not to use your cell phone any more than you must under these circumstances. You don't want to exhaust the battery and lose your means of communication.

Automobile accident or theft. As with a breakdown, you should deal with an accident or theft involving a rental car in much the same fashion as an accident or theft involving your own car. Again, however, you must contact the car-rental company at the emergency number you will find with your contract. Report the accident or theft to the police and try to get a police report. Otherwise, try to let the police and the car-rental company handle the situation.

Even if the car appears drivable and undamaged after an accident, it is in your best interest to have a record of the accident with the car-rental company. You may want to request a replacement car in order to avoid responsibility for some damage that appears later. Again, be sure to note the name of the car-rental company representative(s) with whom you speak and note what they tell you.

As with a breakdown, treat your own safety and security as the paramount concern. In case of theft, you will be much better off if you have the rental agreement with you—a good reason to avoid just leaving it in the vehicle.

There are no cars available. Occasionally, you'll show up at the car rental counter with a reservation and be told that no cars are available. When this situation occurs, it's usually at an airport in a major city hosting a convention or similar event, and customers are simply not returning their cars as scheduled. If you wait, eventually someone will turn in a car that the agency will make available to you. If you don't want to wait, you're pretty much on your own.

If you're at an airport, you can check with other car-rental companies that may have counters nearby. You can check at other locations of the same company or other companies in the same city. The rental companies often have locations downtown, at hotels near the airport, or at other locations that may be reasonably convenient for you.

Need to extend a reservation. There are times when you'll need to extend your car rental reservation. Contact the car-rental company as soon as you become aware that you need the car for a longer time. Be aware of the fact that your daily rate may also change when you get the extension.

The car-rental company has no record of your reservation. You should have your confirmation number with you so that you can prove you're entitled to a car when you arrive. If you are traveling from city to city, though, and renting a car in each one, you may be going to the car-rental desk or remote car lot of one company by habit. You may be surprised to find that someone made a reservation for you with a different company (and maybe you're that someone). On one trip, Deborah was in five different cities in five days, renting a car in each city. She typically rented from the same company and never checked her reservation. But for some reason, one of her reservations was with a different company; she discovered this fact after she had boarded the rental agency's bus, gone to the lot, looked for her car, and hadn't found it. She went back to the airport and stood in line for her car at the correct company; of course, since it wasn't her regular company, she wasn't a member of its club and the process was a lengthy one. Check your reservation before you get in line at the rental desk or board the bus to be sure you're in the right place. If you have your confirmation number, the only reason that the car-rental company might have no record of your reservation should be that you're asking the wrong company!

Woman Road Warrior Checklist

__ Join car-rental company's club program.

__ Have a valid driver's license that won't be expiring during your trip.

__ Have paper evidence of your reservation and your confirmation number.

__ Be sure vehicle and features match reservation.

__ Obtain insurance through your own sources or car-rental company.

__ Be sure proper credits recorded to frequent-flyer/reward programs.

__ Before leaving lot, check:

   __ Rental rate and terms correct

   __ Gas tank full

   __ No damage to car

__ Keep the rental agreement with you when you are not in the vehicle.

__ In case of breakdown or accident:

   __ Contact rental company

   __ Make sure you are safe

   __ In the case of an accident, call the police and get a police report

CHAPTER 5

Alternative Ways to Get Around

To Fly or Not to Fly: That Is the Question

Until the events of September 11, 2001, most business travelers flew on all but the shortest trips. Since then, airline travel has become much less hassle-free and much more time-consuming. Although flight durations haven't changed, the time it takes to get through the airport to the flight has increased dramatically. When you add the time on the airplane, the time it takes to get from home or office to the airport, the time spent in the airport, and the time to get from the destination airport to your hotel, meeting or office, travel by some other means becomes increasingly attractive. The practical alternatives are the following: driving your own automobile, driving a rental car, or taking a train or a bus.

Car Trip

If your destination is close enough, traveling by car is probably the simplest and most convenient means to get there. You can just load your luggage and drive directly to wherever business takes you. There are few places where you cannot park with reasonable convenience. Of course, you still have to find your way around unfamiliar places, fight any traffic, and figure out parking logistics. But you will have to confront these issues whether you drive or not, and the difficulty should be relatively minor if your entire trip is by car.

If you decide to make your trip by car, you need to decide whether to drive your own car (if you have one) or to rent a car. Your own car is more familiar to you, and you will avoid the inconvenience of going to the car-rental agency location to pick up and drop off the vehicle. So you will probably want to drive your own car if your company or your client will reimburse you for doing so at a reasonable rate. Otherwise, rent a car (see Chapter 4).

> **WOMAN ROAD WARRIOR TIP:**
>
> If you do utilize your own car and if you are filling out a time and expense report, make sure you note your mileage and tolls so you will receive reimbursement.

If you are driving and if you haven't ever really focused on the equipment you need for proper car safety, be aware that the American Automobile Association (AAA) recommends that you keep a spare tire, a jack and tire-changing tools, jumper cables, a blanket, and a safety kit in your automobile. The safety kit should include:

- Water
- Bandages
- Flashlights
- Spare batteries
- Flares (in case of accident or flat tire)
- Cell-phone charger (if your car battery is dead, the charger will not work)

You may also want to be a member of an automobile club, such as the AAA. If you are a member of AAA and need roadside assistance, you can call a toll-free number and within a promised time period (usually an hour or less), someone will show up to help. Many cell-phone carriers also offer roadside assistance for a monthly fee.

If you are driving your own car, make sure you know the way to your destination. Directions can be obtained online through map websites such as MapQuest (www.mapquest.com) or Rand McNally (www.randmcnally.com). These kinds of website directions, while usually (but not always) accurate, do not always recommend the fastest route. You can also get directions the old-fashioned way—using paper maps or a road atlas, which can usually be purchased at a gas station or a bookstore. Using a map or atlas, of course, requires you to determine the best or most appropriate route on your own. If you can, it's a good idea to inquire about the best route with your client or someone else at your destination.

> **WOMAN ROAD WARRIOR TIP:**
>
> Either periodically check in with someone throughout your road trip or tell them you'll call when you reach your destination. Doing so will alert that person more quickly should something happen while you are driving.

Train Travel

Most train stations, unlike airports, are in downtown locations convenient to offices and residences. You also won't need to spend the kind of time in the train station that you will in an airport. Thus, if your trip is a short one, the train may be an attractive alternative. Some of the faster trains get from city to city much more quickly than a car. And since you're not behind the wheel, train time can be used to work, read, or just relax. I have heard that some harried business travelers use a long train trip—possibly even overnight—to unwind in relative isolation after meetings and conferences.

I have traveled some, but not a great deal, by train. Helen, an investment banker, prefers the Amtrak train (especially the high-speed train) to the airplane for most of her trips up and down the Boston-Washington corridor. Amtrak serves many other parts of the country as well, of course.

Be aware, however, that train travel is not inexpensive; the cost can rival that of an airplane. Many train routes have been consolidated and eliminated recently due to financial troubles. You can get information and make reservations through a travel agent or on Amtrak's website (www.amtrak.com) or over the phone.

In most of Europe and parts of Asia, business travelers routinely use the excellent train service. See discussion in Chapter 7.

Bus Travel

I have hardly traveled at all by bus in recent years. People who do travel by bus tell me that buses are much more comfortable and better appointed than they used to be. Buses tend, however, to make a lot of stops between cities and, since they use the same roads as our cars, can't go any faster. Thus, travel by bus is usually even more time-consuming than driving. On the other hand, on a bus, like on a train, you also can use the time to work, read, or relax in relative isolation.

Greyhound is the only national bus company, but there are a number of regional lines serving different parts of the country. Buses tend to be a relatively inexpensive means of travel. Much like train service, many bus routes have been eliminated and consolidated recently. You can obtain information and make reservations through your travel agent or by going to Greyhound's website (www.greyhound.com).

Transportation to the Airport

Assuming that, like most of us, you do not live close enough to the airport to walk, the alternatives for getting out to the airport are driving your own car, riding public transportation, taking an airport shuttle bus, and using a livery (limousine or taxi) service.

> **WOMAN ROAD WARRIOR TIP:**
> Be prudent in choosing how you'll get around in any city, especially one you don't know well. Don't risk your safety to save money.

DRIVING

Driving your own car is probably the easiest and, overall, the most convenient way to get to the airport. You do, however, have to bear the cost of parking and the inconvenience of getting from your car to your flight. You'll probably also have to carry your luggage from your car to the terminal. Depending on the airport, there may be several parking choices, varying in convenience and cost: onsite, onsite remote, and offsite. Of course, the longer your trip, the more parking will cost if you park your car at the airport, and thus the more cost-effective a taxi or some other means of transportation will look.

Onsite remote and offsite parking are less expensive, but generally come with a significant nonfinancial cost: You will spend more time traveling to and from the terminal and may have to carry your luggage a greater distance. Some remote and offsite lots are a long way from the airport terminal, and, depending on when you are traveling, you could find yourself alone and unprotected in a far-away parking lot at night.

The operators of some remote lots at some airports provide a bus that will transport you from your car to the terminal when you depart, and from the terminal to your car when you return. This obviously alleviates many security concerns. If this service sounds attractive to you, check with the airport. If you are checking your bags and have the time, check them at curbside check-in before you go to the remote lot to park so you don't have to carry them through the remote lot and onto the bus.

You'll probably start your trip and park your car in the morning or during business hours, when security is less of a concern, but you're likely to return after business hours and often after sunset. Consider the time of your scheduled return when determining where to park.

My own preference (and the preference of most veteran travelers I know) is to get in and out of the airport as quickly and painlessly and with as little risk as possible, even if I have to pay more. Therefore, I always park on the airport grounds close to the terminal, regardless of the services offered by the remote lot operators.

Wherever you decide to park, make sure your car is in a well-lit area and, if you're in a garage, as close to the elevator bank as possible. You can then get into your car and out of the airport as quickly and safely as possible.

Since the events of September 11, 2001, some airports require that each automobile be inspected before entering the parking garage. The definition of inspection varies between locations, so be prepared to spend additional time to respond to whatever is asked.

Once your car is parked and you're about to leave the vehicle, check and make sure:

- All valuables left in the car while you're away are stored in the trunk. It is best to put your valuables in the trunk before arriving at the parking garage. You never know who is watching.

Even better, take your valuables out of the car and leave them at home.

- Note where you parked your car. Write the car's location on the ticket you received upon entering the parking facility and bring the ticket with you. Doing so not only makes it easier for you to remember where your car is parked when you return, but having the ticket with you makes it harder for someone to steal the car while you're gone. Large airports typically offer assistance to travelers who don't remember where they parked their cars. Airport garages are periodically patrolled, and if you are there more than 24 hours, the car's location will probably be recorded with garage security. On one trip, I forgot where I parked and, worse, forgot to follow my own advice on writing down the car's location. It was a relief when I contacted garage security, gave them my automobile license plate number and was immediately told the car's location. I went straight to my car and drove home.

To reduce the amount of time you spend in the garage when you return to your car and also to protect yourself, consider doing the following while heading to the car:

- Have your keys out and ready before you get to the car. Remember, safety is your main concern. You do not want to have to put your bags down while trying to find your keys. Doing so not only takes your eyes off the car and surroundings, but it allows someone to sneak up behind you undetected. *Don't give anyone that chance.*
- When walking up to the car, look around to see if anything seems out of place. Before getting into the car, look into the front and back seats to make sure there's no one in them. If anything looks wrong, turn around and get to a secure, well-lit place as quickly as possible. Contact security immediately and let them handle the situation.
- Request an escort to your car if you are the least bit uncomfortable. A number of large airports provide escort services, which are there for your safety. Don't feel uncomfortable or silly about asking for help. Trust your judgment and intuition. If you are uncomfortable about something or someone, then get out of

WOMAN ROAD WARRIOR TIP:

If you find yourself running late for a flight and the airport's main parking lot is full, look to see if the airport has valet parking available. It may cost you a few dollars extra a day to park using this alternative, but it will probably be preferable in the long run to missing your flight.

the situation and ask for help. Most of us woman road warriors feel that we can conquer anything, but we also have learned that there are times when going it alone is unwise.

PUBLIC TRANSPORTATION

If you live in a large city, public transportation can be a good and inexpensive way to get to and from the airport. Public transportation can be a train (called in different cities the "metro," "T," "subway," "el," et cetera) or a bus.

You still have to get from where you live or work to where you can pick up the train or bus, however, and then get back to your home or office upon return. If you have any significant amount of luggage, you may find it a real strain to lug it between home or office and the place to get on and off the train or bus and between the train or bus and the airport terminal. The distances could be substantial. During rush hour, taking the train can be a lot faster than going by automobile, while the bus would probably be slower.

If you choose public transportation, make sure you know the schedule and the routes, and try to travel only during busy times (such as morning and evening rush hours). Don't put yourself in a potentially dangerous situation in order to save a few dollars by not thinking ahead, especially if you are arriving home at night and traveling alone. Although public transportation is inexpensive, be sure any increased risk is worth the dollars you'll save. If you are short of cash for a cab, limousine, or airport shuttle, automatic teller machines (ATMs) are located at all airports and train and bus terminals. If you can't get cash that way, most livery services will accept credit cards.

AIRPORT SHUTTLE

In most large cities, a shuttle bus service will transport people to and from the airport. The shuttle will typically circulate through several downtown locations, usually hotels, and each shuttle will normally pick up passengers at most of these locations. There are some shuttle companies that offer to pick passengers up at their homes.

The airport shuttle will take longer than driving your own car or taking a cab or limousine, and it may take longer than the train, depending on road traffic and number of stops. The shuttle service is usually less expensive than parking at the airport or taking a taxi or limousine.

LIVERY SERVICE—TAXI OR LIMOUSINE

Although any kind of livery service is more expensive than public transportation and could be more expensive than parking your car at the airport, it usually provides the greatest convenience and safety.

Most major cities are served by a number of limousine companies. Find out if your company recommends or requires that you use a particular limousine service; your company may have negotiated lower rates or favorable terms. Otherwise, ask friends or your travel agent for recommendations. You should be able to arrange to have the limousine pick you up at a specified time and drive you directly to the airport. Try to make the arrangements at least a day or two in advance, but many companies will respond in a few hours. But remember that no limousine service will provide as rapid a response as a taxi.

Many people have been able to find a limousine company that they like and trust, and have built a rapport with a particular driver who will regularly drive them to and from the airport. It's nice to have someone you know taking you to and picking you up at the airport. Drivers can be very flexible, so if your plans change, you can usually count on them to adjust their schedules for you.

Patricia, a consultant with a software company, had a wonderful experience that illustrated the value of such a relationship after she sprained her ankle while out of town. She was in Montreal, Canada, at the time, but lived near Ottawa. After getting her crutches from the hospital, she decided that she did not want the hassle of going home by plane as planned. So she called her limousine driver in Ottawa instead. He not only drove the two hours to pick her up in Montreal, but also brought her coffee and her favorite roll for the drive back home! Drivers like to have regular customers that they can count on, so look to find someone who can be your driver if you plan to use this kind of service regularly.

If you live in a large metropolitan area, taxi services are readily available. Taxi service is usually less expensive than a limousine, and each company has many drivers and vehicles. Some companies are more reputable than others, so ask around for recommendations if you are just starting out.

If I'm going to the airport by taxi, especially from home, I like to call the cab company the night before and arrange for a driver to pick me up at a specific time. As with limousines, it may take time to find a favorite company or driver, but it is well worth it in the long run. These drivers are entrepreneurs who have built up a clientele over the years. They act like limousine drivers with smaller vehicles and a meter, and when they are not with a regular customer, they pick up fares on city streets.

I had a regular driver from a local cab company for years. It was reassuring knowing that when I arrived home, I would not have to stand in the airport cab line, and I would know who was driving me, especially if it was late at night.

Transportation at Your Destination City

Once you get to your destination city, you will need to get from the airport (or train or bus station) to the hotel, office, or meeting. Here are your likely options:

RENTAL CAR

A rented car can take you both from airport to hotel and then from place to place in your destination city. See Chapter 4, Renting a Car, especially the opening section, for the advantages and disadvantages of car rentals, and the entire chapter for an explanation of the process.

AIRPORT OR HOTEL SHUTTLE

Airport and hotel shuttle services will take you from the airport to a specific destination in a city or to a hotel. These shuttles run on a schedule throughout the day. Depending on the time of day, traffic can make airport shuttles a slow means of transport. If you are at the airport and want an airport shuttle, inquire at the information counter, which is usually located in the baggage claim area. Most airport shuttles circulate among a number of different destinations, usually hotels. Thus, in addition to spending time en route, passengers have to wait for shuttles to make the rounds among their different stops.

Hotels (typically hotels located close to airports) may run their own shuttles from the airport. Unlike the airport shuttle, the hotel shuttle is usually free of charge. You can find information on a particular hotel's shuttle by using the hotel's telephone in the bank of phones in the baggage claim area. Just pick up the phone and the operator will give you instructions as to where to board the shuttle. If you have the luxury of planning ahead, check the hotel's website for shuttle information and make a reservation for transportation.

PUBLIC TRANSPORTATION

For the most part, the same rules apply for public transportation at the destination city as they do at home. Your destination city, however, is probably much less familiar to you. Thus, it is even more important that you check out the train or bus schedule and routes before you embark. Schedules and routes can be found by asking at the information counter or public-transportation counter (located where the trains and/or buses depart) or by checking them on the Internet or through your travel agent.

The last thing you need is to find yourself uncomfortable with your surroundings in an unfamiliar city and have your safety compromised because you do not know your way around. This is especially true at night. Do yourself a favor: If you don't know the route or the city, especially if it's nighttime, spend the extra money for a different mode of transportation (e.g., livery). You are worth every penny!

LIVERY SERVICE—TAXI OR LIMOUSINE

There are taxi stands at nearly every airport and bus and train station throughout the United States. A taxi is generally the easiest way to get around, although not necessarily the least expensive. You simply need to get into the cab, tell the driver where you are going, and pay at the destination. Fares are generated either by meter (which is a charge based on distance and sometimes time traveled) or a flat fee. Rates are usually posted at the airport line or in the cab itself.

Taking a taxi in an unfamiliar city is one of your most trusting acts when on the road. After all, you are getting into a car driven by a complete stranger taking you to a destination that you may never have seen before. If you are uncomfortable with the surroundings, the driver, or anything about the process, it's best to get out of the cab right away and ask for help. At the airport taxi stand, there are usually supervisors from the cab companies or police officers around for assistance. If you can't find anyone to help, then go back into the terminal and look for help, starting at the information booth.

Even the most experienced road warrior can feel the need to ask for help. Andrea once got into a taxi when leaving an airport and the driver became belligerent before the car had gotten to the last terminal. She told him to pull over, got out, and informed the attendant in the cab line about the situation. The supervisor told the driver to leave the premises and not come back.

If you want to use a limousine, you should prearrange the service if possible. Ask your client or check with your company for recommendations, or have your travel agent arrange it. You may be able to take advantage of prenegotiated lower rates. Your travel agent should be able to tell you the standard rate for this type of service.

If you have not prearranged limousine service, don't get into a car without verifying its legitimacy. At most large airports, you will find a number of uncertified and unregulated private drivers who try to approach passengers and solicit fares. If you get into one of these cars, you may discover an unlicensed livery driver who charges more than the normal driver; worse, you could be putting yourself in jeopardy.

If your final destination is far from the airport, then taxi or limousine service may be very expensive. If so, you should inquire into the cost of a one-way car rental, which may not involve the usual charge if the pickup and drop-off points are in the same metropolitan area. You may be able to save a significant amount of money without much loss of convenience.

Ultimately, choosing a means of travel to and from an airport or while in the destination city comes down to personal preference. But take into consideration the size of the city (and how long it takes to get around), ease of public transportation, and timing (when you have to get where you need to be). Here are a few additional tips from veteran road warriors:

- Whenever she travels to New York City, Janet always takes a taxi into Manhattan from the airport but arranges for a limousine to take her back to the airport. She has found that it can be difficult to flag a taxi on the street, especially at rush hour, which can be maddening when you have a plane to catch.
- You may find that taking a taxi to your final destination from your home is easier and more cost-effective than alternatives, even if the destination is pretty far from home. As more demands are made on your time, looking for flexible and easy travel alternatives becomes more important. Danielle once took a taxi from Chicago to an appointment in Grand Rapids, Michigan, which was 180 miles away. The driver waited for her and drove her back home.
- Don't assume that the process of hailing a taxicab is more or less the same in all major cities. For instance, taxis in Las Vegas will pick up unscheduled passengers only from cab stations at hotels, airports, or convention sites.
- Andrea always puts her luggage beside her in the cab and not in the trunk. Her experience has been that it's easier to get out of an uncomfortable situation when her bags are next to her than when the driver has to pull over and open the trunk so she can retrieve her luggage.

Getting around a city in another country presents other considerations, because you may be unfamiliar with the customs, language, and rules, as well as with the geography. See discussion in Chapter 7.

Tipping

Not all modes of transportation require a tip. For instance, you don't tip anyone when taking public transportation or when renting a car. Generally, you should give a taxi or limousine driver a tip of 15 to 20 percent of the fare. You should give the driver of a hotel or airport shuttle a tip of a dollar or two per piece of luggage. If you park your car in a valet parking garage, it is appropriate to give a modest tip (a dollar or so) to the attendant who brings your car when you are ready to leave.

If Things Go Wrong

I had been taking the same company's taxis to and from the airport for years without incident until one day when I'd arranged a 6:00 a.m. pickup. Then, once we were on the expressway, the driver decided to show me his handgun, and bragged about pointing it at a passenger's temple the night before.

Needless to say, this behavior certainly got my attention; if I hadn't been fully awake before, this did the job! We were traveling on a major expressway at the time and it was dark. This incident occurred before cell phones became common and I didn't have one. It wasn't practical to have him pull over and let me out, even if he would have done so had I asked. Instead, I tried to remain calm and distract him, hoping to get to the airport safely.

I talked about everything other than the weapon in his hand. We made it to the airport and I proceeded to get on the plane and get out of town. I should have told the police immediately, but instead notified the cab company after I got to my destination. I felt safer knowing that I was in one city and he was in another while his employer investigated the incident. There is no telling, however, what his next passenger might have experienced.

Here's what to do if you are ever faced with a situation like this:

- Try not to panic, or at least try not to show it. I firmly believe that if the driver had known how petrified I was, the situation would only have been worse.
- Collect as much information as you can about the cab: the vehicle license plate number, cab number, driver's name.
- If you have a cell phone and can use it without putting yourself in danger, do so. Call the police, the cab company, or a friend; let anyone and everyone know that you're in danger. Use text messaging if you can't or don't want to talk.
- If you have wireless e-mail or text-message capability, use it to communicate your need for help.
- If you choose to do nothing until you get to your destination, alert security or the police the first chance you get.

Cell phones are very handy in these types of situations. They are the quickest way of reaching out to someone when you are in trouble.

You can also use mace, pepper spray, or some other similar chemical for personal protection, although I don't recommend using something like this in a moving taxicab on an expressway. These items can typically be purchased from the local police station or specialty store. Remember that you may not carry any of these items on an airplane, and they must be checked with your luggage if you are traveling by plane.

You can also use a whistle or other device that makes a loud noise to attract attention if there's trouble. These items can be put on a key chain and will also make it through airport security. Remember that intruders and attackers do not wish to draw attention to themselves, so anything that will throw them off guard will work to your advantage. Amy, an international flight attendant who has received extensive safety training, has been taught to yell "STOP" to distract an assailant and throw him off-guard.

As soon as you can, remove yourself from danger and get to a secure, well-lit, crowded area. Contact security, the police, or whoever can help you immediately. If you need medical attention, ask for help in getting you there, if you cannot take care of yourself.

Woman Road Warrior Checklist

___ Don't compromise your safety to save money.

___ If traveling in your own car, be sure it is properly equipped.

___ If you park at the airport, take the ticket with you and note the location.

___ Prearrange any desired taxi or limousine service.

___ Be sure you know routes and schedules if you are using public transport.

___ Build a rapport with a livery company and/or driver in your hometown.

___ Keep luggage in the taxi with you, instead of in the trunk.

CHAPTER 6

What You Should Know About Packing

Business travel that requires an overnight stay means packing. Deciding what to wear and what to bring with you on a trip can be a big challenge.

Dress for the business world has certainly changed, especially for women, over the past decade. On the first day of orientation on my first job in public accounting, I received the book *How to Dress for Success*. During that time period, suits with bow ties were the "in" look for professional women. For the most part, all traces of femininity, style, color, or individuality were out the window. This style of dress even made it difficult to pack lightly. Each suit needed a matching blouse; mixing and matching was not an option. Luckily for all of us, not only has this style of dress gone out of fashion, but individuality is encouraged and casual dress is much more acceptable.

Every individual has a different definition of what it means to pack light, but if your clothing does not fit in one bag (preferably a bag you

WOMAN ROAD WARRIOR TIP

When it comes to packing for a trip, there is one basic rule: **PACK LIGHT.**

can carry onto an airplane), then you've probably packed too much. Think about it: In the age of constant and continuous accessibility, we are now carrying around computers, briefcases, and cell phones before we even consider clothing.

When I first started traveling, I would have a garment bag (suitcases on wheels weren't an option) on one shoulder, a purse and briefcase (later, with a computer inside as well) on the other, and I was usually wearing high heels. Well, I may have looked good (or at least, that's what I thought), but many years later, back problems continue to haunt me. Now I do not leave home unless my luggage is on wheels. I also avoid carrying too much weight on my shoulders, and I wear flat, comfortable shoes whenever possible.

Of course, if you are packing for an airplane trip that will keep you away from home for much more than a week, you may need to bring more than you can fit into one carry-on bag. If you think you may have more luggage than you want to carry and don't want to check any, consider using a luggage shipment service. Some additional luggage limitations have arisen since the events of September 11, 2001 and August 2006, and limitations on (or additional charges for) extra luggage that were once widely ignored are now being enforced. As a result, there are now services that will pick up your luggage at your home or office and ship it to your destination for your arrival. This service may be more costly than just checking or taking your luggage on the plane, but the convenience may be worth the expense. The service may even save you money if there's a possibility you might exceed the limit for weight or number of pieces.

International travel poses its own packing challenges because of the distances involved, the potential length of trips, and the possibly very different customs and rules in other countries. See discussion in Chapter 7.

Luggage: One Size Does Not Fit All!

If you are just starting to travel, do yourself a favor and get a good piece of luggage. There are as many choices as there are prices, but before you start looking, have an idea of the type of luggage you want. Some things to think about as you decide:

- **To wheel or not to wheel.** Truly functional wheeled luggage has been available for about 15 years now, and it's increasingly versatile. Wheels allow you to pull or push your luggage without a lot of lifting and potentially straining your back, arms, and legs. You can also fasten your briefcase or computer on top of your wheeled luggage and save your back. Wheeled luggage comes in a variety of types, from overnight-sized bags to larger bags that can accommodate multiple sets of clothing.
- **Garment bag or suitcase.** Clothing can be stored on hangers or folded during transport. If you wish to keep your clothing on hangers, a garment bag may be preferable; otherwise, go with a suitcase. Just to confuse the issue more, some suitcases include a place to store hanging items inside. This feature, though, means you won't be able to get as much into the suitcase. Both suitcases and garment bags may come with wheels or without.
- **Leather, canvas, plastic, nylon, and vinyl.** Name the type of material, and chances are you'll be able to find it. Some material is naturally heavier than others, and luggage of that substance will only get heavier when filled up. But the heavier the material, typically the more durable and long-lasting the luggage.
- **Size.** Unless I'm packing for a long trip, I always prefer luggage of a size that I can carry on the plane. Sometimes I may elect to check it, but at least I have the choice. Carry-on luggage must fit under an airplane seat or in the cabin's overhead compartment. Luggage stores and other sellers of luggage will know whether any item you might consider purchasing is small enough to be carried on the plane.
- **Durability.** Remember that to baggage handlers, all pieces of luggage are created equal, regardless of cost or material. The baggage handler's objective is to move luggage from point A to point B without regard for preserving its exterior. A bag costing thousands of dollars will be treated the same as one costing a small fraction of that amount. Luggage needs

to hold up under all weather conditions while being tossed around like a ball.

Whatever type of luggage you use, make sure that you securely attach your identification to it. As a precaution, affix a business card or some other type of personal identification somewhere on both the outside and the inside of the bag. Most luggage tags require an address. Since I do not want to allow strangers to see my home address, I use my work address on any outside luggage tag. You may also want to do the following:

- Keep a photo of your luggage with you when you travel. You need a description of your luggage when you file a lost claim report. A picture may make your bag easier for airline personnel to identify. Use your cell phone or PDA to take a picture of your luggage (if it has the capability). This way you always have the picture with you, you don't have to worry about losing it, and you can pull it up if you need to show it to anyone while you are on the road.

> **WOMAN ROAD WARRIOR TIP:**
>
> If you are checking your luggage, include a copy of your itinerary in your bag. If the destination tag is dislodged and a baggage carrier has to open your luggage, he will know where you are going and be able get it to you much more easily.

- If you are traveling with someone and you are both checking your luggage, exchange an outfit with your traveling companion. If one piece of luggage gets lost or delayed, you will each have at least one change of clothes.
- Put something on the outside of your luggage that is a unique identifier for you. You can, for example, tie a ribbon to the handle or place a sticker on the outside. Since so many pieces of luggage look alike, such an identifier provides a good way to differentiate your bag from others. I'll always remember a trip over the Easter holiday period, when I arrived at baggage claim and picked up what looked exactly like my bag. Hours later, I opened it to find it filled with chocolate candy.

Packing 101

No one likes to pack, and doing it more frequently doesn't make it more pleasant. Although packing is tedious, it is also something of an art, and there are things you can do to make it easier. Since there is no right or wrong way to go about packing, as you do it more frequently you will eventually build your own routine and incorporate your own style.

Some people prefer to pack while they are dressing in the morning on the day of departure. They just go through their clothes and pick out what they want to take. Others have preprinted lists that identify the items that they may need, and they just pick items from the list. Some veterans I know have the following routines:

- Danielle always packs the night before she leaves on a trip. If she is leaving for a week, she starts with two main outfits and mixes and matches from there. She packs things tightly and thus rolls her clothing, instead of folding it, to maximize the use of space. She will place a piece of plastic bag or tissue paper on top of each piece of clothing.
- After all her years of travel, Janet refers to a list when she's packing; she has forgotten something important (for example, nylons or underwear) one time too many. Janet also stresses that one should not make assumptions as to what the hotel will provide. For example, Janet always brings her own hair dryer with her. Although most hotels provide hair dryers, each hotel provides something different, and, contrary to my own experience, she has frequently found herself dissatisfied with the hair dryer provided by the hotel.
- Vicki packs in the morning when she is getting dressed. She mentally runs through her schedule of meetings for her trip and picks her wardrobe in order to have appropriate clothing for each meeting. She builds off the primary color of black and packs for comfort.
- Elizabeth has three small children at home and packs the

> **WOMAN ROAD WARRIOR TIP:**
>
> If you are traveling for a short trip (1 to 3 days), consider packing only business clothing from the same color family. This will allow you to bring one pair of shoes (the one on your feet).

night before her trip. She finds that her schedule is too tight in the morning to pack at that time.

Whatever your style, you need to do some planning to pack quickly and well. Here are a few ideas to make the process easier:

- Remember that the Transportation Security Administration (TSA) rules require that all your liquids and gels (other than essential prescription medicine, breast milk, and formula) be in containers of three ounces or less and must fit into one quart-size zip-top bag. Keep a separate traveling set of liquids and gels in those kinds of containers in that kind of bag, and keep that bag in or near your carry-on bag.
- Keep a duplicate set of makeup and toiletries (other than your liquids and gels) in a separate case or other container. If you usually travel with a particular suitcase, you can put these items in that suitcase or nearby. Although these items are typically small, they can eat up space quickly, and if they are not all in one place, you can easily forget something.
- If possible, keep a duplicate set of medicine for travel use as well. Like the duplicate sets of liquids, gels, makeup, and toiletries, keep it in or near your suitcase. Of course, you need to be aware of the expiration dates on these items, especially if you are not traveling regularly. Since medicine can directly affect your health and can be difficult to replace quickly on the road, you should take special precautions to be sure you don't lose or forget it. Therefore, once you start packing for a particular trip, consider keeping your medicine either in your purse or brief-case for safekeeping while you're actually traveling.
- Similarly, keep a spare set of some clothing items that you can dedicate to a "travel set" (such as gym shoes, sleepwear, workout clothes, bathing suit) with your luggage. The fewer items you need to be concerned about on the day of packing, the better.
- Have a portable clock in your travel bag, preferably one that illuminates. All too often the clock in the hotel room is located in the television set across the room, which makes it very difficult to see in the middle of the night, especially if you wear glasses. Travel clocks have become very light and adaptable, and for me it's reassuring to know that I have one next to my bed at all times. Although I typically arrange for a wake-up call, I

use the alarm on the travel clock as a backup. Too many times hotels have forgotten my wake-up call. Remember to check the clock batteries frequently.

- Have a flashlight in your travel bag. It's nice to have with you in a dark, unfamiliar hotel room where you may be unable to find the light switches. Just check the batteries periodically.
- Keep a spare hair dryer near your bag. Most hotels, however, other than small ones in secondary markets, have hair dryers either in the room or available at the front desk. Contrary to Janet's experience, I have always found these hair dryers eminently satisfactory, and so I never bring a hair dryer with me unless I am certain that the hotel will not provide one. I don't want to carry the extra weight or take up valuable space in my luggage if it's not necessary.
- Always bring an umbrella. There are plenty of small models that take up very little space in your bag.
- Don't forget the charger for your mobile phone. Better yet, have a spare charger that you can keep near your travel bag.
- Take earplugs and an eye mask with you on every trip, especially for use on an airplane. They will help you ward off noise and light when you are trying to sleep. Keep them in or near the bag you usually use as a carry-on.
- Take a sewing kit and stain remover; again, keep them in or near your regular travel bag. I remember traveling with Mary, a colleague, who spilled a liquid on the skirt she planned to wear to an important meeting the next day. We unsuccessfully raced around looking for a way to remove the stain. If the clothing you planned to use for business is absolutely unusable and you have no other alternative, ask the hotel for the use of a uniform, which is usually a pantsuit (remember this advice from Chapter 2 on dealing with lost luggage).
- Take a zip-top or similar plastic bag and fill it with spare plastic bags. These bags can be very handy in all kinds of circumstances—to hold a broken watch or jewelry, ice, stationery, and store snacks. Teresa also found them very useful, unfortunately, when dealing with her morning sickness while on the road.

For those who need a reminder of what to bring, two examples of packing lists are included in the appendix.

Wrinkles

Certain types of clothing material travel better than others. Cottons, polyesters, and knits tend to weather the traveling storm well. Silk and linen, on the other hand, have a tendency to get wrinkled very quickly and will typically need attention before you can wear them after they've been folded up in a suitcase. You can minimize wrinkles by wrapping clothing in plastic bags. Of course, plastic bags don't to-tally prevent wrinkles all the time, but I have had a lot of luck using this technique. Or you may want to consider using them only for those items that require more care and handling. Plastic bags can even help minimize wrinkles for those items that are placed in a hanging or garment bag.

When you get to your destination, take your clothing out of your luggage as soon as you can, especially in hot weather. If you have a long drive from the airport to your hotel, you might take some cloth-ing items out of the bag and hang them up or spread them out in the car during the drive (assuming you have a rental car). For security reasons, you may be better off putting them in the trunk. If your trip is completely by car, you should definitely lay some items out flat in the trunk or hang them up in the car. Doing so will minimize wrinkles and lighten your luggage.

For clothing items that come out of your suitcase wrinkled and in need of attention, there are a number of options:

- Iron them yourself (most hotels provide irons in the room or will send one up to the room if requested).
- Send them out to be ironed (you'll have to pay for this service).
- Hang the clothing up in the closet and hope the wrinkles will fall or minimize.
- Hang the clothing in the bathroom while taking a shower and let the steam smooth out some of the wrinkles.

Carry-on Restrictions

Being aware of what is and isn't allowed on an airplane can be almost a full-time job. Certain items aren't allowed in your checked or carry-on lug-gage; other items are allowed in your checked but not your carry-on bags. Given the security measures implemented at airports since the events of September 11, 2001 and August 2006, these rules not only have a direct impact on whether or not you'll check your bag, but also on what you may want to pack. The TSA's website, www.tsa.gov, lists prohibited items, but most of them are what you would already expect. Each airline also has its own policies, which may prohibit items that the FAA would allow.

The rules pertaining to what you can carry on and what you can't frequently change. After the events of September 11, 2001, the rules prohibited many useful items that we take for granted, such as knives, scissors, nail files and nail clippers. More recently, the TSA has liberalized its rules, so you may now carry on your nail file and nail clipper, but not any knives (other than plastic or butter knives) or long-bladed metal scissors. However, people I know have either had to check various prohibited items, send them a different way, or abandon them before boarding. The lesson: Keep up on the rules, and check the TSA website for changes if you are ever in doubt.

Of course, people are responsible for applying these rules, and two different people may apply them inconsistently. The applications may even be inconsistent with the rules themselves. For example, tweezers were never a prohibited item, but Mary once had her tweezers confiscated during a search at security before the rules were changed to permit passengers to carry on tweezers specifically. If there is any doubt, either check the item or leave it at home.

Now you know what you *can't* carry on; what *should* you carry on? I suggest that you always keep the following items with you:

- Prescriptions or any over-the-counter medical items
- Personal hygiene items (those that can't be easily replaced if lost)
- Passport or identification documents
- Important documents such as birth certificates or legal documents (anything considered difficult to replace if lost)
- Valuables (such as jewelry, cameras, computers)
- Cell phone and cell-phone charger
- If possible, anything for which the airline is not responsible if it gets lost or stolen in your checked luggage
- If possible, whatever you need to get by if your luggage is lost or stolen.

Mary once traveled to a small town in North Carolina on a Sunday in shorts and a tank top. She arrived safely, but her luggage did not. In this small town, she had no way to buy any replacement clothing on a Sunday and, obviously, was not comfortable appearing at a business meeting the next day in such casual attire. Fortunately, her luggage was retrieved in time for her to dress properly for the next day's meeting. If her luggage had not arrived, she would have had to cancel or postpone the meeting. If your carry-on will not hold a change of clothes, then be sure you travel in clothes that you will not find embarrassing if your luggage is lost, even though for comfort your traveling outfit might be more casual than you would otherwise wear for a business meeting.

The federal government now requires that all checked luggage be x-rayed and, if necessary, searched. Therefore, you must assume that someone will be opening any bag you have checked and looking at everything in it. You cannot lock your suitcase; if you do, someone may open it forcibly and ruin it. You may also find that the airline has bound the zippers on your checked suitcase together with a plastic clasp that can be opened with scissors. You, of course, must pack any scissors in your checked suitcase and not in your carry-on. Janet has successfully used a key to pry the plastic clasp apart; otherwise, you may need to wait until you arrive at your hotel and use borrowed scissors. I also suggest that if you're going to check your luggage, pack your toiletries and other nonclothing items in clear packaging, so that security personnel can inspect them easily.

You Forgot Something— Now What?

Replacing forgotten items is a lot easier than it used to be. Of course, the ease with which you can accomplish the replacement depends on the item, the time of day, and where you are. The first question to ask yourself is whether you really need this item before returning home. If so, then here are a few options you should consider:

> **WOMAN ROAD WARRIOR TIP:**
>
> If you are giving an important presentation, don't leave all of the hard copies of the presentation in your checked luggage; take one with you. Even if the document is saved on your computer's hard drive, you never know when your computer might "have a moment"!

CLOTHING

- Ask someone at home to courier or express-mail it to you.
- Replace it in the hotel gift shop (if possible).

- Find the nearest shopping area and replace it there.
- Ask the concierge to help you replace it. Sometimes you might realize that you're missing something important late at night or very early in the morning. If this occurs, contact the concierge and see what can be done. It's amazing how resourceful concierges are. Of course, you can also ask for the concierge's help under less demanding circumstances.
- Borrow a hotel uniform as a temporary substitute for forgotten business attire.

MEDICINE

- See if there is a pharmacy nearby that is part of the same chain that you use at home. If so, call the pharmacist and see if she can refill the prescription or at least assist you in getting it refilled. Many major pharmacies share the same database and can access your file. I have had prescriptions refilled in this manner many times.
- Contact your pharmacy at home and ask for assistance.
- Determine (1) whether you can wait for the medicine to be sent from home, and (2) whether someone at home can send it.
- Ask the concierge for help.
- Some hotels have medical staff on premises. If so, the doctor may be able to assist you in getting the item replaced.
- Contact your doctor.

WORK-RELATED ITEMS

- Have someone back in your office send the item to you by courier or express mail.
- If the item is a digital file, have it e-mailed to you. You should be able to access your e-mail from your hotel room if you have a laptop, from your hotel's business center, or from an Internet café. If you don't have access to your e-mail, have someone e-mail the file to a colleague or the hotel manager, who can download the file for you.
- Open a free webmail account (such as Yahoo! Mail or Hotmail) as a backup to your office or personal e-mail account, and have the file sent to that account.
- If the item is a document that's not too long, have someone fax a copy to you.

Woman Road Warrior Checklist

___ Proper identification is attached to luggage, including a ribbon, sticker, or other simple identifier.

___ Copy of itinerary is included on top of clothing in checked luggage.

___ Packed items are complete in accordance with check-list or personal list.

___ If traveling with someone, have exchanged outfit in checked luggage.

___ Critical personal items are in carry-on.

___ Review TSA website to determine security changes.

___ No forbidden items in carry-on.

___ Photograph of luggage.

___ Checked luggage is prepared for search: not locked, items in clear packaging.

CHAPTER 7

The Global Traveler

If you travel abroad, your travels will involve greater complexity, and often greater burdens. Distances are often much longer. If you get antsy on a 6-hour plane flight from New York to San Francisco, try a 25-hour flight to Sydney. Cultures and often languages and customs will be different. Rose, probably like any other American who travels to Australia, says that the people may speak English there, but you will feel as if you are in another world—and for the most part, you are. The time difference from your home could be as much as 12 hours or more, you will probably cross the International Date Line, and you will have left home in one season only to have arrived in another. If you decide to rent a car, you'll be driving on the left-hand side of the road, and if you order a white coffee expecting coffee with cream, you'll be surprised when you receive plain black coffee. And then consider going to Europe, South America, or Asia, where almost everyone speaks your language as a second language, if they speak it at all.

Global travel will push you out of your comfort zone quicker than you can imagine. At times you will feel isolated and will react to things in ways that may surprise you. Cathleen, a seasoned traveler before she started going abroad, was surprised by the difficulties she encountered in dealing with the emotional side effects of international travel. Although she was constantly with her business and professional colleagues while abroad, she found herself in a very different time zone and experienced moments of isolation as she realized that everyone she loved was on the other side of the world. If you aren't ready for it, you can be caught off-guard by the impact this type of travel may have on your physical and emotional state.

And yet this type of travel, if you let it, can open up your world tremendously. I first traveled to Europe many years ago, and I vividly remember the beauty of the architecture and its impact on me; I was awed by its history and the realization of just how young America is by comparison. The pace of other cultures is different from ours, and you can either adapt to it or bring your old habits with you. Believe me when I say that your trip will be much more enjoyable if you take a step back and let the experience unfold. The one comment I heard over and over again from women global travelers was "you're in their land—accept it and enjoy it. Leave the aggressive, impatient, I-want-it-*now* attitude we have in the States at home." If you can pack this type of curious and almost carefree attitude, you'll find yourself laughing at the absurd, accepting the unacceptable, and telling great stories to your colleagues upon your return.

Planning for the Mechanics of Your Trip

Global travel requires even more planning than domestic business travel. You need to plan the mechanics of the trip—how to get there, where to stay, what to pack, how to get around. You also need to deal with the issues created by being in a different country—language, business climate, currency, time zones, etc.

Making reservations and buying tickets. You have many of the same resources for making travel arrangements abroad as for making travel arrangements domestically that were discussed in Chapter 1. You need to remember, however, that the people you would normally consult on domestic travel—such as your corporate travel department, internal travel agency or external travel agent—may not have a lot of experience with planning a trip to the particular places abroad to which you are going. So you may need to do even more of the planning yourself than usual.

The international traveler also has an additional resource available for booking airline flights—the consolidator. A consolidator is an independent travel company that purchases a group of seats from a major airline at a heavily discounted price and then sells them, typically through another travel agency, at a discount to the passenger. A consolidator can save you and/or your organization some money. You can find a consolidator only through your own travel agent; if your travel agent doesn't know about consolidators, you should tell him/her to find out about them, or you should find a different travel agent.

International travel can be very expensive, especially when booking a ticket at the last minute. There are just not as many options available as there are for domestic travel, and airline fares reflect this fact. Even if you can't save money getting to a country (or continent) because the choices are so few, you may be able to find cost-saving choices for travel within your destination country (or continent). Discount airlines are a growing business in many parts of the world. These airlines typically fly from smaller airports with fewer flights, but if you can be flexible, maybe with the help of a creative travel agent or by searching online, you may be amazed at what you will find.

One word of caution: In other countries, discount airline really means discount. Ryanair (www.ryanair.com) is Europe's leading discount airline, and, like Southwest Airlines, it does not assign seats. In addition, the seats are closer together, there are no magazines in the seat pocket in front of you because there is no seat pocket in front of you, and *anything* other than your seat comes at a cost. You will pay extra to check your luggage or to obtain coffee, a soft drink, or food.

Your company's travel and entertainment policy may have a separate section that addresses the issues associated with global travel. For example, some companies may allow their employees to fly business or first class on trips over a certain number of hours. Other issues that may be addressed include: currency conversion rates, per diems (which may be higher than the domestic rate), hotel accommodations (including extra nights that allow you to adjust for jet lag), cell-phone charges (which might be higher than the normal rate depending on the type of service you are using) and dry-cleaning charges (if you are staying for an extended period of time).

As discussed in Chapter 1, travel and entertainment policies may require that you travel with the same airline for all your flights. Mary Ellen, a marketing executive, recommends that you really do your homework and check on flights and schedules before you speak with your travel agent. She was flying on a multileg Asian trip and realized that if she stayed within the

> **WOMAN ROAD WARRIOR TIP:**
>
> When you are speaking with your travel agent, recognize that you are probably better traveled than they are and that you'll need to guide them in order to get what you want.

guidelines of the policy and traveled on the same airline, she would add an extra 16 hours to her trip. Before she approached the travel agent, she went to her supervisor to get approval for an exception to the policy and then made her flight arrangements.

Reciprocal or partnership airline agreements. A number of the United States-based airlines have "partnerships" or reciprocal agreements with international carriers based in other countries. The good news is that if you fly on one of these "partner" airlines, you will be complying with your company's travel and entertainment policy if the policy requires that you travel (or at least permits you to travel) on that airline's domestic partner. The bad news, if you have attained elite status in your home airline's frequent-flyer program, is that the foreign partner will normally not recognize that status and will treat you like its own non-elite passengers. So you may find it difficult to get an upgrade, you may not be able to get a preassigned seat, and, if the foreign partner has an "economy plus"-type seating, you may not be able to sit there. You will receive credit for the miles flown, but otherwise you won't derive much personal benefit from flying on the partner airline.

Coach, business, and first classes; upgrades. International flights are typically longer than domestic, so you will want to sit in business or first class if you can. Check your company's travel and entertainment policy to determine if it permits you to sit in a section other than coach. It is also not uncommon for business travelers to use their air miles to upgrade to business or first class. Airlines will designate a certain number of seats in each cabin to accommodate these types of requests.

WOMAN ROAD WARRIOR TIP:

On an international flight, you must buy a certain class of coach ticket—not the cheapest—in order to upgrade, even with miles. If you want to upgrade, ask the airline or your travel agent whether the ticket you intend to buy will qualify.

Seat assignments. Whether you're sitting in first, business, or coach class, you still want the best seat you can get. In particular, if you are sitting in coach, given the length of most international flights, your comfort may depend on it. If you are unfamiliar with the aircraft on which you will be flying, check the website SeatGuru (www.seatguru. com) to get an overview of the seating.

Unfortunately, it may be difficult or even impossible to receive a seat assignment before you check in at the airport unless you are an elite member of the airline's frequent-flyer program. If you have difficulty getting a preassigned seat, keep trying and be persistent, but you may not be successful. Jennifer, a travel agent, explains that the airlines don't do this just to make your life difficult. They want to be able to verify that you have all the proper travel documentation (passport and/or visa) before they assign you a seat. She tells me that they can be heavily fined if they allow passengers to board without proper travel documentation.

Travel documents. Global travel requires one, and possibly two, additional pieces of paper—a passport, and possibly a country-specific visa. Now, a passport is also required to return to the United States from Canada, Mexico, and the Caribbean, in addition to countries outside North America. Most countries also require that you have a passport to enter. Thus, if you are an American traveling outside the United States and United States possessions, you need a passport. United States passports are issued by the U.S. Department of State (http://travel.state.gov/passport/passport_1738.html). You can apply for a passport in various places: directly with the State Department, at your local post office, or with companies that specialize in processing passport requests (see the appendices for a list of some of these companies). If you need to get your passport quickly, you can pay an extra fee and receive it a few days after you file your application.

Some countries require you to have a visa from that country's government to enter that country. You can obtain a visa most easily through your company's travel agent, if you have one, or through your own travel agent. If you aren't using a travel agent, then you can go directly to the country's embassy or consulate in the United States. The same companies that will obtain passports for you will also obtain visas (see appendices for a list of some).

Some countries may require vaccinations against various diseases. Check with your travel agent, human resources department, your health-care provider, or airline to determine if you need any type of vaccination for the country to which you are going. There can be stringent rules as to when these vaccinations need to be administered, so don't wait until the last minute to begin this process. The World Health Organization (www.who.int) is also a good resource if you don't have other assistance.

Planning for the International Aspects of Your Trip

Planning for the distances you'll travel and the cultural differences you'll find is just as important as planning your travel arrangements. This kind of planning will help you acclimate quicker, be able to conduct business more easily, and enjoy yourself more. I'm not suggesting that you have to be able to speak the language fluently, but consider the following:

Time zones. International travel often sends you to a time zone many hours different from the time at home. Most international business travelers will have meetings during the business day in the country where they're staying, and then call back to their home country for meetings or catch up on business during the business day in their home time zone in other ways. All that makes scheduling challenging. You can't plan to hold a conference call with people in your home office when it's the middle of the night there, and you always have to be aware of the time differences. I keep two master calendars for any foreign trip—one for the time zone I'll be in, and the other for the time zone at home. When I'm setting up my schedule for a trip, I'll use the calendar for the time zone I will be in, whether I'm scheduling meetings there or calls home. I transfer those dates and times to my home-time-zone calendar, which I leave in my office with my administrative assistant. She makes sure it is updated as my schedule changes. I leave another copy at home so my family can keep track of me. Cynthia prints out a listing of the time differences between the different countries where she's going to be and her home country. The websites WorldTimeServer (www.worldtimeserver.com) and Time and Date (www.timeanddate.com/worldclock/full.html) are also helpful in this regard.

Holidays. Every country has different holidays, and people there generally assume everyone knows about them. What your client may think is public knowledge may catch you off-guard. You don't want to show up in a foreign country expecting to conduct business and find that your client or customer—and everyone else—is on holiday. Even if your client or customer is willing to do business on the day of the holiday, you certainly don't want them to think that you didn't know about it. Furthermore, transportation and other services, such as railway travel, may be very limited during a holiday. Your travel agent should be able to assist you finding out about holidays at your destination. Wikipedia is a good source for holidays in a number of countries: http://en.wikipedia.org/wiki/List_of_holidays_by_country. Your client or customer may also give you some guidance.

Weather. Let's face it: Packing for a two-day trip in the *same* time zone can be tough. International travel means potentially adding weeks and crossing the world. Check the weather (www.weather.com) in every location you'll be visiting. Packing for this type of trip will be discussed later in the chapter. Remember that much of the world tracks and reports their temperatures in degrees Celsius, while the United States generally uses degrees Fahrenheit. When checking the weather, be sure you note which is being used and convert Celsius temperatures to Fahrenheit if you are used to seeing them reported that way.

Currency. Global travel, like domestic travel, requires heavy expenditures, and most countries will use a different currency than what you use at home. In order to really understand what something costs, then, you will need to know what the local currency is and convert each amount from the local currency into your home currency. The Bloomberg website offers a currency converter (www.bloomberg.

com/invest/calculators/currency.html) that will identify the local currency for the country(ies) you are visiting and convert any amount into your home currency.

You still need to decide how much local currency you want to have and where to get it. One way to simplify the entire process is to use your charge card whenever possible. You will get a more favorable conversion rate, with a minimal fee, and the charge will show up on your charge card statement already converted into the currency in which you pay your bill. This is a particularly good practice when paying for large items, such as hotel rooms, plane tickets, and meals. You will still need some local currency for expenses like taxis and incidentals. Your options for getting local currency include:

- **Exchange home currency for foreign currency.** You can typically buy foreign currency at a large bank at home, a bank or currency exchange at the destination airport, the hotel at your destination, or a bank or currency exchange in the destination city. You will be carrying cash in a possibly unfamiliar place that could also pose different security risks from what you are accustomed to at home, and you may not want to take the risk of carrying a large amount of cash. Typically, the exchange rate from a bank or currency exchange will be less favorable than if you use a charge or ATM card, and the processing fee will be higher. It's not a bad idea to bring some local currency with you from home in case you arrive at off-hours, when everything is closed. Everyone finds their own way of dealing with this problem, however. Wendy, who lives in Hong Kong and travels all over the Asia-Pacific region, prefers to exchange home currency for local currency at a bank or currency exchange at the destination airport. She finds exchanging currency at the airport easy, with a minimal service fee, and gets a good exchange rate. She cautions against waiting to exchange money at hotels or in the city center, because she finds that the exchange rates aren't as good and the service fees are too high. She typically arrives at her destinations during the business day, when airport services are open.
- **Purchase travelers checks before you depart and use them when traveling.** If you lose travelers checks, you can easily replace them. However, you may not get the best exchange

rate, and the issuer of the travelers checks will often charge a processing fee to purchase the checks and, later, to convert them to local currency.

> **WOMAN ROAD WARRIOR TIP:**
>
> Avoid freestanding ATMs, if possible. Machines that are associated with a bank or building have proven to be more secure and less vulnerable to identity theft.

- **Use your ATM card.** Just about anyone with a checking account has been issued an ATM card, and these cards work just about anywhere in the world. Just like at home, you can visit the nearest ATM and withdraw funds from your account; the ATM will normally issue you local currency, usually at a favorable exchange rate with a minimal fee. When Janet was picking a bank for her checking account, an important criterion was how many monthly "out-of-network" withdrawals she was allowed, because she knew she would be traveling abroad. She uses her "out-of-network" allocation exclusively for obtaining foreign currency in her international travels.

  Natalie tells a story about using her ATM card at a freestanding machine in Amsterdam. When she got home, she discovered that the ATM in Amsterdam had been used to withdraw all the funds from her account. Now, she only uses bank-based ATMs.

Today, charge cards and ATM cards have pretty much supplanted travelers checks as a means of obtaining and carrying cash in other countries.

Language. Although it isn't necessary to have much knowledge of the language of the country you are visiting, many business travelers have noticed that they are treated much better if they know a few basic terms—at least in part because people know they are trying. Leah, an international patent attorney, says she always learns the basics: please; thank you; yes; no; and the numbers one through ten. In her experience, it makes a huge difference. She will also try to pick up some local slang words while she is visiting. She doesn't always get the pronunciation right, but it's a great icebreaker with some of her clients. There are tapes and books that can help you, but the important point is that you try!

Risks/warnings/sanctions. We are all pretty comfortable that we know what to do and what not to do to maximize our safety and security in our home country. Things change on a moment's notice; where or what is safe one moment may not necessarily be safe the next. In some parts of the world, crime is rampant, and foreigners are seen as particularly desirable prey; women in particular should take extra precautions. Many women who work for global firms have their employer hire a local company to advise them on security issues before and during their trip. Often, these firms will also drive the client to and from the office and appointments—even dinners—and act as personal bodyguards whenever the client leaves her hotel or residence. If you are not part of a large organization and are doing your own research, a few resources for you to look at include:

- Travel warnings: http://travel.state.gov/travel/cis_pa_tw/cis_pa_tw_1168.html
- U.S. Treasury sanctions: http://www.ustreas.gov/offices/enforcement/ofac/
- Country Risk Forecast: www.crg-online.com

Risks, warnings, and sanctions should be taken seriously. Alice, an international risk management consultant working in a large commercial center in the Middle East, began each day with a security briefing from her local security firm; if there were any type of threat, she and her team would not leave the compound. They would vary their routes to client sites, and would never stick to the same schedule.

Sometimes safety and security risks may dictate whether you or your company will take on an assignment that will require you to reside in a foreign country—even temporarily. Catie, a leader of a team that implemented enterprise resource-management applications worldwide, used the "McDonald's" factor. Before she would agree to send a team into a foreign city for five months to assist with the implementation, she checked to see if the city had a McDonald's. She believed that if McDonald's had determined that the city was safe enough to do business, it should be safe enough for her and her people. The presence of a McDonald's also would mean that the country had had some exposure to Americans and American culture. If there were no McDonald's in the foreign city, then she would find a local firm to handle the implementation.

It's all about the sports. Okay, not really, but the point is to learn something about the country's business, economy, politics, and even its sports climate. Think about how important sports are to the culture of your home country—it's just as important elsewhere. The whole world plays football, but not American-style. What is known as soccer in the United States is football in the rest of the world. Soccer's World Cup is played every 4 years—the next one being in 2010—and it is the biggest sporting event to most of the world, even though the Super Bowl is much more important in the United States. Cricket—a game between two teams, with 11 players each, that is a little like baseball—is revered in certain parts of the world, but most Americans are unaware of it. Wikipedia (www.wikipedia.org) is a great site to get a quick overview of these and other sports. You can find out which sports are popular in which countries and a little bit about each sport.

Having some knowledge of the country's business climate and issues will be very helpful as well. You probably need to do your own research for each country, but some resources are:

- World Fact Book (https://www.cia.gov/cia/publications/factbook/index.html)
- MSU's GlobalEDGE (http://globaledge.msu.edu/)

Also, the *Financial Times* (www.ft.com) is a daily newspaper published in London and contains a great deal of country-specific business news.

WOMAN ROAD WARRIOR TIP:

A little knowledge can make all the difference in a business or personal situation, and a naïve comment or question may reflect badly on you. Rosemary, a book publisher from Sydney, Australia, marvels at how many people ask her if she has a pet kangaroo!

Etiquette. Perhaps the most important subject you should examine (even more important than sports!) before you travel abroad is business etiquette—the business customs and procedures for your destination. A faux pas could cost you business; some cultures treat proper etiquette as a much more serious subject than you might at home. As Leslie, a Chinese national in the United States, says, in China "there is strict protocol in meetings as to who speaks first (the senior person), how a business card is presented and received (with both hands), and from which part of the body one should bow." The last thing you need is to have spent years cultivating a relationship with a company in China only to start a meeting and have the junior member of your team speak first, or offer and take a business card with one hand. A meeting could end before it begins if protocol is not followed properly.

Cathleen recommends doing research to determine the cultural background of the people you will be doing business with and then taking a conservative approach. Sometimes it pays to take someone else's lead.

Business etiquette covers subjects like gift giving, tipping, meeting protocol, food customs (for instance, it is considered rude to eat all the food on your plate in China), segregation (unmarried men and women do not eat or socialize together in Riyadh), and even hand gestures. Other countries may have very different views of the proper role of women in business, and in society in general; you must learn what to do to adapt so you can effectively do business in those countries. Obviously, the subject of business etiquette is complex and specific to different countries (and maybe even to different regions within a single country). Books have been written on the subject, but I suggest that you find someone to teach you before you depart. One of my

> **WOMAN ROAD WARRIOR TIP:**
>
> Don't assume everyone speaks English. You'll find that you'll be able to communicate in English with most people at airports and hotels, but not necessarily with the people you've come to do business with. You could be embarrassed, not to mention unproductive, if you don't find out whether you need to bring a colleague who speaks the local language or an interpreter to a meeting or business dinner.

favorite resources for business-etiquette training is CultureConnect. As Claudia Jaccarino, a partner at CultureConnect, says, "Even the savviest businesswomen face challenges when confronted with foreign cultural customs, values, and requirements of protocol and etiquette." If there is one area where you do not want to come up short, it is business etiquette. Take the time and get the training.

Entertainment. Client and customer entertainment can be a critical part of any business trip overseas, and it shouldn't be taken lightly. You must be sure that you know what is expected of you wherever you are going. If you have colleagues in your host country, ask them. Your company's human resources department may be of help. If you take business etiquette training, your trainer should focus heavily on entertainment and dining expectations and customs. Whatever the source of information, you should be prepared.

It is hard for me to imagine a business trip overseas that doesn't include some kind of client or customer entertainment. Indeed, there are entire trips planned around "the meals," and in some cultures, a successful social gathering is essential to a successful business relationship. Find out what is expected. Don't wait until the last minute to make the arrangements. You won't be alone in trying to get a coveted reservation or table at the best restaurant in town.

Maneuvering through the Airport

Most airlines require that you be at the airport at least two hours before the scheduled departure of an international flight in order to get through the entire check-in process. You can only check in at the front ticket counter for an international flight; you cannot use a kiosk, curbside check-in, or check-in online. Your class of ticket—first, business, or economy—will determine which line you will enter. At the counter, you will be asked to present your ticket, your passport, and, if necessary, your visa. Once the agent determines that your travel documents are in order, you will be issued a boarding pass, your luggage will be checked, and you will proceed through security.

The rules for flight check-in and seat assignments for international flights are established by each airline in each country. As a general rule, your seat will be forfeited if you have not checked in and received a seat assignment one hour prior to departure. Although this is a general rule, double-check with the airline the day before your flight to verify that there are no changes to security and check-in procedures.

Security lines and procedures for international travel are different from those for domestic travel, and the time to get through the process may be longer. Each country sets its own rules for airport security, and you should not assume that the same rules apply abroad as at home. For example, for a period of time after August 2006, passengers boarding in the United Kingdom could not have any carry-on luggage, but no other country had this rule. Thus, it is important to check the rules before you embark on your trip. The security lines for international flights can move more slowly than for domestic flights, and many international flights depart around the same time, so if you are running late, asking people to allow you to move ahead in line won't get you much sympathy (or movement).

Even if you check luggage, you will probably be bringing onboard a briefcase and perhaps a carry-on or cabin bag. While you are going through security, you will be required to show your passport and ticket, so keep them in a place where they are easily accessible and secure. Consider using something like the A-Way Ticket Tote (www.awaytravelgear.com) to hold your ticket and identification. Given the length of some of these international trips, what you pack in your cabin bag can be very important. A detailed discussion of suggestions is found later in the chapter.

It is not uncommon that you will have time to spare at the airport once you've passed through security. A few suggestions on what to do with that spare time include:

Airport lounge. Each airline has an airport lounge for members; the value of that membership was discussed in Chapter 2. If you are currently not a member of a lounge, seriously consider becoming one if you will be doing a lot of international travel. As much as one tries, flight schedules do not always allow you to arrive at your destination a day in advance of your meetings. There are times when I have arrived in a foreign country in the morning after flying all night long, gone to the airport lounge, showered, changed clothing, and conducted a full day of business. That's just one example of the benefit of this type of membership. If you do not have a membership but are flying business or first class, ask the airline if you can have access to the lounge for this trip. It is not uncommon for them to allow it.

Duty-free. International flights offer a shopping opportunity (we can always use more of those!) that domestic flights do not—the duty-free shop. Prices can be lower in duty-free shops than in the country where the airport is located, because the store doesn't pay the normal customs duty on imported goods. A number of clothing items and pieces of luggage are usually available at duty-free shops, and it's a great place to

> **WOMAN ROAD WARRIOR TIP:**
>
> If you purchased bottles containing liquid from a duty-free shop or while onboard during flight and are connecting to another flight, be sure to pack those items in your checked luggage. The current security rules may prohibit you from carrying those items onboard the next flight.

pick up last-minute gift items. You must keep your receipts, because you will need to declare these items when you go through customs and immigration when you arrive at your final destination.

Airplane Comfort

Boarding. International flights typically board through two doors—the front of the plane for first and business class and the middle for economy/coach. International flights typically have more passengers than domestic ones, so they need two doors for boarding efficiency. The gate agent will direct you to your access point.

International flights by their nature are usually longer than domestic ones and require additional planning on your part. You will be sedentary for an extended period of time, and you need to plan for that. Unlike most domestic flights, the airline will serve you food, but you will be eating meals that have been prepared well in advance, and you will have no idea what ingredients were used. If you have any type of food allergies or intolerances, be prepared, and perhaps bring your own food.

Preparing. What should you do to help you get through the long flight? First, dress in layers—it's a lot easier to take off clothing than to add something you don't have. Wear comfortable shoes that are expandable or have shoelaces, because your feet will probably swell. Many people take their shoes off during flight, and the swelling can create a challenge when you try to put your shoes on after landing. If you decide to remove your shoes in-flight, bring something to cover your feet. This is very important if you get up and walk around the cabin, as things get dropped on the floor, and you never know what you might step on. Try A-Way Travel Treads, a nylon spandex sock with a nonslip, waterproof sole (www.awaytravelgear.com).

I've stressed the importance of drinking water while on an airplane (see Chapter 2). The longer the flight is, the more important it is to replenish the moisture that you will lose. Regardless of what class of service you are in, you cannot be sure you will get the amount of water your body needs. It's important to bring enough water onboard with you (purchased after you go through security); try to drink a minimum of eight ounces of water an hour.

Another important part of any traveling woman's routine is to moisturize—especially on long flights. Many flight attendants carry a bottle of moisturizer and eye cream in their pockets, and whenever they remember, they put some on their face (over their makeup). If this is what the veterans are recommending, it's good enough for me!

Kate, an international flight attendant, says that United States carriers (but not necessarily overseas carriers) provide a blanket and pillow for each passenger. She stresses that there are no extras, so if you like to have a pillow for your head and another one for lower-back support, you'll need to bring an extra.

If you are anxious when you fly and are concerned that you will not be able to sleep, talk to your healthcare provider. There is no need for you to be uncomfortable. A number of natural supplements are available, and some prescription drugs can also be of assistance.

Although movies and music will be available throughout the flight, many travelers download their own movies and music onto their computers or iPods and bring them onboard with them. You can also use long flights to catch up on reading and much-needed sleep.

> **WOMAN ROAD WARRIOR TIP:**
>
> Don't take any sleep aid until at least 30 minutes after the flight has taken off. Trouble with an airplane typically occurs within the first hour after takeoff and/or the last hour before landing, and as a passenger, you need to be able to respond to any type of emergency.

If you have any type of food allergies or intolerances, be sure to check with the airline and inquire about the food service. Ask about special meals, and when in doubt, bring your own food with you. If you don't eat all the food you bring with you, remember that certain countries do not allow visitors to bring some food items into the country. You probably don't want leftover food to delay you at customs and immigration after a long flight.

If you are flying an airline that is not based in your home country, don't be surprised if the primary language in which announcements are made is not your own. It is not uncommon for airline employees to make announcements in the language of their home country first and then the language of the country that is the point of origin or destination. If you are flying in a country where your language isn't spoken, make sure you identify the emergency exits on the aircraft before departure; if you have any questions, ask the flight attendant if someone on board speaks your language.

The other thing you need to do for yourself is *move*. Staying seated in a small, cramped chair for an extended period of time is not good for your body. Do whatever you can do to get your muscles moving and your blood flowing. In-flight magazines usually include some exercises, and you can visit www.womanroadwarrior.com to get more ideas.

Customs and Immigration (or Customs and Agriculture)

Arrival at your destination in a foreign country can be bewildering if you aren't prepared. You have just been on a plane for a long time, you're in a country where you may not speak the language, and you have arrived in what seems like an underground passageway that later turns out to be a maze, and you find yourself following groups of people and ending up in a large room with more lines. It's not as bad as it appears, but can be unsettling if you aren't prepared. For every new country you enter, you must go through immigration and customs. Immigration checks your passport and visa and makes sure you are allowed to come into the country; customs makes sure you are bringing in only goods that you are allowed to bring into the country. You will go through the same process when you return home.

Normally, after you have retrieved your luggage, you will go through immigration first. The immigration officer will check your passport (and sometimes stamp it), review your visa for completeness (if applicable) and the country's immigration form (if it has one). In some countries, the immigration form comes in two copies; the officer will

WOMAN ROAD WARRIOR TIP:

If you arrive on an international flight and are connecting to another flight within the country of arrival, you will still need to collect your luggage, go through the immigration and customs process, and recheck your luggage for the next flight before boarding that flight.

retain one and give you back the other, which you will surrender when you leave the country. After immigration, you proceed to customs.

If the country has a customs declaration, you present it to the customs official. The official may ask you if you have any goods to declare. If you don't, he or she will probably wave you through. On occasion, however, the official may open your luggage and search it. Customs agents will remove and hold anything that you shouldn't be bringing into the country. I've heard that people who are caught bringing something into the United States that they shouldn't (like Cuban cigars) are more likely to have their luggage searched on subsequent trips.

During the last hour of the flight, you will be given a customs declaration form (each country may call it something different) or an immigration form, or both, to complete before entering the arrival country. The customs declaration forms are distributed by a flight attendant onboard the aircraft. Some airlines have a flight attendant whose only duty is to distribute and monitor completion of these forms; for other airlines, it is part of the regular crew's duties. Complete the forms in their entirety, and triple-check them to make sure that you didn't miss something. Natalie, an international flight attendant, observes that it is easy to miss checking some small box or signing on the appropriate line. Also, she advises that you should write down everything that you are bringing into a country that fits in a category that you may need to declare (for example, gifts purchased, food, and wine). You may take a chance that the customs agent will take it away from you, but she thinks that's better than having them find the restricted item and then search all of your bags.

Jet Lag

I always wondered what the official definition of jet lag was, so I looked it up. According to *Webster's Dictionary*, it is:

*a condition that is characterized by various psychological and physio-
logical effects (as fatigue and irritability), occurs following long flights
through several time zones, and probably results from disruption of
circadian rhythms in the human body.*

To me, jet lag is that lightheaded feeling I get in the middle of the
first few days after I arrive at a destination. At those moments, I can't
keep my eyes open and just want to get some sleep, mostly because I
was up in the middle of the previous night counting sheep or doing
anything else to counteract my insomnia. When you travel outside of
your time zone, your body clock gets out of sync, and you find yourself
getting tired in the middle of the day or waking up in the middle of the
night. There are a lot of theories (and products) designed to combat
jet lag, and everyone will tell you they have the answer to this nagging
problem. Just as every person's physical makeup is different, each person
responds differently to a lack of sleep and may combat the change in
sleep pattern differently. The following is a list of common techniques
to minimize the effects of jet lag, some of which I've used myself:

- Drink plenty of water on the flight.
- Avoid alcohol and caffeine during the flight.
- Set your watch to the time zone of your destination country as
  soon as you get on the plane, and act accordingly. For example,
  if you are heading to Italy and it's 2 a.m. in Rome at the time
  your plane departs, put some eyeshades on and try to sleep.
  You'll miss the dinner service, but make sure you are awake for
  the breakfast service in the morning, which would probably be
  the right time for breakfast in Rome.
- Some people try medication to help them sleep. If you do, make
  sure you know all of its effects prior to the flight. Don't try something for the first time when you're 40,000 feet in the air.
- On the first day you arrive, make sure that your activities (especially sleep) take place at the normal time for the time zone you
  are in. If it's morning when you arrive, try to stay up the entire
  day, go to bed after a normal (or early) dinner, and get a good
  night's sleep.
- Monica, an international flight attendant, believes that having
  direct sunlight on her retinas helps her adjust more quickly to
  a particular time zone. Therefore, she will walk around outside
  without sunglasses on her first day in town.

Getting Around

It's tough enough to decide how to get around when you're away from home in your own country. Add unfamiliar signs, different traffic patterns, perhaps a different language, and driving on a different side of the road, and getting around at your destination becomes an even more complex challenge.

GETTING TO AND FROM THE AIRPORT

You've just gotten off a 12-hour flight and walked what seemed like a mile to stand in the immigration and customs lines for an hour; you are now faced with figuring out how you are going to get to your hotel! If you haven't done your homework, you could end up incurring unnecessary costs, taking a method that could make the trip take twice as long as it should, or, worse yet, ending up in the wrong place. For example, Wendy, a frequent traveler in Tokyo, knows the route from the airport to the city center is congested with traffic, and taking a taxi is cost prohibitive. She therefore takes a subway that costs $16 U.S. and gets into the city a lot faster than the alternatives. These resources can help you plan:

- travel agent
- concierge at the hotel where you will be staying
- information desk at the airport
- airline flight crew

If you are not renting a car (car rental is discussed in more detail later in this chapter), then bus, rail, and taxi are the most common ways of getting from the airport to a city center. In most large cities, bus and rail (which are also known as subways, tubes, metros, and other names) options can be very convenient and economical ways to travel. Since many international flights arrive at airports around the same time, you should have plenty of company if you choose to get into town this way. You can purchase tickets for bus or rail services at the airport, but you may need local currency for the transaction. (Acquiring local currency was

WOMAN ROAD WARRIOR TIP:

The first time you travel to a new city or town, arrange transportation from the airport to your destination in advance. Doing so will reduce your stress upon arrival. After the first trip, you can look for more economical alternatives.

discussed earlier in this chapter.) Whenever possible, have the currency in your hand or in a pocket when you purchase your ticket. It's better to keep your wallet secure in a public place like an airport.

If you take a taxi, make sure it is licensed; don't risk taking a "gypsy" cab in a foreign city. That doesn't mean you must pick up the taxi at the airport, though. Amy, a physical therapist who frequently travels abroad, avoids congestion at the airport by taking a complimentary bus to an airport hotel and then finding a taxi there for her trip into town.

Returning to the airport requires planning as well. If a travel agent arranged your transportation from the airport, she should have also arranged your transportation back to the airport. If not, ask the hotel concierge for a recommendation, and if you are taking something other than public transportation, have him make a reservation with the limousine or taxi service. If you are taking a taxi, ask about the approximate fare. Kate, an international flight attendant, was on a personal trip and arranged for a taxi to take her from her hotel to the airport in Frankfurt. She was shocked when the fare was $30 US more than she had anticipated. The driver informed her that he had turned the meter on when he started his trip to go to the hotel to pick her up. She renegotiated the fare, but still paid more than she should have. The more questions you ask and the more information you get, the better. Don't be shy.

> **WOMAN ROAD WARRIOR TIP:**
>
> International flights returning to the United States often depart in the morning. If you are leaving for your flight from the center of a major city, allow for rush-hour traffic delays if you plan to take a taxi or limousine, and consider staying at an airport hotel the night before your departure.

IN-COUNTRY TRAVEL

In foreign countries, your transportation choices are much like the choices at home—car rental (see below), taxi, limousine, rail, subway, or bus, and walking—and your considerations also pretty similar. You can flag a taxi in the downtown areas of most major cities. Most taxi drivers, even if they don't speak your language, will know enough to figure out where you are going and tell you how much you will pay. Limousines might be a better, but more expensive alternative: You probably won't have to worry about communication problems, and they will take you where you want to go and wait for you. If you want to walk, just be sure it's a manageable distance and that it will be safe.

Foreign countries, on the other hand, can have certain security and safety risks that you don't normally find at home that can affect your choices of transportation. If your travel will take you into a "high-risk" part of the world, you may want to hire and work with an organization in that area that specializes in business traveler safety. Beth, an executive with an international manufacturing organization, works with such a firm whenever she travels to certain areas in South America. She recalls the first time she went to Sao Paulo and arrived on a very late flight. While driving in from the airport, the limousine driver supplied by her security firm slowed down at a red light, and, once he determined it was safe to proceed, continued through the light although it was still red. When she questioned him on this practice, he commented that it was safer for them to keep moving. You are only going to get these types of safety tips from an insider, and you will get the best advice from someone hired to protect you. The bottom line is to do your homework. A healthy dose of paranoia may serve you very well when traveling to some areas of the world.

Rail service. Europe and parts of Asia have wonderful rail service that many other countries don't have. Rail service allows travelers to pick up a train in the middle of the city, travel a few hours to their destination, be dropped off in the center of the destination city, and get on with their business. If distances are short enough, it's an easy way to get around without dealing with the lines and delays at the airport. You will usually find food and bar service that offers more variety than airplane fare. A few popular websites are included in the appendices to help you get started. If you will be traveling by rail to multiple cities or know that you will be taking more than one trip, investigate a multiuse pass.

A bullet train is a high-speed train, such as the Eurostar that runs between London and Paris, the Shinkansen of Japan, and the KTX of Korea. These trains can travel at speeds exceeding 300 mph and are a great way to travel between certain cities. Service areas are limited, however, so check with your travel agent for availability, schedules, and costs.

Although rail travel is typically very convenient if distances are short, remember that discount airlines are available around the world, so you can no longer assume that rail travel overseas is less expensive than air.

Subway. Most major cities have subway systems that are a great way to get around. Check with the concierge at the hotel or the information desk at the airport for a map. Wendy, who travels to Tokyo quite frequently, usually takes the subway. She finds it to be elaborate, but quite manageable. In Hong Kong, Wendy says, the subway system is also very reliable, and because Hong Kong is smaller than Tokyo, it is more manageable and easier for an outsider to maneuver. Hong Kong also offers a direct train that is the fastest way to get from the city center to the airport. Shanghai also has a bullet train between the airport and the city center, and Wendy has made the trip from the city center to the airport in as little as seven minutes. Using the subway is especially practical during rush hour in almost every city. Leslie mentions that there is a shortage of taxicabs in Shanghai, which makes it very difficult to hail a cab during rush hour.

Exercise your normal safety precautions when traveling by train or subway. Regardless of how safe you feel, you will most likely be wearing different clothing than the locals; your skin tone, facial features, and haircut may be noticeably different, and you may be noticed as a visitor. Exercise caution and use your judgment when choosing a mode of transportation—particularly at night. Further safety tips are included later in the chapter.

When traveling internationally, Jessica usually hires a car and driver depending on her needs. She has her hotel's concierge set up the service and negotiate a discounted rate for an extended contract. Alice, on the other hand, likes to walk between her office and her hotel, and she usually picks a hotel close to the office for that reason. Her trick is to print out a map with directions from the hotel to the office and the office to the hotel on the same page. She folds the paper in half, so it's easy to flip from one map to the other. If she decides to take a taxi, she will show the driver the map, which comes in handy if there is a language barrier. She finds this process gives her comfort, and she doesn't look like a tourist by unfolding a big map to find her way.

Another tip is to have your hotel's concierge write down your destination on the reverse of a hotel business card when he summons a taxi for you. The business card will come in handy when it's time for you to return to the hotel.

However you choose to get around, train yourself to look for visual markers to help guide you in unfamiliar cities. These markers come in handy no matter what manner of transport you are using. If you are concerned that you may have gotten lost, markers can provide a sense of calm in that moment of panic. Mary, who loves to shop, tells the story of how this helped her with a trip to Munich. She had blocked out an afternoon for shopping during a hectic business trip. Although she didn't remember the street name, she knew that the store at one end of the street began with a "K" and a store at the other end of the street began with an "N," so she tells everyone she shopped everywhere between kindergarten and Nordstrom.

Car Rental

Chapter 4 discussed car rental in great detail. International travel isn't much different. The major differences include:

- Have all the arrangements negotiated ahead of time, including the daily (or weekly) rate and other charges. If you prenegotiate the terms and conditions, you won't have any surprises from last-minute price changes.
- International flights generally arrive around the same time, so prepare for a long wait when renting a car at the airport.
- Bring all the documentation about your rental (reservation confirmation, etc.) with you to the counter. Keep your rental contract with you, and don't leave it in the car.
- Fully research your insurance coverage and options before you rent the car, and even before you leave home. It is not uncommon when renting a car domestically to decline the car insurance because your credit card or personal car insurance will cover any damage that occurs. However, this can be unwise when you are renting internationally. Too many travelers have declined the insurance on the assumption that they are covered, and only after having an accident have they discovered that their existing policies and coverage did not cover driving in a foreign country. That can be an expensive lesson. I know of some travelers who have accepted the car-rental company's insurance coverage because they were uncomfortable driving on the opposite side of the road, or just worried about driving in a foreign country, and have walked away without paying anything but the rental charges after having an accident. Assume nothing when it comes to insurance coverage. If you intend to rely on your personal car insurance, credit card, or some other

coverage, make sure it covers you when you are driving wherever you are.

• Do not leave the car-rental lot without thoroughly looking over the automobile and noting any problems (dents, dings, paint chips, etc.) and reporting them to the clerk that checks you out. Unfortunately, too many international travelers pay dearly for not making a detailed inspection when renting a car.

• Avoid leaving anything (including the rental agreement) in your car, even if the car is locked. Don't even leave anything in the trunk if you can avoid it. Rental cars are a magnet for thieves. Even if you are diligent about locking the car doors when you are away from the automobile, many people have lost luggage and valuables from locked rental cars, even from the trunk. Don't become a statistic.

Hotels

You make a hotel reservation abroad much the same way you make them at home. You will probably first determine a general location and then check with a client or other source (fully described in Chapter 3) for recommendations of places to stay. Next, you search for a specific hotel.

Your client may offer to set up your accommodations and have the invoice sent directly to them. Seriously consider accepting this gracious offer. Since you probably won't know the area, the customs, and perhaps the language, you will have one less item on your list to worry about. You may obtain a lower-quality room than you would like, but it will most likely be adequate, and your client will be happy.

If you are making your own reservations, your external or internal travel agent (assuming you are using one) and the Internet are still very good options for finding and securing a room. Try to be sure you have a reservation, as many rapidly growing foreign cities don't have enough hotel rooms to accommodate the demand, so you shouldn't risk not having a room if you can avoid it. Leslie, a Chinese national, frequently scrambles for reservations if she is flying to Shanghai at the last minute.

Today, most large hotel chains (Sheraton, Hilton, Marriott, etc.) have properties in major foreign cities. So, when you travel internationally, you will have a choice between a chain hotel or a smaller boutique hotel that may not advertise on major travel websites. Either way, be sure you obtain a written confirmation of your reservation. If you choose the boutique-hotel route, be sure to note your hotel's cancellation policy; it may be less generous than that of a chain hotel.

A few other differences in the hotel experience overseas:

Room size. Hotel rooms are usually smaller overseas, even if you are staying at a property with the flag of an American company. Wendy, our Asian traveler, remarks on how spacious hotel rooms are in the United States; she's accustomed to much smaller rooms when traveling in the Asia-Pacific region.

Bed size. Not all hotels have king-size beds. If you are staying in a boutique hotel, you probably won't have a bed that large.

Smoking. If you want a smoking room or a nonsmoking room, make sure you say so. You should know, however, that it is not as routine outside the United States and Canada for hotels to designate rooms as nonsmoking. In many countries, smoking is a much more popular and public habit than it currently is in North America. If you need a nonsmoking room, it may take some searching to find a hotel that has one, and, even then, there may be smokers nearby. Monica, a nonsmoker who travels to Greece and other parts of Europe for film shoots, says that smoking is so prevalent in many parts of Europe that she finds it difficult to escape the smell.

Lighting. Overseas hotels, especially smaller boutique hotels, may have less lighting than you are used to. You may find it more difficult to apply your makeup, for example.

Elevator/lift. Most overseas hotels have elevators that are much smaller than those in domestic hotels. If you're staying at a hotel in a small town, don't be surprised if the elevator can only accommodate one person, or that there isn't one at all. By the way, what you might call an elevator is often called a "lift" in other parts of the world.

Utilities. When traveling abroad, keep in mind that some hotel rooms may not have heating or air-conditioning that you can control, and in some cases there may be no heat or air conditioning at all. Also, electrical outlets and power sources may be different from your home country. If you are uncertain, check with the concierge or front desk to make sure you have the right adapters before plugging anything into the wall.

Amenities. You should not assume that your room will have a hair dryer or iron. If it doesn't, you can probably obtain either of them if you ask. Washcloths are also not a staple in every room. I know of a number of travelers who bring their own washcloths in a plastic bag when traveling overseas.

Service. Travelers to Asia always mention the efficiency and attentiveness of service in Asian hotels. Wendy notes how much more quickly she can check into or out of an Asian hotel than a similarly-sized hotel in the United States. Natalie, an international flight attendant, is often impressed by staff at Asian hotels who go out of their way to be attentive and efficient in all aspects of the hotel experience.

Check-in. Some hotels will ask for your passport when you check in, and the staff may insist that they keep it until you check out; if so, get a written receipt before you leave the front desk. Ask if it would be sufficient for them to make a copy of your passport and keep that instead; if they insist on keeping the passport, have them make a copy for you to keep.

Although you are in a different country, don't change your normal routine when settling into your room. Follow the same safety procedures that you would follow at home (see discussion in Chapter 3). Just as at home, if you don't like the room location or something else about it, request a change. Cathleen, a frequent international traveler, once changed rooms four times at one German hotel before settling in—the reasons varied from room lighting to location.

Concierge service. In a foreign land, you will probably find yourself relying on their knowledge more than usual. My own experiences and those of every other international woman road warrior I know demonstrate the value of hotel concierges. We all ask the concierge to help us with questions from the most mundane (where to find an ATM) to the all-important (telling us where to take a client to dinner and then making a reservation). The concierge is the one constant throughout an international business trip. We sometimes take concierges for granted when traveling domestically, but we certainly can't live without them when going abroad.

Packing

We've discussed the art of packing in Chapter 6, but global travel presents some extra challenges. The old adage of doing more with less applies even more to international travel. Whatever your packing routine—packing from a list, waiting until the last minute, or gathering outfits while you dress—take as little as you can. However, given what you will probably need and taking into account the latest security guidelines (3 ounces of hair spray, hair gel, or facial cream may not be much), it may be unrealistic to carry on all your luggage. Assume that you will check at least one bag, and plan your packing accordingly.

Carry-on (also referred to as a cabin bag). Include any items that you cannot live without: medicines (you won't be able to go to your local pharmacy for a replacement if you forget your prescription); travel documents; laptop; work files; a change of clothing; essential toiletries; snacks (especially if you have food allergies); earplugs; an eye mask; something for your feet other than your shoes, like A-Way Travel Treads (www.awaytravelgear.com); and valuables (jewelry, camera, laptop). Your travel outfit should be one that wouldn't embarrass you if you were wearing it when you ran into the president of your company. At the same time, it should be something that will look presentable after you've been in it for over 12 hours. The change of clothing should be something you can wear to a business meeting if your luggage ends up in Istanbul while you're waiting in Melbourne. Remember, again, the 3-1-1 rule: You can only carry on liquids and gels (other than drinks you buy after you pass through security) in containers of 3 ounces or less, all of which must fit into a single one-quart, clear zip-top bag. You cannot bring a 6-ounce tube of toothpaste with only 3 ounces of toothpaste in it; the container itself can hold no more than 3 ounces. The Transportation Security Administration (TSA) (www.tsa.gov), a government agency, has established this policy, so it does not necessarily apply to non-U.S. airlines. Thus, if you are flying Singapore Airlines from Hong Kong to Singapore, TSA rules may not apply, but other rules might. You should contact the airline directly to understand the applicable rules. A list of large international airlines is included in the appendices. You need to be ready to change what you have in your carry-on, and there may be times—such as in England just after the thwarted August 2006 terrorist attacks—that you will not be allowed to bring any luggage on board with you.

Whenever possible, do *not* check your valuables, such as laptops, cameras, and jewelry. If you can, leave your jewelry at home. If you must wear jewelry, be sure to invest in some costume pieces that would not be devastating to lose.

Checked luggage. On international flights, there are strict rules governing both the number of pieces a passenger may check and their permitted weights. Jennifer, our travel agent, cautions that the weight and piece restrictions for American carriers may not apply to carriers based in other countries. Of course, you must comply with the restrictions for every airline you use, so be sure to check the baggage restrictions for the airline for each leg of your journey. The current rules for luggage on most U.S.-based carriers are:

- Economy class: 2 checked bags, 50 pounds each
- Business or first class: 2 checked bags, 70 pounds each
- Elite status: 3 checked bags, 70 pounds each

A non-U.S. based airline will state its weight restrictions in kilograms, not pounds. One kilogram is equivalent to about 2.2 pounds. For exact conversions, visit one of any number of conversion websites, such as http://www.metric-conversions.org/.

In order to get by on a minimal amount of checked luggage, some general guidelines to follow include:

- Bring a good raincoat with a lining (preferably one that zips in and out).
- Keep your gym and/or walking shoes to a minimum.
- Try to avoid wearing gym shoes (especially white ones) when sightseeing. Everyone will know you're an American.
- Lisa, a meeting coordinator from a major pharmaceutical company, brings an exercise CD with her on the road so she doesn't have to leave her room and bring full workout gear.
- It's all about accessorizing—European women in particular do some wonderful things with scarves. Don't leave home without at least two; they will change the look of any outfit and reduce the number of outfits you'll need to bring.
- Don't assume business casual is acceptable in all countries. Bring a few good business suits (including skirts). Dress conservatively, and add color with your accessories. Don't dress too provocatively, as you might create the wrong impression.
- Proper dress for women varies tremendously from one part of the world to another, and you may have difficulty doing business if you do not dress appropriately for the area. You can learn what is considered to be appropriate business dress for

the places you'll be traveling by taking the business-etiquette training discussed earlier in this chapter.

- Your business-etiquette trainer will also teach you when you should bring a gift for your business host and, if so, what gift is appropriate. If you need a gift, bring a small but appropriate one that won't take up too much space in your luggage.
- A travel steam iron can come in very handy, is very small, and can be lightweight. Not all overseas hotels will be able to provide you with use of an iron.

Don't forget the precautions discussed in Chapter 6 that can minimize the risk of lost luggage. Review them before zipping up your suitcase.

Gadgets. Gadgets are great unless they don't work. Two types of gadgets can have problems overseas: communication devices, such as cell phones, BlackBerry devices, and other PDAs, and basic electric appliances, such as curling irons and hair dryers.

- **Cell phone/BlackBerry/PDA.** Don't assume that your cell phone will automatically work in the country in which you are traveling. And if it does work, there is usually a very high per-minute charge in addition to what you normally pay. Check with your company's IT department or your local cell-phone provider to determine what your options are. Each country has different cell-phone capabilities, so if you are traveling to multiple countries or regions within a country, make sure that your solution will work within each different area. You may need to rent or buy a cell phone for use in a particular country; again, check with your IT department, your cell phone provider, or Internet resources on the topic. If you find that you are going to be traveling frequently to a particular country, consider purchasing a cell phone in that country, which will provide you with a local phone number. Leslie points out that in Asia, many meetings are set up using cell-based instant messages, and that her clients appreciate the fact that she has a local cell phone, so they don't have to make long-distance phone calls to reach her. BlackBerry devices and other PDAs use cellular technology (and often include a cell phone), so the same issues apply to them.
- **Electrical voltage**. There are 2 different voltage types in the

world (100-125 and 220-250). U.S. electrical outlets operate within the 100-125 range, but much of the rest of the world uses 220-250. If you bring appliances that operate on one voltage type to a place that uses the other, one of two things will happen: Your appliance will not work, or you will do serious damage to the appliance so that it may never work. Bring an adapter or converter, and remember that you also need the same adapter or converter to operate the battery charger for your cell phone, BlackBerry/PDA, or laptop computer. Most travel-supply stores or airport shops will have what you need. And no matter what anyone tells you, I have yet to find a universal adapter or converter. No converter or adapter will work in every country.

Safety

In a foreign country, you need to be even more alert to security and safety risks than at home. Events or situations that you would regard as totally innocent at home may be quite different abroad. For example, the simple experience of stopping and looking at a street mime or an acrobatic act in a piazza or on a street corner could be a setup for a band of pickpockets or other thieves. People who live in the community know and are aware of this kind of risk, but, as an outsider, you may not be.

> **WOMAN ROAD WARRIOR TIP:**
>
> Carrying a purse or wallet can be a risk. Keep valuables in inside pockets and away from public view.

High-risk areas are train stations, markets, and heavily traveled tourist areas such as cathedrals and public/government offices. Pickpockets and thieves typically travel in groups. One person will act as a decoy, while the other will take your items without your knowing or feeling anything.

General rules to follow for your own safety:

- If you're working with a security firm, follow their advice. If they tell you to avoid a certain area, don't go there.
- When taking the subway or any type of mass transit, know how much the fare will be and either have your money out or

in a place for easy access. These areas are prone to have a lot of tourists and thus are frequented by pickpockets.

- If you are taking a taxi and don't speak the local language, have the concierge give you a piece of paper with the name and address of your destination so you can hand it to the driver. As an extra precaution, you can get printed directions so you can follow the route. Inquire as to the cost of the ride before you leave the hotel.

- Don't carry a lot of cash—it attracts attention. Use your credit card whenever possible.

- American chain restaurants are tourist traps, and locals know that. Keep all your valuables close to you. If you are carrying a wallet or purse, don't put it down on the counter or floor.

- Travel with as few credit cards as possible. Keep a photocopy of these cards at home and be sure to have quick access to the credit card numbers in case you need to cancel them in a hurry. Credit card companies monitor their customers' accounts for suspicious activity. Your credit card company may see a series of charges overseas as suspicious activity and suspend your account if you haven't notified the company in advance that you will be traveling outside your home country. You will probably find it difficult to conduct business, stay in a hotel or buy meals, among other things, if your credit card has been suspended.

- Keep your passport in a safe place. While in another country, I store my passport and travel documents in the room's safe or with the hotel's front desk. Some travelers feel more comfortable having these documents with them at all times. Decide what works best for you, and don't deviate from your routine; that way you won't forget where these documents are. If you are keeping your items in the room safe and are concerned that you'll check out of the room and forget them, put one shoe (preferably one you'll be wearing while traveling) in the safe with your items. When you get dressed on the morning of your departure, you'll remember to check the safe.

- Do not leave anything of value in your hotel room. If you don't want to carry it with you, put it in the room safe or with the front desk.

- Refrain from offering your political opinions to strangers.

Kate, an American, was on a train in Europe when a group of well-lubricated individuals got on the train, noticed her group, and started taunting them about American politics. Rather than engage in a discussion with a rowdy bunch of foreign drunks—with a possibly unpleasant outcome—she and her group quickly changed cars.

- Trust your instincts. No rules or guidelines should override what your instincts are telling you. If a situation makes you uncomfortable, do what you can to move away from it.
- Don't be too embarrassed to take extra precautions, especially in high-risk areas. When Inez goes out in São Paolo, she carries two handbags, hiding one under her coat. If she were to get mugged, she would surrender the visible one, in which she keeps a small amount of money.

It is not uncommon to see armed security guards with machine guns while traveling abroad. The guards are typically at the airport, train depots, malls, and public buildings. Remember that they are there for your protection; feel free to ask for their assistance.

Although security is a serious subject, it's important to put things in perspective. Yes, you have to be careful and aware, but don't let that stop you from getting out and enjoying a country you've never seen before. Body language, mindset and demeanor will determine how others perceive you while you travel abroad. Don't act like a victim and you're less likely to be one. No matter how you feel on the inside, walk with confidence with your head held high—and be vigilant.

Entertainment

When you travel abroad, you'll probably pack your schedule with meetings and other business tasks, with very little downtime. However, you may never get the opportunity to revisit the place you are. So, I suggest that you take what little free time you have to get out and enjoy the opportunity and see some sights, try the local cuisine, and experience something of the local culture.

Every city and every country has something unique to see or experience, whether it be pearls in China, glass in Venice, or cathedrals all over Europe. As I have said, complete a little research before you arrive to get the flavor of the region. Even if you just purchase a guidebook before you leave, throw it in your carry-on, and skim through it on the plane, you will at least get a feel for the area. Once you arrive, you can ask the hotel concierge for ideas.

Food. A woman has to eat, but when it comes to food, try to get out of your comfort zone and experience the local cuisine. Remember, you are in a different country and are eating local cuisine, so don't expect the same flavors and tastes as you've experienced at home. That isn't a negative—but I guarantee you the pasta you eat in Italy isn't what you get in Australia. So enjoy! At the same time, familiar foods from home may taste different overseas. A cheeseburger at a McDonald's in Greece will probably have feta cheese instead of American.

> **WOMAN ROAD WARRIOR TIP:**
>
> Looking for that gem of a restaurant or the place to buy pearls in Beijing? Ask a member of the airline crew. Airline crew members fly repeatedly to the same destinations and usually have hours of downtime between flights. They can be a great resource for the traveler.

You pick a restaurant in a foreign country much as you would at home. Acquaintances, guidebooks, and, of course, the hotel concierge can give you ideas. I have often found that, if I pick the neighborhood carefully, I can often stumble across a wonderful restaurant in a foreign city just by walking around until I find a place that looks good.

Different countries have different sanitation standards and different techniques for storing and processing food. Although those standards and methods may be perfectly proper, your body may react to the difference. Everyone has heard of "Montezuma's revenge," the stomach problems that Americans can experience when drinking tap water or eating fresh vegetables in Mexico. When traveling overseas, Annette always brings plenty of straws. She enjoys a soft drink from a can, but she knows that the canned soft drinks she buys from street vendors are stored in ice. Tap water overseas produces an uncomfortable reaction in her stomach, so, to avoid swallowing any of the melted ice on the can, she drinks the cola through a straw.

If you have food allergies and are traveling to a country where you don't speak the language, ask the concierge to write down what you can't eat in the local language so you can take the information with you. The appendices include a reference to a website that can be of assistance in this regard, as well.

Tour. I know what you're thinking: Tour? You don't have time to get though the business day and answer e-mails and phone calls back home, and now I'm talking about a tour! However, if you happen to come in the day before you have to start your business or you have an extra day at the end of your stay or, who knows, something happened and you find yourself with an afternoon free, a tour is a great way to see a city or some other area. You can go on a group/planned tour, or you can hire a driver to take you around. On my first trip to London, a colleague and I had limited time and hired a driver for an afternoon. We worked with the driver to plan our itinerary and stops. Not only was it a great way to see London, but at the end of a few hours I felt as if I had my bearings and could maneuver through the city with relative ease. To find a group tour or a driver, ask, of course, your hotel concierge.

Shopping. This can be a fun and different experience overseas. You can find things to buy and places to shop that you would not see at home, and often you can find things you can't afford at home overseas at a lower cost. And, besides, who wouldn't like to be able to get a great deal on a unique strand of pearls in Beijing? Knowing where to go is another issue. Natalie, our international flight attendant, has advised many passengers on where to go to buy pearls in Beijing and how to pick them out. Colleagues who are or have been where you are and our all-purpose hotel concierge can give you ideas of where to shop. You can also shop with a business purpose. When Catie was on her worldwide implementation-project tour, she would buy candy in one country and bring it to her colleagues and client in the next. It was a great icebreaker! Shopping also gives you a way of bringing something home to share your experience with family and friends. Brenda, a CEO of an import/export company, will always ask her hosts, "What can I bring back to my family/office that best represents your culture?" Armed with the answers, she goes out and gets something to bring back with her.

Exploring. Since it seems as if our lives are run by calendars and to-do lists, every so often it's nice to be able to walk around just to see what you run across. Exploring a city on foot can be a great experience. You are bound to happen upon shops, cafés, and neighborhoods that you might never have found otherwise. You need to take the usual safety precautions, but that shouldn't hinder you. Get a map (at least so you can find your way back) and perhaps some suggestions from your work colleagues, a guidebook, or the concierge. Walking can be good for jet lag and can help with some homesickness as well.

Tipping. In most countries, the restaurant will include a service charge in your bill computed as a certain percentage of the charges for your food and drink. This service charge includes what Americans call a "tip." If the bill includes a service charge, you are generally not expected to leave a tip or add any additional gratuity to the bill. If the restaurant does not include a service charge, generally you should include a 10 percent gratuity. Your business-etiquette training should cover the subject of tipping, or, if you didn't receive such training or if you are otherwise unsure of the practice in any particular country, ask the hotel concierge. You should also review the discussions of tipping in the earlier chapters of this book; you can expect tipping practices abroad not to be that much different from those at home.

Dealing with the Unexpected

It seems much worse if things go wrong when you're overseas than if you're in your own country. I'm not sure whether it's because you're in a different culture, facing a different type of surroundings, a different language is spoken, all of the above, or what. If you stay calm and treat solving these problems as just part of the experience, however, you'll find that you can deal with them as well.

The transportation systems went on strike. Airline, subway, bus, or rail strikes, which are not uncommon, especially in Europe, could have an impact on your ability to get around, and even to get home. Generally, the public is given notice of these strikes before they occur, but there are occasions where people are caught off-guard. If you learn of a planned airline strike and you are scheduled to fly out on the day of a strike, contact the airline and see if you can get your flight changed so that you will be able to depart before the strike (without financial penalty of course), assuming you have the scheduling flexibility. Public-transportation strikes may require a lot of time on foot; ask the concierge or local friends and colleagues (who also have to deal with the strike) for advice.

You lost your passport during your trip. You cannot return home to most countries without a valid passport. If you lose your passport, contact your country's nearest embassy or consulate for help. If you are a United States citizen, you need to complete the lost-passport application or affidavit which you will obtain from the embassy or consulate. You will need to bring proof of citizenship (a copy of the lost passport will help expedite the process), two passport photos (get replacements before you go to the embassy) and proof of identity (driver's license or birth certificate). There will also be a fee for a replacement passport, so make sure you know this amount before you arrive.

You got a traffic ticket in a foreign country. Normally, if you get a traffic ticket in a foreign country, you just pay it when you get home; it's not much different from a traffic ticket at home, except you probably won't be able to contest it. There are, however, countries where the norm is to pay a bribe to the police officer, and where the officer expects it. If you will be driving, make sure you understand the customs of the area. Your business-etiquette training should cover this issue.

Your cell phone doesn't work. Unfortunately, there will be times when technology will fail you. If you are going to be a frequent visitor to the region, it might make sense to have a local number and simply buy a new, local cell phone. If not, ask the concierge if the hotel has a phone you can rent or knows of someone who can rent a phone to you. You can always use a land line with a credit card or prepaid calling card, but you will not be able to make or receive calls in places like a restaurant or vehicle.

Your client takes you to what you thought was a nightclub, and it turns out to be a "gentleman's" club. In certain countries, this type of entertainment is accepted and part of a normal business day. For a woman, it can be uncomfortable and at times embarrassing. Inez has tried two approaches: grin and bear it, only to hear her American male counterparts tell her that she should have left; and just make an exit as graciously as possible. There is not necessarily a right answer (this is where that business-etiquette training really comes in handy), but as a female business traveler, you need to be aware that you can face this dilemma and should be prepared.

You forgot your adapters/converters and none of your gadgets work. The duty-free shops at the airports are a great place to stock up on adapters and converters. If you can't buy adapters and converters there, or, more likely, don't find out that you forgot your own until you get to the hotel, ask the concierge or desk clerk at the hotel; most hotels will have extras that guests can use. If the hotel can't accommodate you, the concierge may be able to send you to a hardware or another store where you can buy them.

You walk into a public toilet and it's a hole in the ground. Toilet and similar facilities throughout the world may not be like what you are used to at home. It's a good idea to always carry tissue that you can use as toilet paper and antiseptic towelettes for situations like these.

You find yourself homesick. Even the most hardened woman road warrior can have moments of homesickness. That feeling can arise at the most unexpected moments. You may find that a little "comfort food" or a familiar brand will make you feel better. For an American, an Egg McMuffin at a nearby McDonald's (even though it may not taste exactly as it would at home) or a latte from a nearby Starbucks may be enough of a touch of home to get you grounded, help calm you down, and keep you going.

Woman Road Warrior Checklist

__ Verify that all travel documents are up to date.
   __ Passport
   __ Visa
   __ Vaccinations

__ One copy of itinerary, travel documents, and credit cards at home, and another with you in a secure place.

__ Make sure all international aspects of trip have been planned:
   __ Key phrases
   __ Local currency
   __ Customs
   __ Sanctions/risks
   __ Business etiquette
   __ Time zones
   __ Weather
   __ Adapters and converters
   __ Gift(s) purchased

__ Carry-on (cabin bag) is well planned and packed.

__ Credit card company has been alerted to international travel plans.

CHAPTER 8

Taking Care of Yourself on the Road: Health, Recreation, and Entertainment

I'm always amazed at the reaction I receive when I tell people I travel a lot—at least, when I'm telling someone who doesn't. People seem to think business travel is glamorous and that I go to exotic places where I get to shop, sightsee, and wine and dine in fancy, expensive restaurants. What they seem to forget is that most business travel is not to Europe or the Caribbean. On the contrary, those of us who travel for business mostly go to different cities in the United States, stay in "adequate" hotels, and hit the ground running when we arrive at our destination. This doesn't mean going to museums, shopping, and lunch, but to client meetings and working dinners. Most of all, it means adhering to business timelines and deadlines. There's not much glamour to this—it simply requires a lot of coordination, determination, and long hours. Even if a business trip is to London, Melbourne, or Shanghai, it will still mostly mean conference rooms, meetings, and client entertainment—the distance doesn't create glamour, just the additional burden of greater time differences and longer flights.

Let's face it: Traveling isn't necessarily good for your health, either. Your eating, exercise, and sleep routines are all disrupted, and the healthy habits you have at home can disappear in the face of temptations on the road. Of course, you may be a woman who can eat whatever she wants without gaining an ounce, needs only a few hours of sleep, and never has a problem with her complexion. If so, please write a book for the rest of us and share your secrets; in any event, skip the rest of this chapter. If you are part of the 99 percent of us who need to be concerned about weight gain, sleep interruption, and complexion, this chapter is for you.

Remember, though, that being on the road doesn't have to mean sitting in your hotel room whenever you're not working. You can and should take the opportunity to experience some of the things a new city or town can offer. You just need to do so sensibly and with an eye toward your health and well-being.

Restaurants and Food

One simple and enriching way to experience a new city or town is through its restaurants. After all, you have to eat, and you may as well do so in a way that enhances your experience! Of course, as a woman who may be traveling alone, you have to be careful where you go. You also have to take some care to eat healthfully.

Anyone who travels extensively will often order meals from room service. I actually find the experience of eating outside the room better for my health and for my outlook. I have found that I don't eat as much when I eat outside my hotel room. Somehow, the temptation to order—or at least finish—that piece of chocolate cake diminishes when I know other people are watching (or I think they are watching)!

I am usually more comfortable when I'm alone in a restaurant if I bring along work or something to read. When you're watching for it, you'll be amazed at how many people in a restaurant are reading, working on laptops, or answering e-mail with wireless devices. I also find I don't eat as fast when I have something to occupy my time, which is good for the calories and digestion.

FINDING A RESTAURANT

Most cities to which you travel will have a whole host of restaurants for you to sample. A good place to start is a restaurant in your hotel. These restaurants will certainly be convenient, and in many cities, certain hotel restaurants are among the best in town. Hotel restaurants are accustomed to solo diners, and you'll probably find other people there eating alone.

The first time I ate alone in a hotel restaurant, I was very anxious that I would be too conspicuous. Instead, I found that I was treated as a professional, that I enjoyed being around people rather than alone in my room, and that the food choices were more extensive than on the room-service menu.

If you want to try some place other than the hotel restaurant, you may have a recommendation of an alternative from a trusted friend or colleague. If not, these are some of the best ways to find a restaurant:

- **Review the in-room city guide for suggestions.** A word of caution: The guide is essentially advertising for the restaurants listed in it and thus may not be the most objective list.
- **Search the Internet.** Certain websites have restaurant reviews by city. Just remember that there is no guarantee that you and the person making the recommendation have the same taste.
- **Read the local newspaper.** Most newspapers in every city publish restaurant reviews, usually on particular days of the week. Unless the newspaper contains a list of restaurants, however, the reviews will probably only introduce you to the latest hot spots. The newspaper's website may also be of help in this regard.
- **Check out guidebooks.** Some guidebooks include restaurants based on the taste of the author or publisher's staff, while others, most prominently *Zagat*, list and rate restaurants based on the comments of readers.
- **Talk with the concierge.** She should have all sorts of recommendations. A concierge will often (as she probably should) start by telling you that the restaurant in the hotel is just wonderful, but if you say you're looking for something else, you'll get other suggestions. The concierge can also give you

directions, make your reservation, and give you advice regarding neighborhood safety.
* **Explore a shopping mall.** Believe it or not, I have found some
wonderful restaurants in malls. Not only is the food good, but
being at a mall can also let me do some walking, even in in-
clement weather. For me, this is a great way to relax after a long
day. Of course, every mall also gives you the option of fast food.

Unfortunately, restaurants sometimes assign women eating alone
to the most undesirable tables—located in the back of the restaurant
or near the kitchen or wait station. If you are assigned to a table you
don't like, assert yourself and request a change to another table or
another area in the restaurant. You should deal with restaurant tables
just as you should deal with hotel rooms—it is your right to request a
change if you don't like what they give you.

EATING RIGHT

It's easy to splurge on food while traveling. Not only is your schedule
up in the air, but the types and amounts of food on the menu can
also vary drastically from what you eat at home. Planning and care
can minimize the consequences. For example, at breakfast have something close to what you have at home or, at least, something reasonably healthy. If possible, determine when and where you'll be eating
each day and plan all your meals for that day accordingly. For instance,
if you are taking a client to lunch or dinner, think about ordering less
when you are alone in order to compensate for the larger amounts you
may consume with a group.

Before ordering a meal, here are a few things to consider:

* You're not limited to what's on the menu. If your diet is restricted, if you don't like how things are prepared, or if you
can't find anything on the menu that you want, ask the waiter
for something you'd like, prepared the way you prefer. After all,
you're paying for the meal and should be able to get something
you want.
* Start with a salad and order nothing else until after you've
eaten it. Often everything on the menu sounds great, and we
order an entire meal. Then, even if we're full after the first

course, we continue to eat. If you wait to order until after you've eaten a salad, you may order less for the remainder of the meal. After all, you don't usually order your dessert when ordering your appetizer and entrée, so why not utilize the same approach with all the courses? Don't let your anxiety about eating alone hurry the process.

- Many restaurants are notorious for serving extremely large portions of food loaded with salt and butter. Here are a few ways to avoid the temptation to consume these large portions:
  - Order an appetizer for your entrée. There is no rule that says the item you select for an entrée has to be from the entrée section of the menu. Ordering an appetizer means you'll eat less but probably won't go hungry.
  - Order two appetizers for your entire meal. If one doesn't fill you up and yet you don't want an entire entrée, order another.
  - Request a half order. Some restaurants will honor this request. I find it's a great way to get what I want but not be tempted to eat an entire portion. Be aware, however, that some restaurants add a charge for half orders.
  - Split an entrée with someone. If you are dining with someone you're comfortable with and the other person is willing to share an entrée, splitting is a great way to avoid overeating. As with half orders, some restaurants may add on a charge for split orders.
  - Remove half the meal from your plate and ask the waiter to wrap it up for you to take with you. Of course, if you take the leftovers back to the hotel, make sure you aren't tempted to eat them in the middle of the night.
- Request that the breadbasket be removed from the table. This approach works if you are eating alone or if the other members of the party agree. If you are eating with a group and don't want to broach the subject, just make sure that the bread stays on the other side of the table, preferably out of your sight. I've always found it too easy to eat a lot of bread while I'm waiting for the rest of my meal, and it's a very easy way to put on weight.
- Avoid or minimize alcohol consumption. Alcohol is one of the

easiest ways to add pounds, retain water, and disrupt your sleep patterns. As with other foods, if you wish to have a drink, then moderation is the key. Among common alcoholic drinks, wine contains the least amount of sugar and calories.

- Regardless of whatever else you drink, try to consume as much water throughout the meal as possible. Water not only keeps you hydrated, which will help your complexion and sleep, but it assists in giving you that full feeling that can help you avoid overeating.
- Health-wise, the best thing to do with dessert is to avoid it altogether. But nearly all of us are moved by temptation, and so if you're like me, dessert is one course you won't want to skip. Some ideas:
  - Split with someone
  - Order one dessert for the entire table
  - Stick to fruit—it's healthier, and its sweetness could curb a craving for something less healthy
  - Avoid chocolate, which is loaded with sugar and caffeine— eating it, especially late at night, can disrupt your sleep.

Regardless of what or where you end up eating, remember that seeking out healthy food options is better for you in the long run. And don't forget, whether you are eating alone or in a group, that you do not have to limit yourself to what's on the menu.

Pampering

I can't think of a better way to spend nonworking time than to indulge in some spa or salon treatments, such as a manicure, pedicure, facial, or massage. If you are fortunate enough to be staying in a hotel that provides these services, so much the better. If not, try to get a recommendation from someone—perhaps a friend, the concierge, or someone at the client's office, or if you work for a firm that has an office in the city you're staying in, someone there.

Unfortunately, the spa and salon industry has not caught up with the demands of the woman business traveler. Thus, it may be hard to find someone to provide these services at your convenience, especially late into the night, so make reservations early. There are some cities, however, where these services are readily available at all hours.

In many places, the services may come to your hotel, which is a real treat. Your best bet is to be aggressive in your search; talk to everyone you know who might be able to give you a suggestion.

Tipping

Tipping practices on the road are no different from tipping practices at home. If you don't have strong ideas on the subject, what follows is a guide, based on my experience and that of other woman road warriors, for large cities such as New York, Chicago, or Los Angeles. At a restaurant, generally, you should tip a waiter 15 to 20 percent of the bill, excluding alcohol and tax, and the wine steward 10 percent of the wine bill. You do not need to tip the headwaiter unless he provides you exceptional service, such as giving you a table when the restaurant is crowded. For spa (pampering) services, you should tip 15 to 20 percent of the bill. Be sure you divide your tip properly among the people who provide the services.

Entertainment

Every city has opportunities for entertainment: from movies to theater to the symphony, opera, museums, sporting events, you name it. You may find yourself in a city with a world-renowned museum or cultural institution. If you have time, taking advantage of these opportunities can greatly enrich your travel experience.

Ticketed events. You can buy tickets for most events in advance. Again, you can do so over the Internet or by working with the concierge, or you can call the entertainment venue directly. Check with a colleague or friend for suggestions. If you work with the concierge, be aware that the ticket price you are charged may be more than the box-office price. The hotel may use the services of a ticket broker, who charges a premium; depending on the event, the actual cost could be as much as double or triple the box-office price, or even more. On the other hand, it may well be worth the extra cost to have someone else do the work for you and to be sure you get the ticket you want.

If you wait until the day of the performance to look for a ticket, and you don't want to pay the extra cost of going through the concierge or a ticket broker, try going directly to the box office at the event. Frequently, presold tickets to a performance are turned back in to the box office at the last minute, and they are usually available on a first-come, first-serve basis. Success with this method requires luck and persistence, but if you have both, you can often see a popular performance without planning—or overpaying.

Movies. Movies are one of my favorite ways to entertain myself while I'm on the road. Movie lists and times are typically available in the local newspaper or with the concierge. If you are unfamiliar with the area, check on the safety of the neighborhood before you venture out.

Bars and nightclubs. Every city has nightclubs and bars, but you may or may not want to venture out to one if you are alone in a strange city. There is definitely safety in numbers, but if you would go out alone at home, you certainly can do the same away from home provided you are careful about where you go. In any event, you need to follow your instincts, whether you're in a fancy restaurant or in a club that caught your eye. If you're uncomfortable, just leave. If you are comfortable, projecting a serious and confident attitude will help you stay that way.

Jody, a training specialist, often likes to go out for a drink after a long day of training. She worked for several years as a bartender when she was a student, and she believes her experience has taught her how to avoid places where she wouldn't be comfortable. When she enters an establishment, she stands at the front door and scans the place as if she is looking for someone. In fact, she is trying to get a sense of the clientele, and especially of the bartender. She looks to see if the bartender is watching his or her customers, paying attention to what they are ordering as well as watching the rest of the establishment. She feels comfortable if the bartender has a keen sense of what's going on in the place and an attitude of confidence and control. She finds that a good bartender can help her deal with an unwanted conversationalist or other uncomfortable situation. She also has found that minimizing eye contact with other patrons will minimize unwanted approaches. When Jody is ready to leave the bar, if someone who makes her uncomfortable walks out with her, she just turns around and walks back in as if she forgot something. She also sometimes asks the bartender or a server to walk her to her car or to call a taxi for her and escort her to it when it arrives.

Classes. If you know you will be in the same city for an extended period and your work schedule will permit it, consider taking a class. The opportunities for learning are almost unlimited in most cities. Indulge a secret passion—you can learn to cook, tango, or write poetry. If you're concerned about your safety on the road, consider a class in self-defense or martial arts. Some types of classes, such as many cooking classes, meet only once, and a new city may provide some type of learning experience, even for one evening, that you can't find (or don't have time for) at home.

Other passions. Other road warriors use their time away from home and family to indulge a passion or to enrich their experience in something they do back home. Remember Deborah, the vice president of sales and baseball fan, who uses her business travel to see baseball games in ballparks she might not otherwise visit. Vicki, the partner in a consulting firm, loves gardens and gardening. During her downtime on the road, she likes to visit flower shops and public gardens to look for ideas she can use at home. Still other road warriors love cities and architecture and use their time to explore new cities, often on foot, and look at buildings and people. Hannah, a business consultant and avid golfer, takes her golf clubs on trips during the golf season. At the end of the day, she can usually squeeze in nine holes at a local course before dark, and depending on her schedule she can sometimes find time during other parts of the day.

Your hotel room. There is also nothing wrong with being a "slamclicker"—someone who goes to her hotel room at night, closes and locks the door, and doesn't come out until the morning. When you are managing a hectic schedule at home, quiet time in a hotel room often looks enticing. Some ways to spend that time are pretty obvious—such as watching TV or reading a book or magazine—but here are some other suggestions:

- **Work.** Well, I guess that's pretty obvious, too, but let's face it—you're away from home because of work, and you might be able to be very productive when you're away from colleagues and your office telephone. Elizabeth feels that if she's going to be away from her family, she'd much rather spend her time working. That way she can enjoy herself more when she's at home.

- **Pay bills.** Technology has given us online bill paying. You can use downtime in your hotel room for this routine task, either online or conventionally, and have more time at home for more enjoyable pursuits. A word of caution—if you pay your bills by check, don't leave your checkbook in your hotel room when you are not there. Natalie, an international flight attendant, has learned that the most common method of identity theft results from someone's getting access to someone else's checkbook.

- **Shop.** Many of us do a lot of our shopping online, and the quiet of your hotel room provides a good place to accomplish that. Melinda orders home-delivered groceries online, so she does not have to go to the supermarket. You can use this time to order gifts, buy something you need for the house, buy clothing, or shop for anything else that you need and don't want to go to a store for when you get home.
- **Correspondence.** Teresa uses time in her hotel to keep up on both her personal and business correspondence. She brings a stack of mail and paper, note cards, and envelopes on every trip. Because she writes so much correspondence by hand, it's amazing how much she can accomplish in the quiet of her hotel room.
- **Keep your travel plans current.** Assuming you have Internet access, you can use your hotel-room time to plan your next business trip, vacation, or other travel. Even if you use a travel agent, this planning may simplify the reservation process and may save you time when you get back to your office. If you have access to a printer, you can check in for your next day's flight.
- **Do nothing (whatever that means to you).** That's a novel idea! When you're away from the office, family, and other responsibilities, it's okay to enjoy a "guilt-free" evening alone. You decide what "nothing" means, but remember—*no regrets.*

Exercise Options

In recent years we've all seen many books and articles describing the benefits of regular exercise. As much as I find I benefit from exercise at home, on the road I have found that exercise reduces the stress of business travel and makes me feel better. At the same time, finding time to work out at home can be challenging enough, and doing so on the road can be even tougher! My routine has changed over the years—and some days I find it a major triumph just to get out of bed and make it to the client or meeting. If you want to exercise, rest assured that most hotels have some type of equipment and facilities for that purpose. You just need to plan your time and be sure you pack the necessary clothing.

- **Running.** If you are a runner, ask the concierge or front desk for trails or suggested routes to follow. Make sure the area is safe and stick to the running path. If you are running after dusk or before dawn, wear light clothing or have some type of reflective device that is visible to others. Also, bring some type of identification and perhaps a small amount of money with you.

  Jody is a serious runner. When she arrives at her hotel, she asks the concierge about where she can run safely, and she also will use the yellow pages to look up a local running-shoe store and ask someone there about the running environment near her hotel and for other advice about where to run. When she runs, she brings a piece of paper with her hotel's name and phone number, and the name and phone number of the hotel manager. She's also had a special identification tag made—like a military dog tag—that lists her name and address and the phone numbers of her mother and her sister (Jody's unmarried). She fastens the tag to the laces of her running shoes. She feels that she is carrying just the right amount of information should something happen to her.

- **Health clubs.** Most major hotels provide their guests with access to a health club. The club will be in the hotel or nearby, and you may be charged for using it; find out when you check in or before. Don't forget that there is a great variation in facilities and equipment among health clubs. Almost all hotel health clubs have some type of aerobic equipment, free weights, and some type of Nautilus, Universal, or other resistance machines. You also may be interested in aerobics, yoga, Pilates, or other classes that might be offered at a health club. If access to a health club is important to you, ask the hotel what is available (including the types of equipment and services and hours of operation) before you book your reservation.

  If you're a member of a health club at home, it may have a reciprocating arrangement with a club in the city you're visiting. This could provide an alternative if your hotel's health club doesn't meet your needs.

- **Develop your own in-room workout.** You might be looking for some type of physical activity without going to a health club or enduring the pounding of a run, or you might not want to face the prospect of encountering your colleagues or boss in the hotel health club. If you work with a personal trainer at home, you can develop a unique routine that is tailored to your specific requirements. Another option is to bring along an exercise video or DVD. If your hotel room's television does not have a VCR or DVD player, ask the front desk or housekeeping to bring you one. Some hotels will even bring exercise equipment to your room.

For in-room workout ideas, you can also check our website at www.womanroadwarrior.com

The Little Things

Adding some small touches to make your hotel room more homey may have a very positive impact on both your stay and your outlook. If you choose not to bring a pillow from home, what about a pillowcase? I'd recommend a color other than white, so you (and the hotel's housekeeping staff) don't confuse it with the hotel's. Take the flowers from your room-service tray and put them on the desk to make the room more cheerful. Bring framed pictures of your children or your pet and display them on the hotel-room desk. Be creative and think of other things you can do to remind you of home or personalize the space. You may be amazed at the effect these or other similar touches may have on you.

Staying Safe

Staying safe on the road isn't much different from staying safe at home. Remember that you're in an unfamiliar place, so you need to be at least as careful as if you were in a strange neighborhood in your home city. Minimize the amount of time you are walking alone, especially after dark. If you are uncomfortable, get into a well-lit building and call a cab, hotel, or friend.

If you are small, you need to be especially careful. Small women are more likely to look vulnerable than tall ones. All women, but especially petite women, need to walk with a sense of purpose and confidence when they are out in an unfamiliar city and need to appear unburdened and able to take care of themselves. Always be able to move quickly away from a threatening situation.

You also always need to be on the alert even in situations that you might not expect to present safety problems. Danielle, a petite woman, learned this lesson when she was going through an ordinary revolving door. The person in front of her stopped the door before the back of her compartment was totally enclosed, while someone behind her grabbed for her purse. She was able to slam into the glass in front of her and startle the person in front so that the door moved and enclosed her, leaving the person behind her unable to grab her purse. As she says, she might not be so lucky the next time.

Also, when I'm walking in a strange city, I always turn my rings and other jewelry so someone who passes me in the street or watches me in a restaurant or similar public place can't see them. Never hang your purse on the back of a restaurant chair. That is just inviting trouble.

Consider taking a self-defense class if you want some additional protection. I know a few veteran road warriors who are also brown belts in karate. That is certainly one way to help you feel more secure. Some women carry mace or pepper spray in their purses. Remember you cannot carry mace in your airplane carry-on, only in checked luggage.

If you are faced with a threatening situation, remain calm. Remember that your safety is all that matters; don't worry about losing anything but your life. This is not the time for heroics. Once, I was robbed at gunpoint after leaving a restaurant and getting into a car. I remained calm and gave the robber what he wanted and was not physically harmed. He took my purse, which unfortunately contained my cell phone and my glasses, but nothing more. I later described the incident to Michael, a private detective. He told me that when someone with a gun demands your purse, your jewelry, or anything else that doesn't harm you physically, give him what he wants. As fast as you think you are, you can't outrun a bullet. He also said that if you are on the street and someone comes up to you from behind with a gun, put your hand out with your purse,

> **WOMAN ROAD WARRIOR TIP:**
>
> It's worth repeating: Always carry ID with you when you leave your hotel. Also, leave a note stating the time you left and your destination in the room or with a colleague and/or tell the front desk or doorman.

drop the purse and keep walking. Usually, he only wants your money and will just pick up your purse and take off.

When traveling, there are also a few things you do *very* differently than at home, which require different security precautions. On the road, you probably use your credit card more frequently than at home, so be particularly careful to guard your credit card receipts. These receipts provide great opportunities for someone to make unauthorized charges or, worse yet, to steal your identity. Never leave your cards or receipts in your empty hotel room, and, above all, don't just throw them in the trashcan. Be sure you've left copies of your cards (front and back) at home in case of mishap.

Maintaining Your Life Back Home

When you travel extensively, keeping on top of your life back home can be extremely difficult. Not only must you try to keep your home clean and well maintained, but you need to pay bills, do laundry, and take care of all the other chores that go along with running a household. When I was traveling five days a week, I could have used a full-time assistant just to help me run my nonwork life!

A few things to consider that can make life a little easier are as follows:

- **Newspapers.** If you're away for more than a day or two, stop the newspaper delivery. If you are gone for an extended period of time, suspend the newspapers completely, even if you come home on weekends. If you want a paper on the weekend, go to a newsstand. Newspapers left on a doorstep simply invite intruders.
- **Mail.** Have someone retrieve your mail for you. If you live in a high-rise, see if management can collect and hold your mail until you return.
- **Home.** Have a friend periodically check on your home. You don't want to come home to the surprise that something has sprung a leak or broken.
- **Pets.** If you have pets, you have a few choices. See if a friend can take care of them while you are gone. There are pet-walking services that will come into your home and tend to your animals while you're away. Boarding them in a kennel or pet

hotel is another possibility. You may be able to take them with you on the road—but before you do, be sure to check with the hotel or corporate apartment to verify that animals are welcome guests.

- **Dry cleaning/laundry.** If you find you'll be in one place for a long time, have your laundry done in the visiting city. Drop it off when you leave for the weekend and pick it up upon your return.
- **Socializing.** Stay in touch with your social and familial circles. It is so easy to drop out of the social scene while you're on the road. Although e-mail and cell phones have made it easier to stay in touch, it's still not the same as being there. Plan activities with family and/or friends for when you're home. The burden rests with you to maintain your relationships. I was on the road every week for several years, and during this time I did not devote sufficient effort to staying in touch. When I stopped traveling this way, a number of my friends had moved on and I had to start over to rebuild my social life. Yes, it can be done, but it's much easier if you don't have to start over again in the first place.

Traveling takes work, coordination, and organization. Do yourself a favor and try to offload as many of the mundane chores (i.e., laundry, cleaning, etc.) as possible. Use your time at home to reconnect with your friends, family, and peers.

Your Family

If you can successfully balance business travel with the demands of a family at home, you can do anything.

When you're a road warrior, you'll find it challenging enough to remain flexible while managing the tight scheduling and other demands of business travel. When you also have to juggle the needs of a family as well, the challenges become that much greater. Organizational skills are tuned to a new level. Managing your children's schedules while taking part in meetings in faraway places and hopping by airplane from one destination to another can be overwhelming at times. Vicki said it best when she stated, "As women we are performing a balancing act between work, family, and the guilt that's in our head." But there are some things we can do to make the whole process easier for our families and ourselves.

MANAGING YOUR HOUSEHOLD

When you make your plans for your trip, of course you'll consider the obvious ways it affects your family—how can you be sure you'll be home in time for the school play in which your child plays the lead? Do you leave early in the morning and get home late at night on the same day, so you're home the next morning to have breakfast with the kids and take them to school?

In addition, though, your organizational skills will be tested in ensuring not only that your family knows your plans—where you'll be and when—but also that everyone knows what has to occur at home while you're gone. Because let's face it: No matter how good a partner your spouse is, it almost always falls to Mom to take the ultimate responsibility for planning for these kinds of tasks, whether she'll be home to do them herself or not. Everyone does it a little differently, but the thread is common—every woman who can manage this process successfully has a system and uses that system to be sure that all family members can be part of it and know what they have to do and when.

Any system starts with the itinerary for your trip. Once you finalize the itinerary, you should give a copy to your partner or other caregiver. You should also be sure you give a copy to a contact in your company, such as your administrative assistant, if you have one, or someone else in your company who is likely to be in the office if a family member has a question. From there, each family's system is a little different.

Teresa keeps "the book": This is a spiral-bound notebook kept on the kitchen counter next to the refrigerator. The book lists everything needed to run Teresa's household. That includes the obvious, such as names and phone numbers of the family's doctors, but also includes the names and phone numbers of her children's friends, what foods her children can and can't eat, and the schedule for all family members for the period of her trip. A copy of her itinerary goes in the book too, of course. She also makes sure her husband and administrative assistant each has a separate copy of her itinerary.

Vicki hangs a calendar on the wall next to the refrigerator in her kitchen. For each of her four children for each day she is away, the calendar lists the activities for that child, such as after-school meetings, sports practices, and games; any homework or special school assignments that require longer-term planning; and play dates, birthday parties, and the like. Both her husband and her administrative assistant have a copy of her itinerary. She also transcribes her itinerary to the calendar, so that any of her children can find out where she is at any time. She also transfers everything on the calendar into her handheld, so that she knows where her children are supposed to be and what they are supposed to be doing at any time. She frequently telephones her children for updates in case the calendar schedule has changed, as so often occurs with anyone's children. Before she leaves on a trip, Vicki also lines up on her dining room table what each child will need for the activities of that day, organized by child and day. For example, if her daughter Meg goes to soccer practice on Tuesday, Vicki will put Meg's shin guards and soccer shoes on the dining room table labeled for Meg and for Tuesday.

Elizabeth's children are younger than Teresa's and Vicki's. They are too young to understand the concept of a schedule, and they couldn't read it if they did understand. Elizabeth keeps a foldout calendar on the kitchen counter next to the refrigerator (note the popularity of the kitchen—your house is probably the same). The calendar lists her schedule, which she copies from her itinerary, and the daily schedules of her children. The children's schedules will identify school days, after-school activities, play dates, birthday parties and similar events, and—for the very young—feeding schedules. In addition to the calendar, which is mainly for her husband and her children's caregiver, she has a map of the United States posted on the wall of her kitchen for her children. Before she leaves on her trip, she puts a smiley face on the map over each city on her itinerary so that the children can get a sense of where she is at any time. This technique has also taught Elizabeth's children valuable geography lessons, especially as they've grown older.

Whether you use a book, a master calendar, a map with smiley faces, or something else, develop a system that works for you and your family and stick with it. It's comforting for you and your children when you have an established system and routine, and it leaves less room for uncertainty and doubt.

KEEPING IN TOUCH

Every road warrior has different ideas when it comes to keeping in touch with her family. We all feel that our family should come first, but we have to work at balancing our desire to be available to our families at all times against the demands of our business agenda. You will develop your own way of keeping in touch, which may evolve over time, but here are some ways other road warriors I know have dealt with these demands.

During the day, Vicki expects her junior-high and grade-school-age children to communicate with her primarily through e-mail. She has a handheld that receives e-mail so she can monitor it throughout the day. Although she carries her cell phone, she expects to be called during the day only in an emergency. If a child thinks there might be a need to contact Vicki during the day, she calls Vicki's administrative assistant, who decides whether Vicki should be telephoned. Vicki believes that this system helps her children distinguish between "want" and "need."

Vicki's children know that Vicki expects them to keep to a schedule when she is traveling. When they come home from school, they start their homework and check in with her by e-mail. At night, the children are free to call her—although the cell phone may be off if she has a business engagement—and she also phones home every night. Vicki also uses nights on the road to schedule one-on-one phone time with any of her children in need of special attention. She says she actually finds it easier to give undivided attention to just one of her four children when she is traveling.

Melinda's children are quite young and can be sleeping at nearly any time of day or night, so she tries to minimize her calls home during the day so she doesn't awaken anyone. During the day, she communicates with her husband and caregiver primarily by e-mail, although they can also call her on her cell phone; she checks her cell phone for messages frequently. She phones home every night after dinner, principally to talk to the older children.

Teresa's children are in high school, and she believes that she teaches them independence by limiting her communication with them while she is on the road. She checks her BlackBerry frequently. She has taught her children over the years to use good judgment and call her only in situations that truly require it. She believes that her children learn better to handle problems on their own if she is accessible, but not too accessible. She does call home periodically when she is on the road, but by no means daily. She also finds that if she doesn't call home so frequently, her teenaged son is more interested in talking to Mom when she does call!

NEW MOTHERHOOD

When you're a new mother, traveling for business presents a unique set of challenges. If you breastfeed your babies, you need to be prepared. If, like most of us, you can't bring your baby with you, you need to pump your breast milk and keep it so that your baby can consume it. Fortunately, many a breastfeeding mother has gone on the road before you and can teach you some ways of adapting.

You will need a breast pump to extract the milk. Breast pumps today have become smaller and lighter, and many run on rechargeable batteries. Be sure you take your charger with you in your luggage. Most breast pumps come with containers for storage and shipping; depending on how long your trip will be, you may need to buy extra containers. Ameda and Medela are two companies that make breast pumps, but your obstetrician may have other recommendations. Several mothers have told me that the pump manufacturer was of great assistance in answering their questions about how to best manage this process. In general, though, you begin by pumping the milk into one of the containers. You then can store the containers in a refrigerator, if you have one in your hotel room, or in a portable ice chest if you bring one on your trip. If you don't have either of these storage choices, ask your hotel to store the containers in its refrigerator. You can then ship the milk home by courier (such as FedEx) or carry it home in your luggage. You will probably want to ship the milk home every couple of days if you're on a trip of any length to be sure that enough is on hand to feed your baby.

Before you leave, you should try to build up an inventory of breast milk stored in your home refrigerator or freezer. Teresa suggests that if you are running low, mix what milk you have with formula and have the mixture fed to the baby while you are gone.

Every breastfeeding road warrior I've known has found the logistics a challenge. Your meeting schedule and your breast-pumping schedule may be difficult to juggle. You may also not be terribly happy about having something as personal as breastfeeding be a subject of conversation in your business day. You may have to plan carefully so that you have some private time to handle your breast pumping and milk storing during the business day. Melinda says that she has mastered the skill of breast pumping while driving a car. She suggests that if you do so, be very careful to observe the speed limit and any other traffic laws. You probably would prefer to avoid the inevitable embarrassment that would result if a police officer pulled you over while you were pumping.

TRAVELING WITH YOUR CHILDREN

Many road warriors take their children with them on business trips. If your children have attained school age, you'll probably need to limit these trips to school vacations and holidays (we all know that a school holiday doesn't necessarily mean a business holiday). And in any event, since you'll be spending time away from your children during the day while you conduct your business, you'll need to be accompanied by a spouse or other caregiver unless your children are old enough (and you're comfortable allowing them) to take care of themselves. But children of all ages can benefit by accompanying you on a business trip.

Some of the benefits for your children seem pretty obvious. They will be spending more time with you than if you are on the road without them. They will see new cities, eat different food, and learn how to enjoy being away from home. They will see their mother balancing family and work demands in a new context and understand how effectively it can be done. The fact that it's Mom's business responsibility that requires them to leave home will emphasize the importance of that responsibility. Vicki feels that her children are learning a valuable lesson by watching her. They see their mother take control of situations, make things work and solve problems. For daughters, especially, these lessons can help them develop the same skills.

Teresa uses a list to pack for a business trip. She has taught her children to use the same technique—each of them (with her help) has developed a packing list for business trips with Mom, and uses that list to pack. She also has always insisted that each child take responsibility for that child's own baggage. That means that no one but the child carries his or her own baggage through the airport and, for a carry-on, onto the airplane. Teresa says that none of her children has needed more than one trip with a heavy backpack or suitcase to be convinced to pack light and adjust the packing list accordingly.

Teresa also uses business travel to teach her children independence in other ways. Sometimes she will travel in first class while her children travel in coach. She believes they can learn techniques for traveling alone when she isn't so readily available. She also allows them to use the airport shops without her. On one trip, Teresa and her daughters were traveling with some of Teresa's colleagues. Her daughters needed food for the trip but the food concession was outside the security gate, so Teresa sent her daughters with her cell phone back into the terminal to buy food. Their only question, communicated by cell phone to the phone of one of the colleagues, was whether the french fries had to go on the conveyor through the x-ray machine! Teresa also uses this kind of travel to teach her children courtesy and thoughtfulness. For example, she insists that her children move out of the airplane aisle as quickly as they can when they get to their assigned rows. She tells them to store any carry-on bags or coats in the overhead bins immediately and take their seats. Teresa has found all this a great way to teach her children how to stand on their own two feet.

Woman Road Warrior Checklist

__ Always carry identification.

__ Look for meal alternatives to room service.

__ Take something to read or work on when eating alone.

__ Don't limit yourself to food choices listed on the menu.

__ Use the hotel concierge for advice and reservations.

__ Take proper steps to get a good night's sleep in the hotel.

__ Don't limit your exercise options to the hotel health club.

__ Don't leave credit card receipts or anything else with personal information in the hotel room trashcans.

__ Leave copies (front and back) of all credit cards, identification, and other important documents at home.

__ Use your time at home to keep up your relationships.

__ Develop systems for managing your family responsibilities while you're on the road.

Afterword

Now that you've finished this book, I hope that you're better prepared to become a woman road warrior—or, if you already are one, better able to deal with the challenges of business travel. Of course, you'll learn even more from your experiences on the road. I hope that, like those woman road warriors whose stories contribute so much to this book, you'll share the trials, successes, and funny stories that will help define your life on the road with your fellow woman road warriors. If you have a story to tell and to share, visit our website at www.woman-roadwarrior.com.

See you on the road!

APPENDICES

Traveler Profile

Name

Company Name

Street Address

City, State, Zip

Company Phone

Home Address

City, State, Zip

Home Phone

Passport Number

Seating:
__ Nonsmoking   __ Smoking   __ Window   __ Aisle

Car Preference

Car Company   ID Number

_____   _____

_____   _____

_____   _____

Car Size

Frequent-Flyer Programs
Indicate how your name appears on each airline's frequent-flyer program

Airline   Account No.

_____   _____

_____   _____

_____   _____

_____   _____

_____   _____

Special Meal/Dietary Requirements:

Other Additional Information

Credit Cards:
Indicate if personal or corporate

Card Company   Number   Exp Date

_____   _____   _____

_____   _____   _____

Pros and Cons of Travel Arrangement Options

OPTION	PROS	CONS
Internal Travel Agency	Works primarily for your company Knows what, if any, prenegotiated rates are available Typically has working relationships with airlines Typically has 24/7 support, which facilitates changes en route Has access to alternatives One-stop shopping for all reservations	Doesn't always get the cheapest airline deals Means competing with the rest of the organization for service Might be tougher to build a rapport
External Travel Agency	Easier to build a rapport with certain people Looks out for your best interest Ability to provide more options Easier to make changes en route One-stop shopping for all reservations	Processing fee applied to transaction You will be competing with other customers for service May not be available 24/7, therefore may be more difficult to make changes
Internet	Cheaper options available Immediate access to resources	Processing fee applied to transaction Inconsistent rules between websites Price differences between sites, which means needing more time to find the best deal May need to contact carrier directly for added amenities (e.g., seat assignments) If change or trouble occurs en route, will require a call to customer service
Solo	Able to negotiate better deals If brand loyal, can build up status	Processing fee applied to initial reservation More time-consuming due to making multiple calls in order to find best option Potential for higher cost

Charge and Credit Card Issuers' Websites

American Express	www.americanexpress.com
Citibank	www.citibank.com
Diners Club	www.dinersclub.com
Discover Card	www.discovercard.com
MasterCard	www.mastercard.com
Visa	www.visa.com

Domestic Hub Cities for Major Airlines

AIRLINE	HUB CITY
American Airlines	Boston Chicago Dallas/Ft. Worth New York (JFK & LaGuardia) Miami St. Louis
Continental Airlines	Cleveland Houston
Delta	Atlanta (Hartsfield) Cincinnati New York (LaGuardia) Salt Lake City
Northwest	Detroit Memphis Minneapolis/St. Paul
United	Chicago Denver Los Angeles San Francisco Washington, DC
US Airways	Charlotte Las Vegas Philadelphia Phoenix Pittsburgh

Airport Club Lounge Locations

AIRPORT CLUB LOUNGE	LOCATIONS	
American Airlines Admirals Club	Atlanta (Hartsfield)	Orange County
	Austin	Panama City
	Bogata	Paris (Charles de
	Boston (Logan)	Gaulle)
	Buenos Aires	Philadelphia
	Caracas	Raleigh/Durham
	Chicago O'Hare	Rio de Janeiro
	Dallas/Ft. Worth	San Diego
	Denver International	Santo Domingo
	Frankfurt	San Francisco
	Honolulu (shared with	San Jose
	Qantas)	San Juan
	Kansas City	Santiago
	London Heathrow	São Paulo
	Los Angeles	St. Louis
	Mexico City	Tokyo
	Miami	Toronto
	New York (Kennedy)	Washington (Dulles)
	New York (LaGuardia)	Washington (Reagan)
	Newark	
Continental Presidents Club	Atlanta (Hartsfield)	London (Gatwick)
	Austin	Los Angeles
	Boston (Logan)	Mexico City
	Chicago (O'Hare)	New York (LaGuardia)
	Cleveland	Newark
	Dallas/Ft. Worth	Panama City
	Denver	San Antonio
	Ft. Lauderdale	San Francisco
	Guam	San Juan
	Honolulu	Seattle/Tacoma
	Houston (Bush	Washington (Reagan)
	Intercontinental)	

Airport Club Lounge Locations (continued)

AIRPORT CLUB LOUNGE	LOCATIONS	
Delta Crown Room	Atlanta (Hartsfield)	New Orleans
	Boston (Logan)	Newark
	Chicago (O'Hare)	New York (Kennedy)
	Cincinnati	New York (LaGuardia)
	Dallas/Ft. Worth	Orlando
	Denver	Philadelphia
	Frankfurt	Phoenix
	Ft. Lauderdale	Raleigh/Durham
	Honolulu	Salt Lake City
	Jacksonville	San Diego
	Kansas City	San Francisco
	London (Gatwick)	Seattle
	Los Angeles	Tampa
	Miami	Washington (Reagan)
	Nashville	West Palm Beach
AIRPORT CLUB LOUNGE	**LOCATIONS**	
Northwest World Club	Boston (Logan)	New York (LaGuardia)
	Chicago (O'Hare)	Newark
	Detroit	Portland
	Honolulu	San Francisco
	Los Angeles	Seattle
	Manila	Seoul
	Memphis	Tokyo (Narita)
	Milwaukee	Washington (Dulles)
	Minneapolis/St. Paul	Washington (Reagan)

Airport Club Lounge Locations (continued)

AIRPORT CLUB LOUNGE	LOCATIONS	
United Airlines Red Carpet Club	Atlanta (Hartsfield)	New York (Kennedy)
	Baltimore/Washington	New York (LaGuardia)
	International	Orange County
	Bangkok	Orlando
	Boston (Logan)	Osaka
	Buenos Aires	Paris (Charles de
	Chicago (O'Hare)	Gaulle)
	Dallas /Ft. Worth	Philadelphia
	Denver	Phoenix
	Frankfurt	Portland
	Hong Kong	San Diego
	Honolulu	San Francisco
	Los Angeles	Sao Paulo
	London (Heathrow)	Seattle/Tacoma
	Melbourne	Sydney
	Mexico City	Tokyo (Narita)
	Minneapolis/St. Paul	Washington (Reagan)
	Newark	Washington (Dulles)
US Airways Club	Baltimore/Washington	London (Gatwick)
	International	New York (LaGuardia)
	Boston (Logan)	Philadelphia
	Buffalo	Phoenix
	Charlotte (Douglas)	Pittsburgh
	Greensboro	Raleigh/Durham
	Hartford/Springfield	Tampa
	Las Vegas	Washington (Reagan)
	Los Angeles	

Detailed Packing List
(FOR MORE THAN A 3 DAY TRIP)

Destination: _____

Dates: _____

Make-up	Umbrella
Jewelry	Chargers (cell phone, PDA)
Underwear	Adapter/Converter
Toothbrush/toothpaste	Flashlight
Brush/comb	Pants
Soap	Skirt
Deodorant	Blazer
Dental floss	Blouse
Vitamins	Shirts
Medications	Belts
Contact lenses/solutions	Shoes
Glasses	Dress
Shampoo	Shorts
Conditioner	Workout clothes
Moisturizer	Tennis shoes
Cologne	Swimsuit
Suntan lotion	Cover-up
Razor	Sandals
Shaving cream	Pillowcase
Manicure set	Zip-top bags
Pantiliners	Towelettes
Tampons	Water
Pantyhose	Snacks
Socks	Ticket
Pajamas	Passport
Bathrobe	Visa
Slippers	Upgrade certificates
Sunglasses	Briefcase
Watches	Books
Travel alarm	List of frequent-flyer numbers

Packing List
(1–2 DAY TRIP)

Business outfits	AC chargers (cell phone, laptop,
Business shoes	Handheld)
Belt(s)	Travel alarm
Underwear/bras	Umbrella
Pantyhose/knee-highs	Flashlight
Jewelry	Towelettes
Pajamas/slippers	Briefcase
Workout clothes/socks/shoes	Tickets
Makeup	Upgrades
Hairbrush	Passport
Medications	Visa
Vitamins	List of frequent-flyer/
Toiletries	hotel numbers
Glasses	Snacks
Contact lenses	Zip-top bags
Pillowcase	Water
Sunglasses	

Websites

AIRLINES	
ANA—All Nippon Airways	(Japan)http://www.ana.co.jp/eng/
Asiana Airlines	http://us.flyasiana.com/
American	www.aa.com
British Airways	www.ba.com
Cathay Pacific Airways	www.cathaypacific.com
Continental Airlines	www.continental.com
Delta Airlines	www.delta.com
Emirates	www.emirates.com
Malaysia Airlines	www.malaysiaairlines.com
Northwest Airlines	www.nwa.com
Official Airline Guides	www.oag.com
Qantas Airways	www.qantas.com
Qatar Airways	www.qatarairways.com
Ryanair	www.ryanair.com
Singapore Airlines	www.singaporeair.com
Southwest	www.southwest.com
Thai Airways	www.thaiair.com
Transportation Security Administration	www.tsa.gov
United	www.ual.com
US Airways	www.usairways.com
CAR-RENTAL AGENCIES	
Avis	www.avis.com
Budget Rent A Car	www.budget.com
Enterprise	www.enterprise.com
Hertz	www.hertz.com
National Car Rental	www.nationalcar.com

OTHER TRANSPORTATION	
Amtrak	www.amtrak.com
European Rail	www.raileurope.com
	www.eurorailways.com
	www.europeanrail.com
Eurail Passes	www.railpass.com
Greyhound Bus	www.greyhound.com
TRAVEL WEBSITES	
Expedia	www.expedia.com
Hotels	www.hotels.com
Orbitz	www.orbitz.com
Travelocity	www.travelocity.com
OTHER	
Airbus	www.airbus.com
Boeing	www.boeing.com
Country Risk Forecast	www.crg-online.com (service for hire)
Currency Conversion	www.bloomberg.com/invest/
	calculators/currency.html
Financial Times	www.ft.com
Food Allergy Translation Sites	www.selectwisely.com
Global Information	globaledge.msu.edu
Holidays	www.en.wikipedia.org/wiki/List_
	of_holidays_by_country
MapQuest	www.mapquest.com
Marriott ExecuStay	www.execustay.com
Metric Conversion	www.metric-conversions.org
Oakwood Corporate Housing	www.oakwood.com
Rand McNally	www.randmcnally.com
SeatGuru	www.seatguru.com
Time & Date	www.timeanddate.com/
	worldclock/full.html
Translation Sites	www.worldlingo.com
Travel Documents	www.traveldocs.com
Travel Gear	www.awaytravelgear.com

OTHER CONTINUED	
Travel Warnings	travel.state.gov/travel/cis_pa_tw/ cis_pa_tw_1168.html
U.S. State Department	travel.state.gov/passport
U.S. Passport and Visa Service	www.passportsandvisas.com
U.S. Treasury Sanctions	www.ustreas.gov/offices/ enforcement/ofac/
Weather	www.weather.com
Wikipedia	www.en.wikipedia.org
Woman Road Warrior	www.womanroadwarrior.com
World Factbook	www.cia.gov/cia/publications/ factbook/index.html
World Health Organization	www.who.int
WorldTimeServer	www.worldtimeserver.com

About the Author

Kathleen Ameche is CEO of Ameche Group, LLC, a company she founded to be the friend and champion to female business travelers. As a senior executive, corporate officer, and business traveler for more than 25 years—closing in on her two-millionth mile—She is the business travel authority. Her corporate experience ranges from being VP/chief information officer of media giant Tribune Company, VP of business development at consultancy West Monroe Partners, and ten years with international consulting giant Deloitte Touche. She is the featured travel expert on CBS 2 Chicago and her work has been featured in the *New York Times*, the *Washington Post*, and CNN. She has made many speaking and lecture appearances with corporations, organizations, and institutions, including the Library of Congress. Her website is www.womanroadwarrior.com.

More Books for Entrepreneurs from
B2 BOOKS

It Pays to Be Paranoid
Securing Business Success by Preparing for the Worst
By Christopher Eiben

ISBN 1-932841-02-4 $14.95

A practical guide to spotting and avoiding business problems before they occur.

Your Lawyer: An Owner's Manual
By Henry C. Krasnow

ISBN 978-1-932841-12-1 $14

A brass-tacks insider's guide to finding, managing, and motivating attorneys.

Brownie Points
Seven Steps To Success For Woman Entrepreneurs From One Who Made It
By Aundrea Lacy

978-1-932841-26-8 $14

Successful strategies for women who want to start and run their own businesses.

The Nia Guide for Black Women:
Achieving Career Success on Your Terms
By Sheryl Huggins and Cheryl Mayberry McKissack

ISBN 978-1-932841-01-5 $12.95

A practical guide to achieving career empowerment for today's black working woman.

The Nia Guide for Black Women:
Balancing Work and Life
By Sheryl Huggins and Cheryl Mayberry McKissack

ISBN 978-1-932841-05-3 $12.95

The black working woman's handbook for maintaining professional and personal harmony.